R O S S I N I

The Man and His Music

by

FRANCIS TOYE

DOVER PUBLICATIONS, INC.
New York

To
THOMAS BEECHAM
in gratitude for
his music and his wit

This Dover edition, first published in 1987, is an unabridged, slightly revised and enlarged republication of the work originally published by William Heinemann Ltd., London, in 1934 under the title *Rossini: A Study in Tragi-Comedy*. In addition to the preface to the original 1934 edition, the present edition includes the preface written by the author for the 1954 edition (a straight reprint of the original text, with fewer, different illustrations) published by Arthur Barker Ltd., London, under the same title as the original. For reasons of space, the illustrations in the 1934 edition have been relocated in this edition. Numerous spelling errors have been corrected.

Manufactured in the United States of America
Dover Publications, Inc., 31 East 2nd Street, Mineola, N.Y. 11501

Library of Congress Cataloging-in-Publication Data

Toye, Francis, b. 1883.
Rossini, the man and his music.

Reprint. Originally published: Rossini, a study in tragi-comedy. London: W. Heinemann, 1934.
"List of Rossini's compositions": p.
Includes index.
1. Rossini, Gioacchino, 1792–1868. 2. Composers—Biography. I. Title.
ML410.R8T73 1987   782.1′092′4   [B]   87-572
ISBN 0-486-25396-1 (pbk.)

CONTENTS

Chapter		Page
	List of Illustrations	iv
	Preface to the 1954 Edition	v
	Preface to the First Edition	vii
	Prologue	3
I	The Curtain Rises	5
II	Opera in Italy	23
III	First Flights	30
IV	Some Reforms—and a Masterpiece	44
V	Three Interesting Operas	63
VI	Potpourri	76
VII	End of an Act	96
VIII	An English Interlude	112
IX	A la Mode de Paris	122
X	William Tell	137
XI	Entr'acte	152
XII	"The Great Renunciation"	166
XIII	A Losing Battle	177
XIV	De Profundis	190
XV	Paris Days and Nights	205
XVI	Final Scenes	222
	Epilogue	239

Mainly for Musicians   243
List of Rossini's Compositions   258
Index   262

List of Illustrations

                                             Facing page

Drawing by Kunike in Vienna   1

A page from the autograph score of *The Barber of*   3
    Seville

Rossini at the time of *The Barber of Seville*, from an   62
    oil painting by Mayer in the Liceo
    Musicale at Bologna

G. Rossini, lithograph by G. Grevedon in 1828   63

The Sala Rossini in the Liceo Musicale at Bologna   180

A photograph given to Arthur Sullivan in 1862   181

A caricature of Rossini by André Gill   234

Rossini, a woodcut engraved by Robert in 1867   235
    from a picture by Mouilleron

PREFACE TO THE 1954 EDITION

DURING the twenty years that have passed since this book was written, things have gone well for Rossini. I doubt, for instance, if I could now have risked the intentionally provocative assertion which opens the original preface. There is a certain amount of new curiosity about the man, his music is better liked and better known. True, so far as England is concerned, the " serious " operas remain as unfamiliar as ever, but several of the lighter works, notably *La Cenerentola*, have joined *The Barber* in public esteem, while all the overtures have passed from tentative to definite inclusion in the normal concert repertory. Moreover, the 1952 Maggio Musicale at Florence was practically an all-Rossini affair whereat to our great delight we were re-introduced to *Armida*, *Le Comte Ory* and *La Pietra del Paragone*. In short, the contemptuous dismissal of Rossini, pilloried in my original preface, would be scarcely conceivable nowadays. The general contentions of the preface, however, still remain valid enough.

Since writing the book I have heard in the theatre several operas for the appraisal of which I had previously to rely on a study of the scores. In two instances at least this has led to a modification of judgment. I did not sufficiently appreciate the interest of *Armida*, whereof the best music, especially the duets and that strange trio for three tenors (surely unique in operatic literature) is very good indeed.

Again I was too kind to the libretto of *Le Comte Ory* which, in performance, seems ineffective as well as silly, with an ending so casual that Rossini did not even bother to provide it with a proper finale ! The music, however, sounds, if possible, even better than I thought; the scoring throughout is a model of its kind, while no one who has not heard the finale of the first act in the theatre can realise how individual, how gay, how irresistibly charming is Rossini's handling of it. *Le Comte Ory* may be operetta ; if so it is the best operetta ever written.

Finally an apology for a stupid slip on page 156. Marguerite Duval should, needless to say, be Marguerite Gauthier. I can only suppose that sympathy with the heroine of *La Dame aux Camélias* led to belated, if unconscious, participation in some wishful thinking on her part.

FRANCIS TOYE

Florence, September 1, 1954

PREFACE TO THE FIRST EDITION

To THE best of my belief there is no demand whatever for a life of Rossini in English. Supply, however, sometimes creates demand, and Rossini as a figure is so fascinating that people may eventually wonder why they were content to remain for so long in ignorance of his extraordinary career. Moreover, there are undoubted signs of a renewed interest in his music other than the immortal *Barber of Seville*. The most important overtures, rescued at long last from the embraces of tired military bands on the piers of depressing seaside resorts, are beginning to creep back once again into the programmes of our more enterprising concerts. Some of the songs, notably *La Danza* and the little trilogy entitled *La Regata Veneziana*, have made many new friends in recent years. Outside England, of course, the signs are more evident still. *William Tell* obstinately maintains its place in the repertory when a cast of singers can be found adequate to sing the music, and sometimes even when it cannot. Two operas, well-nigh forgotten, *La Cenerentola* and *L'Italiana in Algeri*, have been revived with brilliant success in Paris, where the younger generation of French musicians manifested an unexpected enthusiasm not only by their constant attendance at the Opera Comique, but by their laudatory comments in the press. When a composer of the standing of Darius Milhaud, writing in *Le Soir*, can wax so keen as to express his fervent desire for the additional revival of *La Donna del Lago* and *Comte Ory*, there must still be something in Rossini's music that satisfies a modern need.

It is not surprising that this should be so. The more purely musical a composer is, the better are his chances of weathering the storms of successive fashions, and Rossini, whatever his defects as a man and a musician, was one of the most musical of composers. Indeed, it may be doubted whether his natural genius for musical expression was not equal to that of a Handel, a Mozart or a Schubert, though he failed to turn it to such good account as they did, partly owing to the handicap of his early training and the circumstances of his career, partly owing to a certain flabbiness in his nature. If ever public school masters need an example from the arts of the dangers attending the lack of what they call "character," they can hardly do better than cite the case of Rossini. Had the methods and ideals deriving from the late Dr. Arnold been current in the Liceo Musicale at Bologna, the world might have gained an addition to its dozen composers of the front rank. On the other hand, it might have lost its Rossini altogether.

Further, there is a striking parallel between the conditions of the Europe in which Rossini won his triumphs and the conditions that obtain to-day. Europe then was exhausted by the Napoleonic wars just as Europe to-day is exhausted by the war of 1914 and the economic depression consequent upon it. Rossini's gaiety and high spirits, his exuberant vitality and brilliance, provided just the tonic that Europe needed in the second, third and fourth decades of the nineteenth century. Owing to the passing of the convention to which his operas conform, the supersession of his idiom and an entire change of conditions in the musical theatre, we can never recapture wholly the thrill of delight and surprise felt by Rossini's contemporaries. The delicious shock of novelty, indispensable to perfect æsthetic enjoyment, is gone. But there remains behind the idiom and the conventions something permanent that can still give us unique pleasure, as indeed was proved by the success of *La Boutique Fantasque*, which, despite its modern trappings, possessed the merit of preserving the genuine flavour of the original Rossinian ingredients. The twentieth century may well feel grateful for a whiff of that exciting perfume, an echo of that hearty laugh, which Rossini brought into the music of the nineteenth. Was it not Osbert Sitwell who wrote that in Rossini one felt conscious for the first time of a distinctive flavour of modern music?

In any event, whether there is a demand for it or not, an English book on Rossini needed to be written. Our musicology, too often inspired by a *furor Teutonicus* surpassing that of the Teutons themselves, has ever been apt to leave out of account inconvenient phenomena which happen not to fit the Anglo-German pattern of things-as-they-should-be. The most striking of these, perhaps, was the paramount importance of Paris as a musical centre in the middle years of the nineteenth century. It was Paris, not Vienna or Dresden or Milan, that set the tone, especially of course as regards Opera. Another, until quite recently, was Hector Berlioz, whose originality of design and revolutionary experiments in the handling of the orchestra did not at all harmonise with the claims of the extreme Wagnerians or the classical German pedants. Less vital, maybe, but of great importance was, and still is, Rossini.

It was Ernest Newman, I think, who a few years ago

most justly pilloried some tabloid history of music or other for devoting as many pages to the works of Hubert Parry as it did sentences to the career of Rossini. Such an attitude was typical. Since then, however, we have progressed. In one book containing a chapter devoted to opera Rossini's existence and contributions to the form are dismissed as follows: "Rossini wrote *William Tell*"! Yet without some knowledge of the man and his work no intelligent understanding of Opera in the nineteenth century is at all possible, quite apart from any question of his personal importance or the interest of his unique career. The influence of Rossini on his contemporaries and successors is discussed elsewhere. Even, however, had he had no such influence, his own accomplishments would remain sufficiently remarkable to justify a study of his life and his music. Never in the whole history of music has there been anybody quite like Rossini. In view of the trend of the times it is extremely improbable that there ever will be again. How our musicologists can reconcile their summary dismissal of such a man with Wagner's description of him as "the only person I had so far (1860) met in the artistic world who was really great and worthy of reverence" is not for me to determine. Granted even that he was not in reality great or worthy of reverence, to have elicited such a tribute from Wagner, a greater genius and hostile by profession, so to say, to everything he stood for, does prove that he was neither unimportant nor contemptible.

It was partly the hope of dispelling such illusions, partly the fascination of Rossini's personality, partly a great admiration for much of his music that provoked the writing of this book. Other things being equal, a short book is better than a long book, and fortunately, neither the subject nor the circumstances necessitated making this a very long one. There already exists an authoritative biography of Rossini by Radiciotti, the fruit of immense labour and infinite research, to which the eager student can turn for more detailed information. It is unlikely, however, that his three large volumes will ever be translated into English; they are, moreover, expensive and not always easily obtainable. Inevitably, Radiciotti's conscientious scholarship has saved me much trouble by placing before me all the facts duly collated and fully commented upon, though the sifting from this sometimes turgid mass of what seemed to be of real moment was not altogether an easy task. Further, I have not neglected other sources of information, notably two collections of Rossini's letters, Giulio Fara's penetrating study of the composer's morbid psychology in *Genio ed Ingegno Musicale*, a short but excellent French biography by Henri de Curzon and Edwardes' *Life*, which shares with Stendhal's inaccurate but highly entertaining *Vie de Rossini* the advantage of reflecting a contemporary point of view. Still, on the whole, this book is based on Radiciotti, and I am proud to acknowledge my debt to him as regards most matters of fact.

As regards matters of opinion it is otherwise. Radiciotti, in his enthusiasm for Rossini, seems to me to have erred in one direction as much as previous biographers have erred in the other. He is determined at all costs to make Rossini appear as something very like a hero; which, with all due respect, is nonsense. There was nothing heroic about Rossini at all. If there had been, we should be forced to write him down as one of the world's most abject quitters. As Verdi pointed out long ago, he was never the mere buffoon of popular legend; he was not even the flippant cynic that he himself liked to appear. He undoubtedly possessed some of the attributes of greatness, not to mention brilliant genius, but as a man he was timid, self-indulgent, highly neurotic, though gifted with irresistible charm, whom I, for my part, find more interesting thus than in the ill-fitting uniform of an Olympian.

Nor have I always been able to concur in Radiciotti's æsthetic judgments; which is perhaps, not a matter of great importance. My reasons for disagreeing with his and other orthodox views on *William Tell* are set forth in the chapter dealing with that opera, but there are many other places where I have felt obliged to differ from him. This being so, it is rather unfortunate that an inability to obtain the scores has forced me in the case of some of the least-known works to follow him a little more blindly than I should have wished. True, all these are dead, all forgotten as if they never had been; but one likes to feel that the fullest possible justice has been done even to the dead who have no chance of resurrection.

Such I conceive to be the reasons and the explanations necessary to introduce this book to an English reader. When, if ever, he has finished it, he will not, I think, feel any doubt as to the exceptional interest of the subject, whatever he may think about the merits or the defects of the writer. If he has some knowledge of musical history he will find many things that link together events and phenomena hitherto isolated. If he has no knowledge of history and little of music he will at least be introduced to one of the most striking personalities of the nineteenth century, a figure compounded in equal parts of comedy and tragedy, whose sweeping conquests in the field of music can only be paralleled by Napoleon's conquests on the field of battle. For him, as for Napoleon, there waited, if not a Saint Helena, an ineluctable Elba— largely of his own making.

Rossini! For some of us the name still holds something of the old magic, evoking a vision of the great days of Opera and Song, of triumphant successes in one brilliant European capital after another. To the average person, I suppose, it means little but *The Barber of Seville*, the overture to *William Tell*, and *tournedos Rossini*, a characteristic alliance which he himself would have been the first to laugh at and appreciate. The primary aim of this book is to explain the alliance and to enable a greater number of persons to understand the magic. All I venture to hope is that people may enjoy reading it almost as much as I have enjoyed writing it.

Portofino. New Year's Day, 1934.

P.S.—I have to thank Professor Vatielli, librarian of the Liceo Musicale, for his courtesy and kindness in sending me the three photographs from Bologna; also Mrs. Bashford for allowing me to reproduce the photograph given to Arthur Sullivan.

JOACH ROSSINI.

Drawing by Kunike in Vienna

A page from the Autograph Score of *The Barber of Seville* now in the library of the Liceo Musicale at Bologna.

PROLOGUE

On the 29th of February, 1792, a man was pacing nervously up and down a first-floor room of a house in the Via del Duomo at Pesaro, a small seaport on the Adriatic. From an adjacent room came the sound of a woman in travail. At each groan the man turned round and poured abuse on the statuettes of various saints, which, duly bedecked with candles, had been invited to exert their beneficent influence on the labour. The groans grew worse; the man increasingly agitated. Finally he took a stick and, to show the saints his opinion of their ingratitude or incompetence, proceeded to smash the statuettes to pieces. But just as he came to the image of St. James, a new, faint cry was heard from the next room; the child had been born at last. Falling on his knees, the distracted father poured forth his gratitude in terms of adorable simplicity: "Thanks, thanks, my good St. James, the patron saint of my own parish in Lugo, who hast come to our aid from all that way off . . ."

A ridiculous story, possibly untrue; an incongruous mixture of pain and absurdity; the last day of February in a Leap Year! What could furnish a more appropriate setting for the birth of a man who was to become the subject of more spurious anecdotes, the father, real or putative, of more jokes, than any other musician; whose active career was, for all practical purposes, to end on a question mark before the age of 38, with half a lifetime still to run; whose very glory and success

3

were to lead to a greater disappointment; in whom brilliant wit was to be a mask for profound depression, appearance a complete and intentional antithesis of reality, yet so interwoven that, even to this day, no one can tell exactly where the one ended and the other began? Decidedly, God must have relished from the outset the tragi-comedy He intended to make of the life of Gioacchino Rossini.

CHAPTER I

THE CURTAIN RISES

THOUGH Rossini's parents occupied a very humble position in the world, the father, at any rate, Giuseppe Rossini, had some pretensions to family, for one of his ancestors had acted at one time as ambassador to the Court of the Duke of Ferrara. Under the alternative designation of Russini or Rossini the family originally hailed from Cotignola and was entitled to armorial bearings, of which, as if in prophecy of its most famous member, the main device was a nightingale perched on a rose. During the sixteenth century the Rossinis had moved to Lugo. Two hundred years later, however, Giuseppe, the latest descendant of these modestly illustrious patricians, had to support himself in that city, like a kind of Nanki Poo, by combining the professions of municipal trumpeter* and of virtuoso on the horn and trumpet in the local theatre band. On the 29th of April, 1790, then in his 31st year, he transferred his services to the municipality of Pesaro, where, owing to his ingratiating ways and above all to the gay and impulsive disposition which earned him the nickname of "Vivazza," he soon became a very popular figure. In a short time he managed to get himself appointed inspector of the public slaughterhouses, so that his strangely yoked offices combined to bring him in some

*That is to say he acted in the capacity of what we should call a Town Crier, the trumpet taking the place of our familiar bell.

two hundreds crowns a year, not a bad income for a young man in those days. At any rate it permitted him to indulge in the typically Italian passion for collecting his family round him by the transportation from Lugo of his old mother and sister. It also enabled him eventually to assume the responsibilities, as well as the privileges, of matrimony.

As fellow tenant of the house in which he lived there dwelt a baker who had an only daughter, Anna, at the time a girl of nineteen. She earned her living as a dressmaker and was considered one of the prettiest girls in the town. The composer himself, who adored his mother in life and worshipped her memory in death, later described her to an intimate friend as "tall and well proportioned, with a fresh, rather pale complexion, perfect teeth, and magnificent black curly hair. She was always cheerful and good tempered, a constant smile on her lips, and on her face an expression of truly angelic sweetness". According to many witnesses she preserved the characteristics of her spiritual attributes to her dying day. A weak heart, seconded, perhaps, by the unattractive habit of taking snuff, had impaired her physical charms considerably earlier.

Such, in brief, were the personalities of the two principal actors in the tragi-comedy of the 29th of February, 1792. The third actor, then making positively his first appearance on the world's stage, bore, in many ways, a remarkable resemblance to both, and heredity counts for much in the explanation of his extraordinary career.

The first few years of the Rossinis' married life passed quietly enough, but the heady doctrines of the French Revolution, to say nothing of Napoleon's military

6

successes, soon began to affect in increasing measure the impressionable and highly excitable Vivazza. He frequented secret republican meetings, conspired with ardour, and took a prominent part in welcoming the entrance into Pesaro of the French General, Victor, and his troops on the 5th of February, 1797, his enthusiasm going so far as to make him write upon his door, "Here lives citizen Vivazza, a true republican." Scarcely a month later his transports were effectively moderated by the Peace of Tolentino, which restored Pesaro to the Papal Government, for the authorities, to mark their disapproval of the extreme views of their employee, decided at the end of the year to dispense with his services.

But Vivazza was not a man to be disposed of so easily. Administrations, whether municipal or national, were no more proof against removal than trumpeters. He joined a band of Pesarese patriots who, a week after his dismissal, penetrated into the city by night, put to flight the Papal soldiers, arrested the Governor and set up a new administration which immediately voted for the incorporation of Pesaro with the Cisalpine Republic. Thus, by means which strike us as somewhat disproportionate to the end, the indomitable Vivazza was able to remain municipal trumpeter and indulge his Jacobin enthusiasm to the full. He could even permit himself the luxury of writing, or allowing it to be believed that he had written, a peculiarly turgid Republican Hymn with a bombastic dedication which informs us that "Citizen Giuseppe Rossini, known as Vivazza, being carried away and overwhelmed by patriotic ardour, dedicates this, his Republican Hymn, to all true democrats. Patriotism rather than Apollo;

7

Liberty rather than the Muses have inspired its composition."

This dedication would establish beyond a doubt the paternity of the work in question but for the fact that both the composition itself and the dedication seem to be incompatible with Vivazza's usual style as exemplified in his letters, which suggest an incapacity for any kind of literary composition, however bad. At any rate, there can be no doubt that both were wholly typical of his mentality and ideals, whether or no we are prepared to deduce from the former, as some writers have done, epileptic tendencies in the family.

Vivazza seems to have realised, however, that it might be advisable to insure against the instability of fortune by finding some means of support for himself and his family less susceptible to political oscillations. He therefore concentrated his attention on playing the horn rather than the trumpet and determined to turn to account Anna's fine natural voice. The couple, then, leaving Pesaro, sought employment in various small theatres in that part of Italy. He played in the orchestra and she sang on the stage, sometimes in quite important parts, which presumably he taught her, because Anna, though exceptionally quick, intelligent and with a natural gift for singing, could not read a note of music and had to learn everything by ear. But it was not long before politics came once more to trouble the humble destinies of the Rossinis. In 1799 the French were chased out of the Papal States, and the police of Bologna were enabled to vent their displeasure on Vivazza by forcing him to exchange the orchestra pit for a gaol. Finally they brought him back to Pesaro for trial whereat he seems to have behaved with conspicuous loyalty to his former associates. Fortunately for him, however, the seesaw of world destinies was soon in motion again. In 1800 back came the French to Pesaro, liberating all political prisoners, so that husband and wife were able to start off once more on their joint operatic wanderings. No question of municipal trumpeting again on this occasion, for the post had in the meantime been permanently abolished.

During these exciting vicissitudes Gioacchino was left behind at Pesaro in charge of his aunt and his grandmother. He was supposed to be learning how to read and to write, even something about the elements of music, but in practice he spent most of his time getting into mischief. He was a lad of uncommonly high spirits and extraordinary vitality, though these were usually manifested in a most undesirable manner. For instance, his practical jokes in churches amounted to something very like sacrilege, and one of his playmates bore to his dying day a scar made by a stone successfully aimed at him by the future author of *William Tell*. As a punishment for these escapades his parents bound the boy apprentice to a blacksmith, with, apparently, small success, for shortly afterwards they felt obliged to make him come and live with them at Bologna. This move seems to have been scarcely more successful. Giuseppe and Anna, owing to the exigencies of their profession, had often to be absent, and young Gioacchino, boarded out with a pork butcher, took advantage of these absences to indulge in exactly the same behaviour as before. Arithmetic, Latin and lessons on the spinet had been added to his curriculum, though with little, if any, practical result.

There can be no doubt that for sheer naughtiness

Rossini's boyhood is unparalleled in the annals of the great masters of music; but there was every excuse for him. So handsome as to be commonly known as "The Little Adonis," he was doubtless spoilt by outsiders if not by his parents, the wildly Bohemian circumstances of his boyhood being hardly compatible with discipline in any event. The qualifications of his various teachers, too, were in all probability by no means such as to inspire enthusiasm. The composer himself has left a most diverting account of Prinetti, who combined instruction on the spinet with dealing in wines and spirits. To begin with, Prinetti's ideas of keyboard technique were extraordinarily primitive, for he taught only the use of the thumb and first finger in playing a scale! More remarkable still was his general manner of life. He never at any time possessed a bed but, when night came, just wrapped himself up in his coat and went to sleep in a corner of one of the arcades that abound in Bologna. Naturally enough, under these conditions, he woke very early in the morning, when he immediately proceeded to his pupil's room, hauled him out of bed and sat him down at the spinet. After the first few notes, however, the teacher invariably went to sleep in his chair; whereupon Rossini went back to bed again, informing Prinetti, when that worthy eventually woke up, that he had played his pieces without a mistake! Strictly limited progress was not surprising in such circumstances.

In 1802, that is to say when Gioacchino was ten years old, Vivazza moved himself and his family back to the ancestral town of Lugo, but this does not seem at first to have effected any perceptible improvement in the boy's disposition. Recourse was had once more to a blacksmith, this time with greater effect, for Gioacchino began to develop symptoms of comparative obedience. Probably this improvement was not altogether due to his Siegfried-like occupation at the bellows. It may well be that the influence of his mother began to make itself really felt about this time. She can hardly have failed to plead and expostulate with her son, who, we know, adored her to an extent that was almost abnormal. Even in his earliest years young Rossini was very susceptible to the appearance of women—he confessed that he would rather have a sound thrashing from his father than be kissed by an ugly one—and he thought his mother the most lovely thing in all the world, alike in voice, face and character. Someone once asked him, when a child, what he would do if he went to heaven and found the Madonna more beautiful than his mother. "I should be so upset," he replied, "I should cry for the whole of the rest of my life."

At last, too, he got some intelligent if sporadic teaching from a priest, Don Giuseppe Malerbi, who used to allow him to come and practise in his own house, and, what is more, finding that his pupil had an exceptionally good voice, gave him his first instruction in the art of singing. As a matter of fact, the Malerbi influence seems to have played a considerable part in the formation of the composer's tastes. Don Giuseppe was a great admirer of Mozart and Haydn; his brother, Don Luigi, was well known for his caustic wit and his brilliant sense of humour. Both brothers were decidedly conservative in politics, with an inborn dislike for political excess of any kind; both, like so many priests, showed a decided partiality for good fare, their excellent dinners being renowned in the neighbourhood. It can scarcely be mere coincidence that Rossini, remarkably assimilative and imitative by nature, should have been notable for precisely similar characteristics in later life.

Sometime in 1804 the family moved permanently (so far as any element of permanence can be said to enter into the life of such vagabonds) to Bologna. Nothing could have been more fortunate for young Rossini. Bologna was one of the main musical centres of Italy. In addition to the Liceo Musicale and the Accademia Filarmonica, immortalised by its associations with Mozart, there were two excellent private musical institutions, one of which, the Accademia dei Concordi, made a speciality of classical music, that of Haydn in particular.

In view of the just pre-eminence of Bologna in musical matters, the limitations of contemporary knowledge and taste there are decidedly revelatory. The operas of Gluck and Mozart were never performed at the theatre; Handel and Beethoven were only known by their most elementary and unimportant compositions; Bach was a legend rather than a reality. Even the music of Haydn, despite the laudable efforts of the Accademia dei Concordi, never attained genuine popularity, *The Creation* being considered a morsel digestible only by persons of the most exceptional intelligence and perseverance. Such being the attitude of Bologna, no effort is necessary to imagine the state of affairs in the average Italian town.

The technical competence of the musical instruction available, however, was probably better, not worse, than is usually imagined. At any rate young Rossini began to make rapid progress with his new master, one Angelo Tesei, a pupil of the worthy Mattei. He could already play the viola tolerably, and, thanks no doubt to Vivazza, the horn decidedly well. He worked hard not only at singing but at the cembalo and was soon able to turn both talents to practical account. At the age of fourteen he was already in some demand in the more modest theatres of the neighbourhood as chorus master and accompanist of recitatives, being paid at the magnificent rate of three lire an evening, which, as evidence of his reformed character, he dutifully handed over to his mother, now incapacitated by throat trouble from singing in public. As a boy singer he was even more successful, though no better remunerated He was continually being asked to sing in various churches, where his beautiful voice and inborn musical taste soon won him considerable popularity, and on one occasion he was engaged at one of the Bologna theatres to sing a child's part in an opera by Paer, the popular composer of the day, whom he was destined so soon to eclipse. Indeed, he showed so much promise that at the age of fourteen years and four months he was elected by acclamation a fellow of the Accademia Filarmonica, the customary subscription being waived. In view of his extreme youth, however, it was stipulated that he should have no vote in the deliberations of that august institution.

In spite of this distinction young Rossini had the wit to realise, or to allow himself to be convinced, that his musical education might be further pursued with advantage. All the more credit is due to him on this score because, as he told Ferdinand Hiller in later life, his sole ambition at this time was to be a singer. In April, 1806, he became a student of the violoncello at the Liceo Musicale, which, thanks to the benevolent despotism of the Napoleonic administration, had been instituted two years before in the buildings of what had

formerly been the Convent of St. James. At the end of
1806 his voice showed signs of breaking and he made his
last public appearance as a boy soprano. It seems to
have been about this time that he began to feel a definite
impetus towards composition. Counterpoint was added
to his curriculum in May of the following year, the
pianoforte in November, both remaining his studies
during 1808, when he seems to have concentrated
exclusively on counterpoint till his departure from the
Liceo in 1810.

But it is not generally realised, perhaps, that Rossini
had begun to write music before he had had any lessons
in counterpoint at all: an agreeable *aria buffa* for soprano
(perhaps himself) called *Se il vuol la Molinara* and
some duets for horn intended for him and his father.
Far more important, however, than these trifles were the
collection of numbers that he wrote for the Mombelli
family, destined to appear some six years later as the
opera *Demetrio e Polibio*.

Owing to their own talents, as well as the important
part they played in Rossini's early years, the Mombelli
family are decidedly interesting. The father, once well
known throughout Europe as a tenor, had in 1805
settled in Bologna with his wife, Vincenzina, a sister of
the famous choreographer, Vigano, who, it may be
remembered, collaborated with Beethoven in *Pro-
metheus*. They had two daughters, Marianna and Esther;
and father and daughters, with the help of an imported bass, established themselves as a little touring
company with a repertory suited to their idiosyncrasies.
Marianna used to dress as a man; Esther was the prima
donna. Stendhal, who heard the family perform at
Como in 1814, considered their performance excellent.

He even had a good word for the looks of the two girls, though typically regretting their reputation for "savage virtue".

Rossini himself has related the circumstances in which he made friends with this talented family. They were performing a little opera at one of the theatres in Bologna, and he, already at the age of thirteen an admirer of beautiful ladies, had been commissioned by one of them to procure her by hook or by crook a copy of one of the songs. The copyist met him with a point-blank refusal; so did Mombelli. The boy, however, not to be beaten, told him that he would get the copy just the same. So, returning to the theatre that very night, he afterwards wrote down from memory the whole piano score, which he then took to Mombelli. The tenor refused to believe Rossini's story, saying that the copyist must have played him false. "Very well then," answered the boy, "I will go to the theatre twice more and write out the whole full score." Mombelli, tickled by his delicious impertinence, made friends with him on the spot, and soon after, when he had become intimate with the family, asked him to write a little opera for them.

The teacher of counterpoint at the Liceo Musicale was Padre Mattei, a well-known academic composer and a pupil of the illustrious Padre Martini. It is to be hoped that he was more satisfactory as a composer than as a teacher. Extraordinarily silent, with a constitutional aversion from explaining mistakes, his sole idea in the matter of instruction was to write out a faulty passage correctly without any comment. At any rate, he succeeded in soon damping the ardour of his amazingly gifted if impetuous pupil. Rossini later told Wagner that he had learned far more from the study of the works of

Haydn and Mozart than from all his counterpoint lessons. That he was a considerably keener student than is usually supposed, is proved by the trouble he took to procure these scores, borrowing them, as he had no money, from a local amateur. What is more, he worked at them with exceptional diligence, his method being to copy out one part, then to supply the others on his own account, afterwards comparing them with the originals. It was these labours, combined with his enthusiasm for Haydn, at that time his favourite composer, which caused old Mattei, who had more respect than love for German music, to nickname the boy, "Il Tedeschino", or the Little German.

Mattei's excessive rigidity at first exercised an almost paralysing effect on young Rossini. For the best part of a year his natural facility seems to have deserted him; he was obsessed by the idea of all the mistakes that his teacher would discover in his music at their next lesson. Gradually, however, self-confidence began to return, perhaps because his study of Haydn and Mozart taught him that some of the licences frowned on by Padre Mattei were by no means unknown in the works of those great masters. At any rate, in 1808 he wrote a Mass to the order of an amateur player on the double-bass at Ravenna, duly performed in that city with a scratch—a very scratch—orchestra, of which, apparently, everybody in the neighbourhood wanted to be a member! He also wrote various songs for friends of the family and, most important of all, five string quartets. Some attention has been paid to these of recent years, and, if they show few traces of the influence of Haydn and Mozart as regards structure in general and independence of part writing in particular, they are decidedly agreeable compositions, with an abundance of fresh, fluent melody and occasional charming harmonic invention.

The official vindication of Rossini's academic ability, however, was a commission to write a cantata for the annual prize giving at the Liceo in August, 1808. This was entitled *Il Pianto d'Armonia sulla Morte d'Orfeo,** and the text inflicted on the young composer was nearly as pompous as the title. Such subject matter, combined with the rigorous pedantry of Mattei, still induced an unnatural stiffness in his music, for, in view of Rossini's habits, the fact that he never made any subsequent use of any portion of it is the best proof of the small regard he had for the composition. Not improbably the most satisfactory feature of the whole business was the award to him of a medal for counterpoint. He was more at his ease during the next year when he wrote, in addition to two sets of orchestral variations and a song for tenor and orchestra, two overtures, the second of which he subsequently attached to *La Cambiale di Matrimonio.* Then, in the autumn of 1810, he bade a definite farewell to Mattei and the Liceo.

The reader may already have noticed that the account of Rossini's studies current in most textbooks is by no means accurate. It is true that old Mattei continued to say for years that Rossini did no credit to his school; but this was due to Mattei's pedantry and Rossini's constitutional dislike of strict counterpoint rather than to any lack of assiduity or capacity. The story of his departure from the Liceo is even less accurate, the impression usually given being that he just walked out one day when, in answer to his question whether he knew enough counterpoint to write an opera, Mattei answered in the

*"The Lament of Harmony on the Death of Orpheus."

17

affirmative. To begin with, young Rossini did not quit the Liceo abruptly; during his last two years or so he absented himself with increasing frequency in order to earn money to support his parents, who seem at this time to have become almost destitute.

This also was the reason why he left his theoretical studies uncompleted. Mattei was satisfied, apparently, with his pupil's knowledge of counterpoint and fugue, but told him candidly that another two years would be necessary to acquire a complete mastery of Canto Fermo and Canon.* Rossini answered with equal candour that he simply could not afford the time, and the old pedant seems to have appreciated, however regretfully, the exigencies of the situation. At any rate this was the version given by Rossini to Hiller in later years. It is not always possible to accept Rossini's account of himself without reserve, but in this instance there is no reason to question its substantial accuracy; the more so because he had also told Hiller that he often regretted not to have been able to continue his studies to their logical conclusion. Whether, in view of his character and the nature of his genius, the extra instruction would have made any difference to his music, remains in any event a matter of doubt. Only the influence of a strong, sympathetic personality, capable of stimulating his enthusiasm and quickening his æsthetic conscience, could have produced any permanent effect on such a boy.

Following the example of Stendhal, whose ambition it seems to have been to link any and every event in Rossini's life with some woman or other, most of the

---

*The professional musician will probably share the author's surprise at this order of studies. Probably Canto Fermo implies what we call Plain Song; but the study of Canon after Fugue seems odd.

biographers have asserted that Rossini owed the production of his first opera to the efforts of a lady who had fallen in love with him. They appear to differ as to the identity of the lady, but on the fact of a lady they remain practically unanimous. Yet they are wrong. Heaven knows, love affairs played a sufficiently important part in Rossini's theatrical life! Extremely good-looking as a young man,* he was always, even in his most tender years, a favourite among women of every class. They found his fresh complexion, his brown, saucy eyes, his delicate hands and, above all, his winning, roguish smile, almost irresistible. But no element of romance entered into the origin of his first operatic commission.

Vivazza and his wife were friendly with a couple called Morandi, employed like themselves in the smaller operatic theatres. Rossini's mother had already spoken to Morandi of the talent of her son, but it was not till the autumn of 1810, while engaged at the San Mosè Theatre at Venice, that an opportunity occurred for Morandi to serve his friends. The repertory of the company consisted of five one-act operas, technically known as *farse*. The composer of one of these had failed to fulfil his contract, so Morandi suggested to the impresario, the Marquis Cavalli, that he might do worse than give an opportunity to the gifted student so well spoken of at Bologna.

Now it happened that Cavalli had an agreeable recollection of Rossini, the story of their meeting, not

*While Wagner was waiting in Rossini's Paris drawing-room his eye fell on a portrait painted of the composer in his 28th year, dressed in a large green coat with a red cap. Wagner, after observing that the witty expression and the ironic mouth were wholly typical of the composer of *The Barber of Seville*, remarked to his companion that such good looks must have worked havoc among the inflammable ladies of Naples. Such judgments by one expert on another are always a pleasure to record.

denied even by the sceptical and austere Radiciotti, being as follows: Cavalli a few years before had been impresario of the theatre at Sinigaglia, where his mistress, Adelaide Carpano, was the leading soprano. Rossini, then earning his three lire a night by playing the cembalo at that theatre, was on one occasion so overcome by Carpano's faulty execution of some florid passage or other that he burst into loud laughter. The furious Carpano not unnaturally complained to Cavalli, who immediately summoned the offender to his presence. When, however, he saw before him a boy of about fourteen he was so struck by the precocity of his talent, his quick intelligence and his evident desire, even in those days, to make his name as a composer, that anger gave way to interest, and he promised, should the occasion arise, to do something for him. So, when Morandi approached the impresario in the matter of the little opera, Cavalli willingly gave his consent, and young Rossini was asked by letter whether he would care to come to Venice.

His answer was to arrive at once; whereupon he was handed the libretto called *La Cambiale di Matrimonio*,* which he set to music in a few days, making use, as we have already seen, of one of the two overtures he had already written at the Liceo. At rehearsals everything went as badly as possible. Some of the singers refused to appear unless the young composer made the orchestral accompaniment less important. Morandi, with whom Rossini was staying, found the boy in tears in his room but, with his practical knowledge of operatic problems, soon showed him how to make the adjustments con-

*Literally "The Bill of Marriage," but "Marriage by Promissory Note" gives, perhaps, a better idea of the story.

sidered indispensable by the singers. At last, on the 3rd of November, the little opera was produced with definite, though not, as has been sometimes stated, brilliant, success, due in large part to the excellence of the per-formance, in which Signora Morandi, a conscientious and versatile artist, seems especially to have distinguished herself.

Apart from the fact that it was Rossini's first opera, *La Cambiale di Matrimonio* is interesting. The libretto, a story of how a rich Canadian merchant, a Mr. Slook, tries, on a strictly commercial basis, to marry the daughter of his English correspondent, Tobias Mill, but is of course obliged to renounce his claims in favour of a genuine lover, is artificial and wholly impossible if not unfunny in parts. Rossini's music certainly made the best of it. Some of the score is rather derivative, notably the overture, which, though fresh and charming, excessively reflects the more superficial characteristics of its classical models. But there are at least two attractive arias, a first-class trio with musical subjects and characters admirably contrasted, and a duel scene which for comic martial swagger could not well be bettered. The most remarkable features of the score as a whole are its gaiety and high spirits. Indeed it may be doubted whether any previous opera, Mozart's *Entführung* and Cimarosa's *Matrimonio Segreto* not excepted, had ever before been characterised by such sparkle, such a wholly irresponsible sense of fun. These, of course, were precisely the new attributes brought by Rossini into music. It is not unnatural that as a boy of eighteen he should already have possessed them; it is remark-able that he should already have known so well how to translate them into musical terms.

CHAPTER II

OPERA IN ITALY

FROM various incidents already related the reader will in all probability have gathered that operatic conditions in Italy were very different from anything that exists to-day. A more detailed picture of the world in which Rossini was now about to make his career seems, however, indispensable to any right understanding of his character as well as of his music, especially in view of the fact that during the best part of twenty years his operas were to sum up practically everything of real moment in his life.

All towns of importance and many towns of no importance at all had their opera seasons, generally three or four in the year, of which the most important as a rule was that known as the Carnival, beginning immediately after Christmas. The big theatres like La Scala in Milan and San Carlo in Naples were much as they are to-day except that in some cases the impresario responsible for the performances was able to rely not only on a handsome Court subsidy, but on the profits of the gambling-rooms attached to the theatre, doubtless well patronised in the entr'actes. But conditions in the smaller towns were very strange. Stendhal gives an amusing account of them, of which the following is a free translation:

"Some rich nobleman or other undertakes to run the theatre of the town of which he is the shining light. He

23

first gathers together a company, invariably composed of a prima donna, a tenor, a *basso cantante*, a *basso buffo* and one or two persons of minor importance. He then engages a composer to write a new opera with due regard to the voices of the company, having in the meantime paid some local hack anything from sixty to eighty francs for a libretto. The business management has probably been entrusted to the gentleman who manages his affairs in private life, usually a lawyer of incredible rascality. Lastly, he falls in love with the prima donna, and the whole town is agog to know whether or not he will give her his arm in public.

"The company, thus 'organised,' eventually gives its first performance after a month of comic intrigues which have been the source of endless gossip for the countryside. It is the greatest public event of the year in the little town; nothing in Paris can be compared with it. For three weeks eight or ten thousand people discuss the merits and defects of the opera with all the acumen that Heaven has given them and, above all, with the utmost force of which their lungs are capable. This first performance, if not blasted by some uproar or other, is usually followed by thirty or forty more performances; at the end of which the company disperses."

A realisation of the preponderant part then played by Opera in Italian life is of importance. To all intents and purposes there was no other amusement whatever available; the attention of everybody was focussed on the theatre, which served as a kind of club where all sections of the population met to discuss their business and their private affairs. Inevitably the composer of a new opera got a great deal of what we now call publicity. On his arrival in the town all the local *dilettanti* vied with each other in asking him to parties, particularly if he was a handsome and amusing fellow like Rossini. A band of acquaintances and satellites followed him wherever he went, and almost the only work he was able to do would be to familiarise himself with the characteristics of the singers and jot down ideas at odd moments. He might allow himself, perhaps, some two or three weeks of comparative or complete solitude before the date of production to compose and score the opera as a whole.

The disadvantages of such a crazy state of affairs are obvious, and explain why so much music written at the time bears the character of improvisation. Without an exceptionally facile and ready talent it would have been impossible to provide the music at all. Nor, it must be remembered, was the score ever printed, so that when a composer moved on from one town to another he was safe, particularly if the opera had been a failure, in incorporating portions of it in his new work. Unless, of course, some member of the audience happened to have been present at the first opera, when there might be some kind of protest.

On the other hand, the very casualness of the system, besides postulating a high degree of technical ability in composers, ensured the production of a vast quantity of new operas every year. Doubtless, ninety-nine per cent of them were worthless, but when, like Rossini, a composer happened to possess genius or even mere talent, he was tolerably certain (unlike his descendants at the present day) to be able to make some kind of a living. Nor was the attitude of the audience quite so nonchalant as is sometimes supposed. It is true that at an ordinary performance, alike in large or small theatres, people only

listened to certain numbers, filling in the rest of the
evening by paying visits and playing cards and having
refreshments. But this was not the case at first performances, which were followed, from beginning to end,
with attention. Moreover, the pit was always considered
a place sacred to those who wished to listen to all the
music, even the recitatives and the *arie del sorbetto* in the
second act. On the whole, however, Rossini's audiences
must be imagined as approximating far more to those at
a musical comedy or a revue than at anything which is
now covered by the term Opera.*

There is this, further, to be said for them: the evening
was extremely long. Convention demanded that every
opera seria and most operas *di mezzo carattere* should be in
two acts, the first of great length. After this first act
there was a ballet, sometimes lasting as much as an hour;
and after the second there was another ballet, mercifully
shorter. The usual duration of an evening's performance, therefore, was from half past seven till well
past midnight. Even with our now ingrained Wagnerian
fortitude it is difficult for us to understand the readiness
with which everybody acquiesced in the tyranny of this
convention; but the whole of Italian Opera was swathed
in conventions which nobody, least of all composers,
dreamed of questioning. Certain kinds of arias had to
come in definite places and be planned in definite forms;
basses were not expected to sing important roles in
opera seria, in which, as in *opera buffa*, the orchestra might
not accompany the recitatives or at any time obtrude
itself excessively on the attention of listeners. The
composer had to preside at the piano at the first three

*Those of maturer years will remember an even more exact parallel in the
behaviour of the audiences at the old Empire and Alhambra theatres.

performances of a new opera, to be hissed or applauded as the case might be.

Added to the tyranny of the form itself was the tyranny of its interpreters. Singers, even at the present day, are notoriously difficult to deal with, but at the beginning of the nineteenth century there was no question of dealing with them at all; they did what they liked. Marchesi, for instance, at the end of his theatrical career, refused to sing unless his first entrance on to the stage was made either on horseback or from the top of a hill, a helmet finished off by white feathers not less than six feet high being indispensable in both instances! Crivelli invariably insisted on her first aria containing the words, "Felice ognora," because she found them particularly convenient for the display of her vocal technique!

These, of course, remained extreme instances but the attitude behind them was typical if not universal. If the singers did not like the music provided for them by a composer they just refused to sing it; even when the music was passed as suitable the composer's troubles were by no means at an end. Rossini himself told Wagner that the composition of *arie di bravura* became a positive nightmare to him owing to the difficulty of satisfying the rival claims of the principal singers. Some of them even used to count the bars, at times refusing to appear if the aria allotted to one of their male or female colleagues was a little longer, contained an extra trill, a greater amount of ornament, and so on.

It is hardly necessary, perhaps, to explain that the reason why singers were able to dictate their terms in this manner was because the interest and attention of the public were focussed on them. Provided that an opera was not too aggressively original or unoriginal and contained two or three attractive numbers perfectly sung, it would generally pass muster. The modern reader who is inclined to feel superior may usefully be reminded that, in some degree, at any rate, a similar attitude on the part of the public is the rule rather than the exception among patrons of the cinema. Moreover, there is this to be said in favour of early nineteenth-century Italy: whereas the modern worshipper of screen divinities is too often satisfied with mere physical attraction in his or her idol, Italian opera audiences demanded a great deal more from their favourites. It was not enough for singers to have good voices; they had to know very well how to use them. Not only that. There is good reason to believe that the standard of their acting was expected to be little if at all inferior to that of their singing, and some of the singers, particularly among the rapidly vanishing race of *castrati*, were admirable musicians, capable of composing not only effective but expressive cadenzas.

The question of the embellishments provided by the singers themselves, and their eventual suppression by Rossini, is discussed elsewhere, but it must be emphasised now that they were not a mere display of acrobatics. Quite apart from definite contemporary statements to the contrary, it is clear from the effect produced on connoisseurs of the period that they were much more than that. Extemporisations of singers evoked an emotional response, not merely gaping admiration for difficulties miraculously surmounted.

Those who are fortunate enough to have heard Rosa Ponselle sing the *fioritura* passages in *La Traviata* and *Norma*, or Conchita Supervia in *L'Italiana* or *La Cenerentola*, will have had a partial glimpse, at any rate, into that strange world, so completely alien to us, in which Verdi was later to be accounted a revolutionary of the deepest dye, where the singers reigned supreme, monopolising, for all practical purposes, every means of expression, dictating terms to composer and librettists alike.

Such then was Italian Opera in the opening years of the nineteenth century. It had the merit of encouraging a certain spontaneity, a certain fluent if rather superficial craftsmanship, and a habit of excellent singing. It had driven Gluck out of Italy and still prevented any real appreciation of Mozart. Rossini dealt some shrewd blows at its most flagrant absurdities, but he possessed neither the character nor the muscle to win a complete victory, so that it eventually sapped his vitality as well as his genius. Not till the iron determination of Verdi finally bound it in chains of his own forging did it acknowledge defeat, a stubborn, wanton, but not unlovable creature.

CHAPTER III

FIRST FLIGHTS

Rossini spent the greater part of the year 1811 at Bologna where, besides conducting *The Creation* and helping to produce various operas, he wrote a cantata, *La Morte di Didone*,* for one of the Mombelli girls, who, however, did not see her way to perform it till seven years later. He also composed a second opera, *L'Equivoco Stravagante.*† It was a failure, mainly, it appears, owing to the idiocy of the libretto, whereof the main theme is the hoodwinking of one lover by his rival into the belief that the lady of their choice is really a eunuch in disguise! However, two of the best numbers, a quintet and a trio, were incorporated later into *La Pietra del Paragone.*‡ In short, Rossini's return to Bologna was by no means wholly successful. He even got into trouble with the police because, during the rehearsal of some opera or other, he became so enraged at the incompetence of the chorus that he threatened them with physical violence. At any rate, before the end of the year he was back again in Venice, where, on the 8th of January, 1812, his third opera, *L'Inganno Felice*,§ was produced at the San Mosè Theatre.

Apart from the fact that it contains some charming,

*Not *Didone Abbandonata* as usually stated.
†"The Absurd Misunderstanding."
‡The vocal score contains the overture that served subsequently in *Aureliano, Elisabetta* and *The Barber*, but Radiciotti gives convincing reasons for thinking this to be a later interpolation on the part of the publishers.
§"The Fortunate Deception."

truly individual music, notably the aria for the soprano and an overture that may be regarded as the first typical example of Rossini's essays in the form, this little one-act opera is of importance in that it was Rossini's first undiluted success. The illiteracy of the press notices was only equalled by their enthusiasm, and the opera remained in the bill until the last night of the season, when, to mark their admiration for the work and the fine singing of the leading lady, some enthusiasts let loose in the theatre a bevy of doves, canaries and guinea-fowl. Nor did its career come to an end with that particular season. It survived for some time both in the Italian and foreign repertory, to the delight of Stendhal, who compared it with the first pictures of Raphael after he left the school of Perugino, full of all the defects and awkwardness of youth, but characterised throughout by the obvious imprints of genius.

While still at Venice, Rossini received a libretto, *Ciro in Babilonia*, half opera, half oratorio, to be produced at Ferrara during the following Lent. The result was a failure, in the main deserved, though the score contains one or two good numbers. Perhaps, apart from some signs of technical progress, the most interesting thing about it is that it contains the first typical example of that storm music which the composer favoured in so many of his subsequent operas. Further, a very peculiar aria well illustrates both the habits of the time and the roguish characteristics of the young composer.

In the second act of an *opera seria* there were always some arias written for secondary characters, known as *arie del sorbetto*, thus called because during these arias it was the custom to serve refreshments in the boxes, with the result that nobody, as a rule, paid the slightest attention to them. Now when Rossini arrived at Ferrara, he found that his second female singer combined extreme ugliness with a very inferior voice, in which, however, according to his own account, there was one good note, the middle B flat. So, entrusting all the melodic interest of the aria to the orchestra, he confined her part to that note alone. The result was so unusual that for once an *aria del sorbetto* was not only listened to with comparative attention, but loudly applauded, the singer, we are told, being delighted with her success.

In the spring of 1812 Rossini was back in Venice, where, on the 9th of May, a new one-act *farsa, La Scala di Seta** was produced at the San Mosè Theatre. The theme of the libretto, based on a French farce of the same name, was considered too similar to that of *Il Matrimonio Segreto*, and Rossini's music, apparently, too elaborate as regards the treatment of the orchestra. In short, the little opera was compared unfavourably with *L'Inganno Felice*, and there seems to have been some kind of manifestation of hostility towards the composer. Nevertheless, the opera remained in the repertory until the middle of June, being subsequently revived on at least two occasions, so that it cannot be considered a total failure. Stendhal and other biographers have asserted that Rossini had packed his score with every imaginable kind of extravagance and buffoonery, but this seems not to have been the case. The overture, at any rate, with its piquant colouring and very individual freshness, is an entirely charming composition, one of the best of Rossini's early essays in the form, particularly interesting, moreover, as showing the genesis of the

*"The Silk Ladder."

crescendo idea which, a few months later, he was accused of stealing from another composer.

On the other hand, there is something rather mysterious about *La Scala di Seta*. In a letter from Rome to the impresario, Cera, of which the authenticity is quite arbitrarily denied by the over-zealous Radiciotti, Rossini wrote as follows:

"MY DEAR FELLOW,—

"In making me write music for the libretto called *La Scala di Seta*, you treated me like a boy, and I in turning out a failure only paid you back in kind. So now we're quits."*

This very characteristic communication appears to lend colour to the oft-repeated story that Cera, distrustful of Rossini's youth or talents, had deliberately given him the worst libretto at his disposal. Wherefore the composer, aware of this fact, had, to say the least, not taken any great trouble except, perhaps, as regards certain orchestral details that happened to amuse him.

Rossini had gone to Rome to assist his friends, the Mombelli family, in the production of *Demetrio e Polibio*, an *opera seria* in two acts with words by Signora Mombelli herself, which he had written for them in Bologna some five years previously. The prudent Mombelli had apparently thought it advisable not to give the music to the world until the young composer had made something of a name for himself. In all probability he acted wisely. Certainly, when *Demetrio e Polibio* was produced in Rome on the 18th of May, 1812, it achieved a definite success. Both the public and the critics liked the per-

*This may very possibly be the origin of the well-known account of Rossini's wanton trifling in the matter of *Il Signor Bruschino*, which, as we shall see, is wholly untrue.

formances of himself and his two daughters as much as they liked the tenderness and warmth of the music. Stendhal, who heard the opera two years later, more than confirmed their favourable opinion, comparing its beauties—a typical instance of his Anglomania—with those of Windsor Park, where one perfection of scenery succeeds another.

It is easy for us nowadays to see the immaturities and the weakness of *Demetrio e Polibio*, defects due in part to the amateurishness of the libretto, which, moreover, the composer never even saw as a whole, receiving (and in fact being paid for) each number singly. Nevertheless, there are some beautiful moments in it, notably the charming duet for the two girls, the finale of the first act and, especially, a quartet, of which the skill in the concluding passage surprised even Rossini himself in his later years. For it must not be forgotten that *Demetrio e Polibio* was the product of a boy of fourteen, a boy, too, only just starting to study counterpoint seriously. We are not told that he made any change in the original score for the Roman production, though he may of course have retouched it in places. In any case the opera remains one of the most remarkable instances of precocity in the history of music.

Rossini had progressed gradually from fourth- or third-rate theatres to those that may optimistically be described as being of the second order, but he had not yet succeeded in securing admission into any of the leading Italian opera houses. In the same year, however, he was enabled, thanks to the warm recommendation of the prima donna, Marcolini, to secure a commission to write a two-act opera for La Scala in Milan, the libretto being provided as usual by the management. It was *La Pietra del Paragone,** undoubtedly the best libretto he had yet had. The touchstone in question is poverty, for the hero, a certain count, pretends to have been ruined in order to find out which of three ladies professing to be in love with him really cares for him and not for his possessions. At any rate, it provided Rossini with several situations admirably suited to the display of his wit and vitality. Indeed, everybody seems agreed that *La Pietra del Paragone* was the first of Rossini's really important works. Not to mention a charming air, "Eco pietosa," a definite forerunner of the famous "Di Tanti Palpiti" in *Tancredi*, and a delicious quintet, the concerted music as a whole is admirable. It is scarcely surprising, in view of the nature of the subject and the characteristics of the composer, that one of the greatest successes of the score was a *buffo* number not only excellent in itself, but interesting as the progenitor of a particular six-eight lilt subsequently much favoured by Offenbach.

It has been said, too, that in the overture Rossini first made an extended use of the famous crescendo device which later became inseparably connected with his name. He was accused, falsely, as we have seen, of having stolen the idea from one Mosca, another musician writing for the same theatre, to the unspeakable disgust of that composer, already sore enough at seeing his opera—and for the matter of that all the other new operas of the season—thrown completely into the shade by the work of a mere lad of twenty. For *La Pietra del Paragone*, produced on the 26th of September, 1812, was a great success, achieving fifty performances during the season. It made Rossini the fashion; some have even

*"The Touchstone."

35

said that it secured as his mistress one of the most distinguished and beautiful women in Lombardy, with a charming country house where he could go to write music whenever he felt so inclined. It certainly had the important practical result of obtaining him exemption from military service, for the general commanding the troops in Milan (not Prince Eugène himself, as is sometimes said) was sufficiently impressed by the composer's genius to make an exception in his favour. Which, as Rossini remarked in later life to one of his biographers, was a clear gain to Napoleon's army.

The success of *La Pietra del Paragone* automatically placed Rossini in quite a new category among composers. He was commissioned almost at once to write two *farse* for the San Mosè Theatre in Venice as well as an *opera seria* for the Fenice Theatre itself. One of the *farse*, a two-act trifle called *L'Occasione fa il Ladro*,* is the merest trifle though an agreeable one. Perhaps the two most interesting things about it are that it was written in eleven days and, after its production on the 24th of November, achieved only five performances.† The second of the two *farse*, known both as *Il Signor Bruschino* and *Il Figlio per Azzardo*,‡ is in reality of little greater moment, but has acquired an adventitious importance owing to a legend that has grown up around it.

According to this legend Rossini, in order to revenge himself on the manager, Cera, for having saddled him with an impossible libretto, deliberately filled his score with every extravagance, every inconsequent and

---

*"Opportunity makes the Thief."

†Subsequently, however, it was revived from time to time, and was, in fact, performed in London in 1929 by the Roman Marionettes, to the delight of almost everybody who heard it.

‡"Mr. Bruschino" and "The Adventitious Son."

inapposite device imaginable. In the overture he made the second violins strike on their desks with their bows; he wrote low notes for the soprano, impossible *fioritura* for the bass, inserted a long funeral march at the climax of the comic action, and so on.

To begin with, as Radiciotti acutely points out, the story depends for its very possibility on Cera never having attended a single rehearsal; which seems extremely unlikely. Secondly, anyone who takes the trouble to spend an hour with the score will soon be convinced that the allegations are not in fact true. The libretto, a typical tangle of mistaken identity, is silly, no doubt, but not more silly than several others, and definitely superior to one or two. As for the score, so far from being an essay in mere buffoonery, it is wholly charming. The funeral march is not long and must, as a matter of fact, produce a very comic effect, accompanying, as it does, the entrance of Bruschino's errant son singing "Son pentito-tito-tito." The *buffo* aria for the bass is admirably, not awkwardly, written and, in fact, exactly resembles many of Rossini's similar arias, being, if anything, above rather than below the average. There is one of the most alluring songs for tenor that Rossini ever wrote, and the main soprano aria is equally good. Most of the ensemble writing throughout is brilliant, often very funny, and occasionally marked by a welcome sense of characterisation. The comic effect in the overture produced by the second violins tapping their desks may or may not be considered felicitous. It was very possibly intended as a kind of parody of the rhythm of the rather impressive subject which opens the overture and plays a leading part in it. At any rate, the overture as a whole, without being in any way a great composition, is the very embodiment of gaiety and light-heartedness. A charming soufflé in fact.

Though *Il Signor Bruschino* (probably produced towards the end of January, 1813) was a failure at Venice, it later won favour in several places. Offenbach had the libretto revised and produced it at the Bouffes Parisiens in 1857, apparently with success. Rossini, then living in Paris, refused to attend either a performance or a rehearsal; he had, he typically said, incurred sufficient responsibility in allowing Offenbach and his colleagues to have their way without making himself their definite accomplice.

Almost immediately after *Il Signor Bruschino*, on the 6th of February in fact, the opera which was destined to place Rossini unquestionably ahead of all his Italian contemporaries was produced at the Fenice Theatre. This was *Tancredi*. The libretto, based on the tragedy of the same name by Voltaire, is one of those essays in high romance so popular at the time. Except that the adapter provided a happy ending* to suit the taste of his audience, it followed very much the lines of the original, being equally devoid of any real action. The story, derived in the first place from Tasso, deals with one of the usual misunderstandings between the hero and the heroine which the opera librettists of the period so greatly favoured, the scene being laid in Syracuse during one of the almost equally popular conflicts between the Christians and the Moslems. It appears to us both pompous and incredible, but it gave Rossini certain situations that seem to have appealed to his

*At a subsequent performance at Ferrara in the spring of the same year Voltaire's original tragic ending was restored, Rossini rewriting the whole of the final scene. But the audience would have none of it, and the experiment was not repeated.

imagination, all the more, maybe, because Tasso was one of the very few authors with whom he had been familiar as a boy.

Tancredi contains what is, perhaps, the only genuine love music, as distinct from the music of gallantry or passion, that he ever wrote. Even in some of the recitatives, not to mention the famous aria "Di Tanti Palpiti" (said to have been written on the day before production to satisfy the demands of the capricious prima donna, Malanotte) and the beautiful andante of the duet between Amenaide and Tancredi, there is a feeling of tenderness quite exceptional in Rossini's music. There is more besides: a very effective overture borrowed from *La Pietra del Paragone*, some fine concerted writing and, above all, a care and an insight in the handling of the orchestra quite new in Italian opera. It is difficult for us to appreciate the enthusiasm aroused among contemporary connoisseurs by the orchestration of *Tancredi*, though some of it, notably the beautiful oboe melody at the beginning of the prison scene in the second act, can be appreciated even to-day. But at the time people were amazed by the new use of the wood-wind in particular and the general ingenuity with which the composer employed his orchestra to reinforce the expressiveness of the vocal line. Stendhal, who thought that the composer subsequently began to attach too much importance to the orchestra, and considered *Tancredi* the high-water mark of Rossini's achievements in *opera seria*, summed up the general opinion in a striking phrase. After comparing Rossini's orchestration and harmonic invention with the descriptive passages in Walter Scott for psychological suggestiveness, he precises his views as follows: "This is not the art, so popular in Germany, of expressing the sentiments of the characters on the stage by clarinets, 'cellos or oboes; it is the far rarer art of expressing by means of instruments that portion of their sentiments which the characters themselves could not convey to us."

The public at large, however, were entranced rather by the new vitality of the music and, above all, by the originality and charm of the tunes. All Venice, we are told, from the gondoliers to members of the aristocracy, sang snatches of "Di Tanti Palpiti" from morning till night. Even in the law courts, it is said, the public had to be ordered to stop humming the tune. Nevertheless, *Tancredi* was not the immediate success usually suggested. It is true that the overture aroused great enthusiasm on the first night and sufficed to sweep away in a moment a certain feeling of resentment that some of the Venetians had undoubtedly begun to feel against Rossini. But the rest of the opera by no means achieved the same success. Indeed, it was not even heard as a whole until the third performance because, till then, it never got further than the middle of the second act owing to the indisposition of both the prima donnas!* Popularity came gradually, in fact, after performances in several other cities. When it did come, however, it endured for very many years and eventually extended to France, England, Austria and Germany. Moreover, despite some weaknesses and absurdities more apparent to us, perhaps, than its considerable merits, *Tancredi* deserved its good fortune, if only for the fact that it first let some fresh air into the stifling, convention-laden atmosphere of *opera seria*.

---

*The hero is a contralto, a concession to the persistence of the *castrato* tradition in *opera seria*. Indeed, the part was subsequently sung by Velluti, apparently the last of his exceedingly talented if unsavoury line.

On the other hand, Rossini's next opera, *L'Italiana in Algeri*, produced at the San Benedetto Theatre on the 22nd of May in the same year, took Venice by storm at the first assault. He had written it in twenty-seven days, some say less; but press and public vied with each other in their enthusiasm for the music, which, as Stendhal well says, could not have been better suited to the pleasure-loving characteristics of the Venetians, the most light-hearted public in the world.

The libretto, based on the well-known legend of the beautiful Roxelana, the favourite slave of Solomon the Second, and already set by Mosca, bears no conceivable relationship to real life, either in Italy, Algeria or anywhere else. This story of an Italian lady (Isabella), who in company with an ineffective admirer (Taddeo) sets forth to rescue her lover (Lindoro) and then, fortunately wrecked on the shores of the very country where he is held prisoner, makes a fool of both Taddeo and Mustafa, the Bey of Algeria, is frank farce. But it is very good farce, abounding in funny situations, wily stratagems, and ridiculous expedients. One of the scenes, where Isabella persuades the infatuated Bey that, if he wants to be really up-to-date in the Italian manner, he must be initiated as one of the *Pappatacci*, an order limited to those who make it their sole duty to eat and sleep well and pay no attention to what their lovers or their wives may do, aroused much enthusiasm on its own account, though there were not wanting Puritans on the contemporary press to protest that the term *Pappatacci* in fact possessed a more questionable significance.

Beyond a doubt here was the best and most important *opera buffa* libretto that Rossini had yet handled, and he made the most of his opportunities. *L'Italiana in Algeri* is certainly the third, possibly the second, best light opera he ever wrote. Though there are still traces in the score of Cimarosa, Haydn and Mozart, the flavour of the whole is unmistakably Rossinian, for here, for the first time, we feel the irresistible appeal of the great laugh that Rossini brought into music. The outstanding feature of *L'Italiana* is the impresssion it gives, as an entity, of spontaneity, freshness and, above all, gaiety. Indeed, the succession of so many numbers tripping along, one after the other, in so sprightly and impertinent a fashion is its especial charm.

One feels loth to dissect even momentarily such a delightful butterfly, but one or two points about the music must be noticed. First, the overture, fortunately still familiar, though not heard in our concert halls nearly as often as it should be, appropriately suggests the "light and tenuous leaf" to which Mustafa's character is compared by the chorus in the first scene. Then, in addition to the grace of Lindoro's cavatina, the bubble and sparkle of his duet with Mustafa, the real inspiration of the whole of the scene in Isabella's dressing-room as well as of the *Pappatacci* initiation scene, there is the masterly handling of the "patter" throughout and the extraordinary success of the comic effects generally. But the high light of the whole score is the finale of the first act, with its sham-pompous opening chorus in praise of "Mustafa, the scourge of the women," its admirable duet between Isabella and Mustafa, her high-spirited outburst when she learns he already has a wife, and the final vivace, which positively takes one's breath away, so madly, so swiftly it rushes along. Youth and genius have rarely been more happily allied than in this delightful opera, which, it is hardly necessary to add, rapidly extended its popularity from Venice, first to the other cities of Italy and soon to those of other European countries. The achievement in the course of one year of two such brilliant and diverse successes as *Tancredi* and *L'Italiana in Algeri* gave Rossini the undisputed musical primacy in Venice, if not in the whole of northern Italy. And he was only twenty-one!

CHAPTER IV

THE triumph of *Tancredi* and *L'Italiana in Algeri* had made Rossini the most popular and famous figure in Venice; the ladies, especially, vied with one another for his favours, and it is said that a certain prima donna even threw over Prince Lucien Bonaparte for his sake. Nevertheless Rossini did not stay there, but went to Milan, where, in addition to an insignificant cantata, *Esle e Irene*, in honour of his patroness, Princess Belgioioso, he wrote two operas for La Scala. The first of these, an *opera seria* entitled *Aureliano in Palmira*, with a libretto dealing with Romans and Persians of incredible high-mindedness, and an exotic queen, Zenobia, of irresistible charm, was produced on the 26th of December, 1813. The main interest of this opera lies in the fact that for it was originally written the overture now attached to *The Barber of Seville*. Its merits, though much exaggerated by Stendhal, were not wholly negligible—in particular the first part of the duet between Zenobia and Arsace is beautiful in itself and interesting as the model from which Verdi was subsequently to draw his favourite device of expressing emotion by the repetition of a note—but it was considered to lack vitality. Moreover, the performance does not seem to have been wholly satisfactory. An attack of hoarseness forced the tenor to throw up his part during rehearsals, and a change of tenor in those days meant a change in the music. Not only that. The famous male soprano, Velluti, who signalised his first appearance in a Rossini opera by plaguing the composer with embellishments that made his music almost unrecognisable, did not even sing particularly well. Small wonder, then, that the opera at first was not an immediate success, though it subsequently met with some favour in Italy.

The second of the two operas, *Il Turco in Italia*, produced on the 14th of August, 1814, for the opening of the autumn season at La Scala, was equally, if not more, unsuccessful despite an unusually fine cast of singers. It seems that this was due not so much to the music, which contains some delightful numbers, notably a quartet, a quintet and a duet between the heroine and her husband that must be accounted one of the most plastic and varied essays of the kind ever written by the composer. The Milanese, always jealous of the Venetians, resented being given an opera supposed to be a mere pendant to *L'Italiana in Algeri*. Superficially they had a certain amount of reason on their side; the story of *Il Turco in Italia* resembles the title in being almost that of *L'Italiana in Algeri* upside-down. Had they listened more carefully to the music, they might have realised that, despite a similarity of style and a slight inferiority of quality, it did in reality possess originality and merit of its own. But they do not appear to have given it a chance, for quite a number of them walked out of the theatre after the first act. Not till seven years later was the unfortunate opera again produced in Milan.

It is scarcely surprising, after two such rebuffs, that Rossini decided to tempt fortune once again in Venice. This time, however, without success. His *opera seria*, *Sigismondo*, produced on the 26th of December, 1814, at the Fenice, met with complete and well-deserved failure, the music being judged to be almost as poor as the libretto. The only people who liked it were the members of the orchestra, who unanimously told the composer at a rehearsal that it was one of his best works! But Rossini himself was never under any illusion about it, and in later life expressed his gratitude to the Venetians, who, notwithstanding their utter boredom, had been courteous enough to refrain from any manifestation of definite hostility. He subsequently incorporated the opening chorus of the second act, as well as a crescendo, in *The Barber of Seville*, this crescendo, in fact, being none other than the famous passage in the song about calumny. Otherwise the whole score remains wholly, irretrievably, dead and buried.

It seems improbable that these misfortunes should have affected Rossini very deeply. In spite of a sensitiveness verging on the abnormal, his exuberant vitality and his naturally happy disposition, his extraordinary facility where work was concerned, his attitude towards his fellows, compounded in about equal parts of indifference and good-humoured tolerance, made him, in his younger days, fairly proof against depression. True, his musical triumphs had been less brilliant during the last year; but his personal triumphs, about which he cared very nearly as much, remained unimpaired. So we need not regard the fact that he elected to spend the spring of 1815 in complete inaction at Bologna as evidence of anything in particular, except perhaps a desire to be near his adored parents.

The times were troubled. Napoleon had escaped from Elba in February, and two months later his troops entered Bologna under the auspices of Murat, who had made himself the protagonist of Italian Independence. Local patriots, taking advantage of the presence in their midst of such a popular composer, urged him to celebrate the occasion by setting to music a Hymn of Independence written by a hydraulic engineer called Giusti, who had done his best to interest Rossini in literature as a boy. Doubtless old Vivazza, mindful of former exploits at Pesaro, used all his influence to the same end. At any rate, Rossini accepted, and the hymn was duly performed in the theatre amidst frantic applause. But the story of Pesaro was repeated only too faithfully. By the 16th of April the Austrian troops were back again, and the more ardent apostles of liberty and patriotism found themselves in considerable danger. There is a legend that Rossini, believing himself to be among their number, hurriedly adapted the music of his hymn to a completely new set of words in honour of the Emperor Francis and presented it to the general in command of the Austrian troops. It is nothing but a legend, always denied by Rossini himself; for the words in question, the work of one Monti, were not in fact written until eight months later. Probably Rossini's reputation for cynical humour, allied with the familiar tragedy of Cimarosa, who was put into prison for a similar offence, gave rise to the story. Doubtless the patriotism of Rossini was never at any time of the kind that makes martyrs. But he was not an ignoble toady, and a recent discovery in the secret archives of the Austrian police at Venice, wherein he is described as "Strongly infected by revolutionary principles," proves that he was considered politically suspect as late as 1821.

In the circumstances it can scarcely have been with any reluctance that Rossini left Bologna for Naples on the 17th of May to fulfil a contract with Barbaia, the impresario of the San Carlo and the Fondo theatres. Little is known about this contract; even the amount received by the composer is variously given as eight thousand and twelve thousand francs. It is certain, however, that Rossini bound himself to write two operas a year, to do a good deal of the executive work at both theatres, including on occasions the engagement of singers, and generally to make himself useful to Barbaia, who seems to have been an exacting taskmaster. "Had he been able," said Rossini in later years, "Barbaia would have made me run his kitchen." Even at the maximum figure Rossini's salary appears small enough, but it is said to have been augmented by a percentage of the profit drawn by Barbaia from the gaming tables in the theatre. Moreover, he was lodged and fed by the impresario and allowed on occasions leave of absence (without salary) to produce operas in other cities.

Domenico Barbaia is one of the most fantastic figures in the whole fantastic world of Italian Opera. He started life, it appears, as a bottlewasher or waiter, in which capacity he presently acquired fame and, perhaps, merit by inventing that mixture of whipped cream with coffee or chocolate which remains to this day so popular in Vienna and Naples. Using the little capital derived from this curious stroke of genius, he next combined speculation in army contracts during the Napoleonic wars with the exploitation of the gambling rooms at La Scala in Milan. These activities made him so rich that he eventually became impresario, first of La Scala itself, next of the San Carlo in Naples.

The most cruel things have been written about Barbaia by imaginative biographers. He has been presented as a kind of super-Falstaff, incredibly gross and fat, whose inability to read or write was only matched by his inability to observe the most elementary rules of decency and honesty. Every woman in all his theatres was said to be a member of his harem; every librettist, conductor and stage-hand was pictured as cowering in terror at his brutality and coarseness. The only people in the world whom he was supposed to treat with any respect were his leading lady and his cook— especially the cook. To a great extent all this is mere libel. It is clear from Barbaia's portrait that his appearance was by no means gross. He seems to have ruled his theatres strictly but not unjustly. He certainly lived with his prima donna, Isabella Colbran; but that was expected of an impresario. His illiteracy, however, comparative or total, remains beyond question. He was one of those men whom nature had gifted with a shrewdness quite independent of any education. They are by no means extinct, even to-day. Far more extraordinary was his natural flair for artistic merit of every kind, for in addition to his discrimination in musical matters, notably where singers were concerned, he had an instinctive taste for architecture. Not only did he rebuild the San Carlo in excellent taste after its destruction by fire in 1816, but he enriched Naples with an admirable church. As an impresario pure and simple, he was undoubtedly one of the most remarkable who ever lived, because, all things said and done, it is very remarkable that one who began his career washing bottles should, before he died, have directed with brilliant success the great opera houses of Milan, Naples and Vienna, and have given to the world Rossini's *Otello* and Weber's *Euryanthe*.

At the time of Rossini's arrival in Naples Barbaia's power and influence were very great. This was fortunate for the composer, because the Neapolitans viewed any musician who had not been trained in their own schools with the utmost suspicion. As Verdi had occasion to remark many years later, they regarded the past possession of so many distinguished composers as conferring upon them a kind of monopoly in musical taste and knowledge. Rossini's triumphs in Venice meant less than nothing to them. This xenophobia in general was rendered all the more dangerous by the intrigues in particular of old Paisiello, now living in retirement, and of Zingarelli, the director of the Conservatoire, who made a point of liking no music but their own and of doing everything possible to discredit younger composers.* In addition to this, a rather different style of music from that which found favour in the north of Italy was expected by the Neapolitans, who, further, demanded from their singers robustness and brilliance rather than subtlety or delicacy. Above all, there was Madame Colbran to be studied and propitiated; for, if Barbaia ruled Naples, Colbran ruled Barbaia and enjoyed, moreover, the especial favour of the Court as well.

A Spaniard, born in Madrid in 1785, she was very handsome in a Junoesque way, with black hair and dark eyes. It seems that she had the advantage not only of a voice of exceptional compass, but of a striking dignity of movement and gesture. By a curious coincidence she had arrived at Bologna to celebrate the bestowal on her of an honorary diploma by the Accademia at the same time as the fourteen-year-old Rossini received the same

---

*Zingarelli, in a conversation with Spohr, actually said that, if Mozart had only studied a little more, he would certainly have ended by writing a good opera!

honour. Her singing then created something of a furore. He may even have known her personally; he almost certainly must have heard her sing. At any rate, owing to this link in the past or natural sympathy in the present, the two seem to have got on well together from the outset. When Rossini's first Neapolitan opera, *Elisabetta, Regina d'Inghilterra,** was produced on the 4th of October, 1815, the principal part could not have been better suited to her idiosyncrasies—a sure passport to the favours of any prima donna.

Barbaia had had the libretto adapted from a play which had been successfully produced in Naples in the previous year, based in its turn on an English novel called *The Recess.* It may be summed up as a highly sentimental reconstruction of the love affair between Elizabeth and Leicester. There is no question here of Amy Robsart. Leicester is secretly and happily married to one Matilda, who is fortunate enough to save the Queen's life from the treacherous attacks of the Duke of Norfolk, thus securing full forgiveness for herself and her husband, while Elizabeth decides to renounce love in favour of politics. The story, written, be it noted, several years before *Kenilworth*, has, of course, little to do with history, though possibly not much less in reality than certain reconstructions of the love affair between Elizabeth and Essex that have passed muster in recent years. Colbran looked magnificent in her sixteenth-century costumes. The whole of Naples raved about her beauty and her talent. In fact, *Elisabetta* may fairly be summed up as little more than a glorification of the Spanish prima donna. Rossini quite deliberately and persistently devoted all his talents to this end. The

*"Elizabeth, Queen of England."

qualities of characterisation and spontaneity, so agreeable in his music, were exchanged for mere effectiveness, showy brilliance and rodomontade. The opera aroused, however, great enthusiasm on its own account. Even Spohr, who recognised its defects, considered it to be one of Rossini's best works up to that time, and Stendhal, who gives a vivid account of the first night (at which he was not present) says that it immediately dissipated all the hostility that the Neapolitans had felt against Rossini as a stranger.

Though Rossini had been at Naples during the entire summer, and *Elisabetta* was not performed until October, its actual production and composition seem to have been undertaken in a hurry. We do not know the reason; possibly the composer had needed all his time and attention to grapple with the various problems indicated above. At any rate, in addition to at least two other numbers from preceding operas, he commandeered for *Elisabetta* the overture he had written for the unlucky *Aureliano*, making use of the crescendo subject at the end for the climax of a duet between Elizabeth and Norfolk. Apart from some tender touches in the music associated with Matilda and a certain dramatic power, the interest of the opera to us lies solely in two historical points of more or less incidental importance.

Rossini, having an excellent orchestra at his disposal, not only produced a score decidedly more elaborate than usual, but for the first time provided the recitatives throughout with instrumental accompaniment. More important still, this was the first occasion on which he wrote out in full all the embellishments to be sung by the singers. He is said to have decided to do this after hearing Velluti's exploits in *Aureliano*, which, as already stated, made the music almost unrecognisable. Apparently Rossini, though he admitted that in Velluti's case the embellishments were musicianly enough, argued that a singer who happened to be less musical than Velluti might, on similar lines, produce a hopeless travesty of the original. But a decision of such a revolutionary nature was one thing; the putting of it into practice quite another, so that the fact that he was successful in getting his way argues an exceptional degree of understanding between himself, Barbaia and Colbran.

At the beginning of November Rossini took advantage of the leave-of-absence clause in his contract to go to Rome, where he had been asked by the management of the Valle Theatre to produce the *Turco* as well as to write a new *opera seria* called *Torvaldo e Dorliska*. Though Rossini's music was popular in Rome, this was a definite failure when it was produced on the day after Christmas, 1815. So much so that Rossini, who was accustomed to inform his mother of his failures by the simple process of sending her a drawing of a fiasco,* on this occasion drew an even larger one than usual. In the main, as is indicated by the press notices, the libretto, a clumsily constructed, dreary melodrama by Sterbini, was to blame. Rossini, with his usual quickness in seizing upon any situation that offered any musical opportunity whatever, achieved one or two good scenes, but everybody seems agreed that the score as a whole is quite uninspired. The orchestral writing, too, appears to have been much less interesting than usual. Rossini was the last man in the world to take trouble for nothing, and, when

*Perhaps it should be explained to those unfamiliar with Italian life that a fiasco is the bulb-shaped glass flask, with straw round the bottom half, traditionally associated with Chianti and other Italian wines. Originally it was made from a bottle that had gone wrong in the blowing; hence the secondary meaning of the word both in English and Italian.

he discovered from a chance remark that the barber who shaved him in the morning was the first clarinettist in the theatre in the evening, he drew his own conclusions, apparently only too well justified, as to the capacity of the Valle orchestra. In spite of its little merit *Torvaldo* was subsequently revived on many occasions and received the honour of production in Berlin, Vienna, Dresden, Paris (where Malibran made her début in it), Madrid . . . and Vera Cruz.

Some biographers have written as if Rossini had gone to Rome with a definite contract to write two new operas, of which the immortal *Barber of Seville** was the second. This is not the case. The contract for what was eventually to be *The Barber of Seville* was signed by the composer and the Duke Francesco Sforza-Cesarini, the impresario of the Argentina Theatre, on the 15th of December, while *Torvaldo* was actually in rehearsal at the Valle. So many inaccurate statements have been made about the production of *The Barber of Seville* that one of such comparatively minor importance seems of little moment. It has not been thought necessary, save in exceptional circumstances, to stress in this book the countless inaccuracies, whether of fact, date or opinion, that have characterised nearly all the biographies of Rossini; a mere presentation of the truth will, it is hoped, suffice. But in the case of a work so important as *The Barber of Seville*, round which, moreover, has gathered such a cloud of fiction, it is perhaps advisable to be a little more explicit.

First, then, it is not true that the Papal censorship had anything whatever to do with the choice of subject. Sforza-Cesarini had originally ordered for Rossini's use

---

*At the expense of logic I have decided to use the English titles in dealing with *Il Barbiere di Siviglia* and *Guillaume Tell*; both seem too familiar to discard.

an *opera buffa* libretto to contain an important part for the Spanish tenor, Garcia. When it arrived, he thought the plot too vulgar and refused it. It was Rossini himself who suggested to the author of the ill-starred *Torvaldo* that he should prepare in its stead a libretto from Beaumarchais's famous play. So far from this being identical with that which Paisiello had so successfully set to music more than thirty years before, both Rossini and Sterbini took great trouble to produce a new libretto thoroughly up-to-date, the active collaboration of Rossini himself in the matter remaining beyond question.

Second, it is not true that Rossini wrote to Paisiello to ask if he had any objection to *The Barber of Seville* being set once more to music. There was not the slightest reason why he should have done so. It was customary in those days for various composers to set the same libretto over and over again, Metastasio being the most favoured source on which to draw. As a matter of fact, *The Barber of Seville* had been used for musical purposes on two occasions before Paisiello's version in 1782; three Germans and a Frenchman had tackled it between that date and Rossini's production in Rome, while, by a curious coincidence, Morlacchi produced another *Barber of Seville* in Dresden at almost exactly the same time.* What Rossini and his librettist in fact did is this: they called their opera in the first instance *Almaviva* or *L'Inutile Precauzione*, informing the public in a preface to the libretto that the change of title was due to their respect for the previous achievement of Paisiello, and

---

*To round off the story, the curious may like to know that in the last year of his life Rossini accepted the dedication of yet another version, writing to the composer, a young man called Dall'Argine, a charming letter full of the praises of "Papa Paisiello" and good wishes for his success. Moreover, as recently as 1929 a final attempt, wholly unsuccessful, was made to supersede Rossini's *Barber*, which has now remained for nearly a hundred and twenty years in secure possession of the field—the best possible tribute to its merits.

explaining various departures from Beaumarchais's original text. In view of Paisiello's well-known attitude towards all other composers, it seems possible that the eminently practical Rossini was making an attempt to prevent any definite act of hostility on the part of the old Neapolitan composer. He might have saved himself the trouble.

Third, it is not true to say, as a distinguished French biographer has done, that Rossini made no use of music from his previous operas in *The Barber*. As we have already seen, he took one phrase and a chorus from *Sigismondo*, making use further of ideas (not whole numbers) from *Aureliano*, *Signor Bruschino*, and *La Cambiale*, as well as the storm music from *La Pietra del Paragone*. But the suggestion in the opposite sense, frequently made, that he handed over certain numbers to other composers, is equally untrue. It is a fact that he allowed the tenor, Garcia, to serenade Rosina with some arrangements of his own of Spanish popular tunes, but he himself had already written music for the purpose, and in fact insisted on its being restored after the first night. Nor is it a fact that a composer called Romani wrote at Rossini's request one of Bartolo's numbers. This number, "Manca un Foglio," was written by Romani when *The Barber* was produced at Florence nine months later. Unfortunately, though Rossini's original number, "A un Dottor," is infinitely superior in every respect, the Italians (not the French) have as a rule sung Romani's ever since, presumably because it is much easier. It has, however, been left in the main to foreigners to substitute for the charming music provided for Rosina's singing lesson a succession of imported show pieces, one more inept than the other. Possibly the reason is that the part is usually sung nowadays by a soprano, not a mezzo-soprano.

Lastly, *The Barber* was not produced, as Stendhal says, on the 26th of December, 1816; nor on the 16th, the 6th or the 5th of February, as stated by other biographers, including the writer of the article on Rossini in Grove's Dictionary. It is now established from documents recently published that *The Barber of Seville* was first performed on the 20th of February, 1816.

The ground having been cleared of definite inaccuracies, a moment's consideration may be given to the vexed question of exactly how long Rossini took to write his masterpiece. He himself specified thirteen days to Wagner, but on other occasions he said twelve. According to Garcia he wrote it in eight days, and various other periods have been given. What is certain is that Sterbini did not even begin to work on the libretto before the 16th of January. Thus, if we allow a week for final rehearsals and presume that Rossini started on the music a few days after the libretto was actually begun, he could not in any case have taken more than three weeks. Besides we do, in fact, know that the first act was delivered to the theatre on the 5th of February, so that a fortnight seems the more probable period of time.

It is, of course, a miracle. The mere writing down of the notes would seem to be an impossibility, quite apart from any consideration of their quality. The reader must also remember, though the overture now associated with *The Barber* was imported from *Aureliano* by way of *Elisabetta*, that Rossini originally wrote an entirely new overture on Spanish popular themes, which has since been lost.* He may, however, have done this during

---

* The score would seem, however, to have been in existence in 1865, when Arditi announced in the prospectus of his promenade concerts at Her Majesty's Theatre an "overture in B flat, originally written for *Il Barbiere di Siviglia* (first performance in England)." Unless, of course, Arditi was the victim, conscious or unconscious, of a hoax.

rehearsals. So far as any explanation of the phenomenon is possible, that suggested by Verdi, who insisted that Rossini must have had the music of *The Barber* in his head for some time before he actually began writing it down, seems the most plausible, especially when we remember that it was he himself who pressed the subject on Sterbini.

Everybody knows that the first performance of *The Barber of Seville* was a spectacular failure. The partisans of Paisiello, not improbably at the instigation of the old man himself, turned out in force to jeer and hiss, but this was not the chief trouble. Apparently the management of the Argentina Theatre was unpopular in Rome, a fact which the rival management of the Valle was not slow to exploit to its own advantage. How strong the feeling was may be gathered by the fact that, during the famous unison passage in the ensemble at the end of the first act, somebody shouted out, "Here we are at D.C.'s funeral," the allusion, with its scarcely credible bad taste, being to the fact that Duke Cesarini had died during rehearsals only a fortnight before. The account of the evening left by the original Rosina, the mezzo-soprano, Signora Giorgi Righetti, leaves no doubt of the determination of an organised opposition to ruin the opera. They roared with laughter when the tenor began tuning the guitar for his serenade to Rosina. They whistled and shouted during the entire first act. Some say that Don Basilio falling through a trap-door inadvertently left open, and a cat wandering across the stage during the first finale, completed the disaster. When Rossini rose from his seat at the piano to applaud the singers who had made such a brave fight against hopeless odds, he was roundly hissed for what was judged to be his insulting indifference to the verdict of the public. The second act was scarcely listened to at all; irretrievable ruin seemed assured. At the end he just slipped out of the theatre and went home.

Signora Giorgi Righetti says that, wishing to show her sympathy, she later went round to his house and found him sound asleep, but Giulio Fara, who has made a penetrating study of Rossini's psychology, justly doubts the truth of this. From what we know of Rossini's sensitiveness and nervousness, it is extremely unlikely that he met such an ordeal with the indifference implied.* Giorgi Righetti may well have thought she was telling the truth, and it would have been typical of Rossini, both at the time and later, to corroborate her story. After all, who is to know whether his sleep was not, in fact, a pretence? Just as he pretended at the second performance to be ill, so that he should not have to appear at the piano and expose himself once more to the hostility of the public. It seems far more likely that we have here the first instance of that nervous shrinking from public criticism which was later to play such an important part in Rossini's life. As we shall see, he was discovered on several occasions in ruses of a similar nature. But this was the first of them, and more likely, therefore, to win credence.

His extreme discomfiture did not, however, last long. After the second performance friends hurried to his supposed sickbed to assure him that the evening had been as successful as the first had been disastrous. The Romans, left to themselves and allowed to listen to the music in peace, were not slow in taking *The Barber* to

*In later life, by way of comforting the young composer, Catelani, who suffered from nerves, Rossini admitted that when he was young he often had to assume a mask of gaiety to hide his nervous terror.

their hearts, though the fact that the season came to an end a week later prevented there being a great number of further performances. Even then, however, Rossini's adversaries do not seem to have thrown up the sponge, for it is not without significance that five years were to elapse before *The Barber*, after a triumphal tour through the rest of Italy, was again produced in Rome.

Nor must it be imagined that *The Barber* won immediate and universal approval elsewhere. The English press dismissed the music as light and careless, and prophesied a short life for the opera! A well-known German musical critic, comparing it unfavourably with Paisiello's *Barber*, found the music too heavy and confused, notably devoid of the spark of genius so evident in *L'Italiana in Algeri!* Some of the French critics also professed their preference for Paisiello; others found the first finale painfully noisy and the opera as a whole lacking in cantabile tunes. Nevertheless, it did not take long for *The Barber* to win the position which it has ever since retained. The musicians, headed by Beethoven, Berlioz, Wagner and Brahms, though they might disapprove of Rossini in general, always kept a particularly warm place in their hearts for *The Barber* in particular. The public in all countries have never shown any sign of wavering in their allegiance. For more than a hundred years *The Barber*, enjoying as much esteem as popularity, has occupied a unique position in musical literature, and the opera is so well known even now that any indication of the nature of the libretto seems superfluous.

Beyond question, it was the most satisfactory, perhaps the only completely satisfactory, libretto that Rossini ever set to music. True, Sterbini, whom there is no reason to suspect of any particular talent, could not go far wrong. It is often forgotten that Beaumarchais's original *Le Barbier de Séville* was interspersed with songs; all he had to do was to follow the main outlines of the original as faithfully as he could. He must have the credit, however, for having performed his task with intelligence, and for having displayed ingenuity in turning some of Beaumarchais's best ideas, not to say actual lines, into quite tolerable verse, the Calumny song being a notable instance.

In practice, however, the glory of *The Barber* remains Rossini's alone, quite apart from any share he may have had in the construction of the libretto. Every situation, almost every idea, seems to have suggested to him one musical train of thought after another, nearly all equally felicitous. Indeed, the spontaneity of the score is such that one has an impression of music spouting from his pen, as it were, under high pressure. There are one or two defects in the second act, notably as regards excessive ornamentation, but the first act is sheer perfection, alike in the quality and the differentiation of the various numbers. One has only to think of the dramatic imagination of "La Calunnia," the sparkling bustle of "Largo al Factotum," the sophisticated ingenuousness of "Una Voce," all household words even to-day. Then there are the deft orchestral touches and, above all, the ingenuity and the mastery displayed in the handling of the various movements of the finale. No comic opera can show anything better.

Some comparison with Mozart's *Marriage of Figaro* is perhaps inevitable. In the matter of recitative and, especially, of the tenderness and the melancholy with which Mozart, reflecting his own personality, invested the characters of Cherubino and the Countess, *Figaro* possesses an undoubted superiority. But it may be doubted whether, as a setting pure and simple of Beaumarchais's text, *The Barber* is not in reality more successful. There is no real passion, much less love, in either of Beaumarchais's plays; there is gallantry, irony, wit—precisely the qualities that Rossini was able to turn into music better than any other man who ever lived. In a sense he was built on very much the same lines as Beaumarchais, both having a good deal in common with the character of Figaro, so that it is not surprising if we get the impression of Figaro's vital, mocking personality dominating everything and everybody in the opera. The naughty Rosina, the dashing Count, the repulsive Bartolo, the unspeakable Basilio, all really move and have their being in the sprightly intrigues of Figaro, who was something of a literary man before he became a barber! Anyone who has seen Beaumarchais's plays on the stage knows that this is precisely the impression conveyed by them. It was Rossini's great achievement and good fortune to have been able, apparently without effort, to convey the same idea from the beginning to the end of his opera.*

*As an indication of the scale on which composers were paid in those days the reader may be interested to know what Rossini received for *The Barber of Seville*. There were no royalties, of course, and no publication rights. According to his own account his remuneration consisted of twelve hundred francs and a nut-brown suit with gilt buttons presented to him by the impresario so that he should look well in the orchestra pit! In his famous interview with Wagner Rossini amusingly analysed this payment as working out at a hundred francs a day for each of the thirteen days employed in writing the opera, the suit being taken as worth a hundred francs. It made him, he said, feel very proud, for two and a half francs a day was all that his father had ever been able to earn by playing the trumpet.

As a matter of fact the accounts of the Argentina Theatre show that Rossini received 400, not 300, scudi as he imagined. But whether the sum total was some sixty or some eighty pounds, it does not seem an excessive price for the world to have paid for a *Barber of Seville*.

Rossini at the time of *The Barber of Seville,* from an oil painting
by Mayer in the Liceo Musicale at Bologna.

G. Rossini, lithograph by G. Grevedon in 1828

CHAPTER V

WHEN Rossini returned to Naples he found the San
Carlo burnt down, so that his next opera, *La Gazzetta*,
was earmarked for the Dei Fiorentini Theatre, where it
was produced on the 26th of September, 1816. Rossini
seems to have passed what, for him, were an uncommonly
lazy spring and summer, because, except for an insignificant cantata, *Le Nozze di Teti e di Peleo*, performed in
honour of the betrothal of King Ferdinand's niece to the
Duc de Berry on the 24th of April, and a supervision of
the first Neapolitan production of *Tancredi*, he did
nothing. Even *La Gazzetta*, originally intended for production in August, was repeatedly postponed. Perhaps
the growing attractions of Mademoiselle Colbran and
the even more insidious lure of Neapolitan macaroni
and Neapolitan oysters (two of Rossini's more particular
passions) may have played their part in the composer's
detachment. Even when *La Gazzetta* did finally appear
it met with a great and deserved failure, not, however,
mainly due to any exceptional inadequacy in the music.
True, most of it was rightly considered to be quite
undistinguished by the local critics, who might have been
even more severe had they known that a whole quintet,
words and all, had been transplanted from *Il Turco in
Italia.* Nevertheless, the opera contains one or two good
numbers, notably a love duet and a soprano aria, while
the overture, which was subsequently attached to *La*

Cenerentola, is one of the best of Rossini's less-known essays in the form. The libretto, a clumsy re-hash of a Goldoni comedy, was chiefly to blame, being voted old-fashioned and stupid. In any case, *La Gazzetta*, after a few performances, died a final death, well exemplifying Stendhal's famous dictum that music in Italy leaves few traces.

Whether from a desire to provide Mademoiselle Colbran with a striking new part, or from pique at the failure of *La Gazzetta*, Rossini was very soon ready with his new opera, *Otello*, performed by the San Carlo company in their temporary home at the Fondo Theatre on the 4th of December, 1816. This work, long considered one of the standard operas of the world, is of real importance, though rendered impossible to us by the nature of the libretto. This was not the production of the usual hack librettist but of a local dilettante, the Marchese Berio, famous in Naples for his culture and his salon, which was frequented by all the most interesting personalities resident in, or visiting the city. The Marquis's beautiful manners and even his culture—he is said to have known most of Homer, Sophocles, Corneille and Shakespeare by heart!—remain beyond question, but his ability as a dramatist can scarcely have impressed anybody outside Italy. When Lord Byron saw *Otello* he was charmed by the music but absolutely scandalised by the liberties taken with Shakespeare. As, indeed, well he might be, for, apart from the spoiling of much of the action, Othello himself is turned into a mere vehicle for one outburst of rage after another, with vanity rather than passion outraged, while Iago becomes wholly conventionalised. Even the famous handkerchief is turned into a love letter!

But the Italian contemporaries of the Marquis thought otherwise, and actually congratulated him on the tactful manner in which he had dealt with "the tremendous catastrophes of the ferocious Shakespeare." As a matter of fact, the talented Marquis must have the credit for considerable originality in having dared to retain at least one of the "tremendous catastrophes," the final suffocation of Desdemona by Othello. An *opera seria* that ended in such gloom! It was unheard of! No ordinary librettist would ever have dared to do such a thing. Berio's local reputation for good taste seems to have anæsthetised the doubtless inflamed feelings of the Neapolitans but his revolutionary boldness was by no means always condoned in the rest of Italy. Indeed, on several subsequent occasions the opera was provided with a new ending in which Othello, instead of killing Desdemona, is unexpectedly convinced by her final protestation of innocence. Whereupon, taking her by the hand, he leads her gallantly to the footlights to sing a sentimental duet conveniently extracted from another opera by the composer!

Rossini's score, though it must have been written quickly (some even say in three weeks), shows traces of exceptional care. This is especially noticeable in the recitatives, which are not only in themselves unusually plastic and expressive, but, for the first time, are accompanied throughout by the full orchestra, not by the strings alone, as in *Elisabetta*. Generally speaking, the opera may be divided into two parts: the first two acts, which are almost exclusively Berio, and the last which is very nearly Shakespeare. Inevitably, it is in the former, where the situations and the psychology are wholly conventional, that we find the greatest inequality in the music, the overture, with its curious mixture of real nobility in the andante and utter triviality in the main themes of the allegro, being more or less typical of the whole. There are fine things, it is true, in both acts, especially in the first. Thus, the duet between Emilia and Desdemona is a model of tenderness as well as of grace, and the varied moods of the finale, besides being in themselves admirably translated into music, are well woven into a musical whole. There are good points, too, about the duet between Othello and Iago in the second act, the final movement of which may well have suggested to Verdi the familiar tune at the end of the third act of *Rigoletto*. Desdemona's scena and aria must be accounted even better, for some of the declamatory passages are quite of the first order as expressive music.

The third act, however, is a masterpiece with only one defect: the introduction of the crescendo from the Calumny Song in *The Barber*, which effectually ruins the otherwise magnificent vigour of the scene between Othello and Desdemona when he comes to kill her. But the Willow Song is lovely, with "Deh' calma o ciel" as a pendant of at least equal loveliness. Another exquisite piece of music is the phrase sung in the distance by a gondolier at the beginning of the act, the words being the familiar lines of Dante, "Nessun maggior dolore, che ricordarsi del tempo felice nella miseria."* The insertion of this was Rossini's own idea, maintained in face of the opposition of the cultured Berio, who not unreasonably objected that gondoliers would scarcely be familiar with Dante. He probably realised the beauty of the melody to which he had wedded the words and

*"There is no pain greater than the remembrance of happiness in times of misery."

would not on any account sacrifice what in fact remains one of the high-water marks of his inspiration.

On the whole *Otello* is one of the very best of Rossini's serious operas. It may be true, as Stendhal wrote, that the composer resembled Sir Walter Scott in being unable to depict the passion of love, but there is much genuine dramatic emotion in the music, much grace and some strength. The very memory of the score has been obliterated by Verdi's great masterpiece on the same theme, and a good deal of it must in any case be unpalatable to us owing to the conventionality of presentation. In all probability we shall never again hear *Otello* as an opera; that is no reason to overlook the undeniable beauty of many of its pages.

With the completion of the two operas due under his contract Rossini was now at liberty again to go away from Naples. As a matter of fact, before leaving Rome, he had already promised the management of the Valle Theatre to return in the autumn to write an opera for production on the 26th of December. For various reasons neither side was able to observe the times stipulated in the contract, and Rossini did not actually arrive in Rome until the middle of December. He found even then that no libretto had been definitely selected, the Papal censorship having objected, apparently with some reason, to the subject originally suggested.

As often happened, Rossini received board and lodging from his impresario as part of his remuneration,* so he and the theatre librettist, Ferretti, spent the second night before Christmas drinking tea in the impresario's

---

*In this case the board does not seem to have been satisfactory. The Valle impresario liked food very highly seasoned, which was not at all to Rossini's taste. It is characteristic of him that he almost immediately decided to eat out at his own expense.

house and discussing possible subjects. Rossini had retired to bed, and Ferretti, who has left a vivid account of the incident, was sitting by his side, half overcome with sleep, when somehow the idea of Cinderella occurred to both of them.

"Would you write me a libretto?" said Rossini.

"Would you really put it to music?" replied Ferretti, in whom the remembrance of being passed over in favour of Sterbini a year before seems still to have rankled.

"When can I have the scenario?"

"To-morrow morning if I can keep awake."

"All right. Good night."

Whereupon Rossini turned over and immediately went to sleep. Nothing could better illustrate the happy-go-lucky methods of operatic manufacture in those days.

Ferretti kept his word. By Christmas Day Rossini had received the first instalment of the libretto known as *La Cenerentola* (Cinderella), the others arriving at regular intervals during the next three weeks. Rossini seems to have set them to music as they came, and in twenty-four days completed the entire opera, a feat all the more remarkable because, except for the overture, which he borrowed from *La Gazzetta*, and the two *arie del sorbetto*, "Vasto teatro è il mondo" and "Sventurata! Mi credea," which he handed over to a composer called Agolini, all the music was entirely new.*

When *La Cenerentola* was produced on the 25th of January, 1817, it met with a reception only less hostile

---

*Radiciotti is not wholly correct in identifying the last allegro with the Count's "Ah, il più lieto" in the finale of *The Barber*. The main ideas are the same but they are treated differently, the very characteristic and delightful run down from top A to low G sharp, for instance, being in fact peculiar to Cinderella. De Curzon and others who have stated that *La Cenerentola* is characterised by many instances of self-borrowing are, it would seem, mistaken.

than that given to *The Barber*. But, according to Ferretti, Rossini, though pained and a little stunned by the apparent failure, never doubted for one moment the eventual success of the opera. "It will be very popular in Rome before the end of the season; in the whole of Italy at the end of a year, and in France and England within two years. Impresarios and, still more, prima donnas, will end by fighting for it," he assured the disconsolate Ferretti. His prophecy showed remarkable acumen, because *La Cenerentola* over a long period rivalled *The Barber* itself in popularity, and shows signs of returning to favour even at the present time. Deservedly so, for it is a delightful opera.

The libretto has been abused by several biographers, including Radiciotti, but by no means with justice. It is true that Ferretti's version of Cinderella has nothing except its bare bones in common with the story as we know it. The fairy element is dispensed with altogether, partly, no doubt, as a concession to Rossini's well-known dislike of the fantastic, the place of the fairy god-mother being taken by an eminently practical philosopher in the service of the prince. Cinderella herself, with her talk of Paris and Vienna fashions, becomes something very like a poor little débutante, bullied by two stepsisters, who in modern parlance would certainly be termed "gold diggers," and a rascally stepfather who has embezzled her fortune. In short, nothing could be more mundane, prosaic if you will, alike in action and dialogue. But, with this reservation, Ferretti's libretto, following in its main lines Etienne's *Cendrillon*, an operatic version of the story which had met with great favour in Paris, is efficient, even at times ingenious. The action moves well and quickly; the situations are effective and often, like some of the dialogue, really funny; the characterisation is excellent, especially in the cases of the stepfather, Don Magnifico, Dandini and Cinderella herself. If *La Cenerentola* has failed to maintain a position corresponding to its merits, the responsibility cannot justly be laid upon Ferretti.

Still less can the failure be ascribed to any inferior quality in Rossini's music. For fun, sparkle and elegance, for almost everything, indeed, except profundity of feeling, the score of *La Cenerentola* could scarcely be improved upon. There is even some genuine pathos in the little song Cinderella sings to herself, and, especially, in the charming scene where she asks to be allowed to go to the ball. But apart from the excellent workmanship of the concerted music, notably the very typical and original sextet in the second act and the finale of the first, perhaps the most delightful characteristics of the opera are its thoroughgoing, unabashed lightheartedness and its astonishing wealth of musical ideas. It is impossible to particularise the excellent things, so many are they; but, as an example of gaiety, all Dandini's music must be mentioned, to say nothing of the splendid scene when Don Magnifico, half intoxicated, boasts of what he proposes to do when he is made superintendent of the princely cellars. Then there is the delicacy of the overture alike in subject and treatment, the vivacity of the opening scene, not to mention the galaxy of "patter" songs and the thunderstorm, happily conventionalised in music which remains suggestive without ever being out of character with the delicious frivolity of the opera as a whole.

In view of all these charming qualities it does seem odd

that *La Cenerentola* should not have survived in the repertory. True, the recitatives are rather commonplace; but then the recitatives of *The Barber* are in no way remarkable. True, *La Cenerentola*, with its comparatively frequent changes of scene, has not quite the direct appeal of its predecessor, apart from the latter's inestimable advantage in the matter of Beaumarchais's wit, still partly enshrined in the opera. In all probability, however, the main reason for the decline of *La Cenerentola* should be sought in the increasing difficulty of finding a cast of singers adequate to deal with it. Doubtless, the elaborate vocal ornamentation must become a trifle monotonous in any case, though there are several passages in the opera, notably where Cinderella makes her brilliant entry to the ball, where it can be justified on strictly æsthetic grounds. Whether justifiable or unjustifiable, however, the fact remains that singers of sufficient competence have during the last fifty years become increasingly rare. It is not merely a question of finding an adequate Cinderella, though, in view of the fact that she is a mezzo-soprano, this is difficult enough.*
Practically the whole cast must be possessed of consummate vocal technique if anything like justice is to be done to the music, which is far more exacting in this respect than that of *The Barber of Seville*. Nevertheless, as a work of art the score of *La Cenerentola* must be rated exceedingly high; it is undoubtedly one of the most happy products of the school of Cimarosa to which it so emphatically belongs.

While *La Cenerentola* was still captivating Rome,

*Since these words were written Madame Supervia's exploits in Florence and Paris have both justified and invalidated them. The admirable performance of herself and the cast that supported her won for *La Cenerentola* the brilliant success it deserved.

Rossini left for Bologna in the company of a friend of his, an amateur composer called the Marchese Sampieri. On the way they stopped at Spoleto to find that *L'Italiana in Algeri* was being given at the local theatre. The whim seized them to take part in the performance, so Sampieri presided at the piano and Rossini tried the experiment of playing the double-bass.

He was, of course, going to Bologna to pay a visit to his beloved parents, but he wished to be in Milan in plenty of time for the opera destined for La Scala at the end of May. He was actually installed there at the beginning of March, undoubtedly feeling a little nervous as to his reception by the Milanese. His last two operas produced in that city had been failures; the taste of Milan was said to have developed considerably, and the inhabitants, who prided themselves, not without reason, on their intellectual superiority, were inclined to be prejudiced rather than impressed by his recent successes in Rome and Naples. Hence the comparatively long period of time allowed for study of conditions generally and consideration of whatever libretto might be selected by the management.

This materialised as *La Gazza Ladra*,* an adaptation by one Gherardini of a play that had been popular in Paris two years previously. It is a half-comic, half-melodramatic story of a little servant girl, who, on circumstantial evidence, impossible to rebut owing to the necessity of shielding her father from arrest as a deserter, is condemned to death for the theft of a silver spoon which has in reality been hidden by a pet magpie. The plot is complicated by the fact that she and her mistress's son are secretly engaged, much to the mother's disgust,

* "The Thieving Magpie."

and that the Podestà,* in whose hands her fate lies, is animated by intentions towards her that are strictly dishonourable. Finally, thanks to the opportune clearing up of her father's equivocal position, the truth is revealed and everything ends happily, but not before the audience has been harrowed by some really emotional, not to say tragic, scenes. If the strange unwillingness of the father to come forward and save his daughter be considered credible, the story is effective enough; up to a point, genuinely moving. It contains plenty of varied incidents and is, moreover, entirely different from anything that had previously come Rossini's way. We know that he was enthusiastic about it and took exceptional trouble with the score. Doubtless, the realistic nature of the situations appealed to his temperament; they were as strong as the characters were well defined. He had never had such a good opportunity for an essay in contrasts.

Rossini, however, would not have been the essentially practical man he was if he had failed to turn to account what he had learnt of the present taste of the Milanese. They had lately shown a liking for German Opera with its greater stress on orchestral values. Very well; the orchestration of *La Gazza Ladra* should be more elaborate. A composer named Winter had just taken Milan by storm with an operatic prayer, then a complete novelty on the Italian stage. His librettist, too, should provide a prayer so that he might show how much better an one he could write. Nevertheless, there is no reason to think that purely artistic considerations did not come first. The style of the libretto was new; he emphasised the fact by opening his overture with two drum rolls, an unheard-

---

*More or less the equivalent of our mayor.

of innovation, which, it is said, so scandalised a certain music student of conservative tastes that he seriously thought of assassinating the composer! It is clear from the result that Rossini had gauged the tastes of his public with exceptional acumen, for, when *La Gazza Ladra* was produced at La Scala on the 31st of May, 1817, any prejudice the Milanese may have felt against him was swept away in an instant. Stendhal, who summed up the evening as the most successful first night he had ever attended, says that they were so excited after the overture that, contrary to custom, everybody began talking to his neighbour; Rossini was acclaimed again and again, and his opera remained throughout the entire season the most popular feature of the repertory.

The long and short of the matter was that *La Gazza Ladra*, owing to the variety of its moods, could scarcely fail to please in one respect or another. There was something for everybody: pathos, tragedy, tenderness and gaiety. Things of startling originality were presented in a manner that anybody could follow and understand. In this respect the overture (possibly, after *William Tell*, the best of all Rossini's overtures) is a synthesis of the whole opera. Apart from the fact that the themes are in themselves excellent, it is characterised by a directness which, though we now take it for granted, was at the time quite new. Moreover, it possesses, for a change, some links, in feeling as well as in actual musical material, with the opera as a whole. The orchestration, too, and even some of the harmonic scheme, must have seemed very bold to the original audiences. For instance, it is not without significance that Stendhal, despite his enthusiasm, singled out *La Gazza Ladra* as the opera wherein Rossini first definitely sacrificed his singers to the orchestra.

Generally speaking, the outstanding quality of *La Gazza Ladra* is the excellence of its characterisation. Thus, the feeling of rustic gaiety that permeates the opening of the first act is admirably conveyed. The lecherous old Podestà, also, is well translated into music, while the sense of trouble in Fernando's aria in the second act, with the almost Beethovenian touches in the coda, is very real. Most of Ninetta's music is highly expressive, and the concerted numbers, the trio and the finale of the first act, and, above all, the whole Judgment Scene, are beyond praise. The last, indeed, is admirable, not only as music but as drama, one of the very best examples of power and dignity in Rossini's writing for the stage. In short, *La Gazza Ladra* is an exceedingly interesting work, with a real dramatic unity between words and music. Its weaknesses and incongruities are few; its merits remarkable. Though it had a long life, especially in France, it seems now to be almost, if not quite, dead. But, of all the forgotten operas by Rossini, it is one of the most likely, perhaps, to repay the trouble of resuscitation.

CHAPTER VI

WHEREAS the operas discussed in the last chapter were all, with the exception of *La Gazzetta*, of definite significance and importance, we now come to a period characterised by numerous works which, with the exception of *La Donna del Lago*, possess little interest. This is not fair, in fact, to *Mosè* and *Maometto II*, but these operas are only known to us nowadays in the revised versions subsequently made by the composer in Paris, so that what may appropriately be termed a Rossinian tempo in dealing with the period as a whole seems to be indicated.

As a matter of fact, the opera which Rossini composed when he returned to Naples after *La Gazza Ladra* is one of the more important, and, according to Radiciotti, has been treated by the biographers in altogether too cavalier a fashion. This was *Armida*, produced at the newly rebuilt San Carlo on the 11th of November, 1817. Apparently Rossini found the libretto awaiting him on his return at the beginning of August. It cannot have been altogether to his liking, for the subject was essentially a fantastic one, as those familiar with Gluck's opera on the same theme will know, and his aversion to the supernatural and the magical has already been emphasised. At that time, however, it was only in exceptional cases that composers had anything to say in the matter of a libretto chosen by an impresario, particularly by an impresario so imperious as Barbaia, with a lady so exacting as Isabella Colbran to consider. Rossini set to work with what seems to have been unusual conscientiousness, taking exceptional care with the choruses and recitatives, experimenting in new harmonies and modulations, and writing for the orchestra with comparative elaboration. He might have spared himself the trouble, for the Neapolitan critics judged the result to be "too German," too learned altogether, disappointingly devoid of spontaneity. Nobody seems to have traced the responsibility of what must have been, in fact, rather a dull opera to its real cause—the incompetence of the librettist, a certain Schmitt. Not only is his version of Tasso's immortal story notably inferior to the other librettos on the same subject as regards poetical imagination, but it is almost totally devoid of action. In practice *Armida* is one long love scene, and its sole merit lies in the fact that it inspired Rossini to write three splendid love duets, with some of the most voluptuous music that he ever composed. Even this may have been due more to the ever-growing intensity of his feelings for Colbran than to any particular talent on the part of Schmitt. The Venusberg quality of this music was duly recognised at the time, for Stendhal says of one of the duets that "ladies were almost ashamed to praise it!" This, however, did not suffice to save the opera, which was never at any time a success in Italy, though it subsequently achieved the honour of a German translation and considerable appreciation both in Germany and Austria.

Incredible as it may appear, Rossini wrote still one more opera in the year 1817, *Adelaide di Borgogna*, an *opera seria* commissioned by the Argentina Theatre in

Rome, and produced there on the 27th of December. This extremely tiresome, medieval melodrama has nothing to recommend it, and it seems for once as if Rossini had really been guilty of the wanton carelessness with which he has often unjustly been reproached. Probably he did not write all of it; he made use of the *Cambiale* overture; he took a definite step backwards in accompanying the recitatives with the piano alone. The performance seems to have been almost as mediocre as the score of the libretto, so after little more than a fortnight the opera was withdrawn.

During the first week of 1818 he was back in Naples, where, stimulated by the desire to please Isabella Colbran or to safeguard his own reputation, he set to work in earnest on a new composition. Both Isabella and he had to look to their laurels. Her voice was beginning to show signs of wear, and, fortunately or unfortunately, her supremacy at the San Carlo had become a matter of politics. The King and the Court party were her enthusiastic supporters, while the constitutional party opposed to them were equally wholehearted in their hostility. Stendhal, whose political sympathies were with the latter, has left us a typically venomous comment on the situation as it developed a year or so later, saying that the Neapolitans would have preferred the removal of Colbran even to the grant of a constitution. As for Rossini, he had always been regarded by the musical conservatives as a wanton revolutionary. They now seized the opportunity of the return from Germany of a composer called Morlacchi to extol him at Rossini's expense. Morlacchi had written an opera entitled *Boadicea* in which they professed to find "the old-time simplicity and nobility" as contrasted with the "vain and false ornaments" characteristic of Rossini's music. It must not be thought that by these "ornaments" they meant mainly, if at all, vocal *fioriture*. It was the new importance of the orchestra in Rossini's operas, the accompanied recitatives, the harmonic audacities, the elaborate concerted numbers, that excited their ire. Probably the composer, like the singer, was too well assured of the devotion and the power of his numerous partisans to be excessively worried; but for him, as for her, a success was important. And, as was usually the case when Rossini, with the still unimpaired vitality of his twenty-six years, wanted something badly enough, he got it.

Barbaia's tame librettist, a certain Tottola, had been ordered to prepare an oratorio* for production in Lent. It was called *Mosè in Egitto*. He had taken as his subject the struggle between the Jews and Pharaoh that culminated in the Exodus. In the main the story runs on the familiar biblical lines, with one important exception. Whereas in the Old Testament Pharaoh's reluctance to let the Jews go is not definitely explained, Tottola invented a motive which had the double advantage of providing a love interest and a part of first-class importance for Colbran. It is Pharaoh's son, Osiris, afraid of losing a Jewish girl to whom he is secretly married, who persuades his father to revoke the promise of liberation twice given to Moses. So in the end the opera becomes practically a struggle between Moses on the one hand, and Pharaoh and Osiris on the other, for the allegiance of the lady in question—a highly ingenious method of making Isabella Colbran the pivot of a story

*The reader must remember that the oratorio in Italy, unlike the oratorio in England and Germany, was actually performed on the stage. It was in fact only an opera on a sacred, instead of a secular, subject.

79

which at first sight seems unpromising. She appears to have risen to the occasion, for, according to contemporary accounts, her performance surpassed anything she had yet done in nobility and expressiveness.

Rossini's success was equally great. Since he subsequently incorporated the major portion of the score in the revised version called *Moïse*, the music can more conveniently be discussed later; but it must be said at once that it possesses a sincerity and a dignity exceptional among Rossini's compositions. Nor did he achieve his success by any concession to the party opposed to him and his reforms. On the contrary. The orchestra plays an unusually important part; the choral writing is unwontedly elaborate; and, more striking still, the part of Moses himself, not to mention that of Pharaoh, is written for a bass. Hitherto convention had demanded that important parts should be assigned to basses only in *opera buffa*. *Mosè* marks the final and complete emancipation of the bass singer (already tentatively begun in *Tancredi* and *Otello*) for the purposes of *opera seria*.*

Mosè drove Naples wild with enthusiasm. Even Stendhal, who disliked equally Isabella Colbran and biblical subjects, and went to the theatre prepared for a good laugh, admitted that he had rarely been so moved. Moreover, the success was later repeated not only in Italy, but in Vienna, Munich, Dresden, Prague, Paris, Madrid and London, where, owing to the biblical inhibitions of the censorship the opera had to be produced as *Peter the Hermit*. The success of *Mosè* in Naples was all the more remarkable because the last scene

*Quite possibly this radical reform may have been due to the accident that Rossini found two exceptionally fine basses at his disposal: just as previously, in *Otello*, he had written for two tenors. Accident or not, Rossini must be credited, if not with a definite zeal for reform, at least with exceptional courage, particularly when the attendant circumstances are taken into consideration.

originally set the audience rocking with laughter. The ingenuous Tottola had apparently overlooked the difficulty of depicting the destruction of Pharaoh and his army in the Red Sea. For that tremendous catastrophe to be in any way visible to the stalls or the pit, the sea had to be raised some six feet above the level of the shore, with the result that the occupants of the boxes and the galleries had a full view of little boys opening and closing the waves at appropriate moments.

To this ridiculous, but apparently insuperable, dilemma was due the composition of the most famous piece of music in the opera, the "Prayer" that was once the idol of our grandfathers and great-grandfathers. This did not figure in the original production; it was written for the Lent performances of 1819. The usual story, that Tottola one day during the winter rushed to Rossini in a wild state of excitement, saying that he had solved the problem of the final scene, and that Rossini wrote the music then and there whilst talking to his friends, is not true. The idea was Rossini's own, for he told his crony Michotte that it was he who first wrote the music, to which Tottola afterwards fitted the words. It is difficult for us, to whom this prayer appears a very simple, though beautiful, tune, to appreciate the effect produced by it on the original audience. Yet, with its changes of key and its use of the chorus, never before employed in a number of this kind, it was in reality highly original. The excitement which it evoked in the theatre was intense. Those who had come to repeat their laugh of the previous year forgot about the Red Sea altogether. A well-known doctor of Naples told Carpani that more than forty attacks of nervous fever or violent convulsions on the part of young women of excessive musical sensibility were directly traceable to it! In England the result was almost equally striking, if less tragic, for the enthusiasm aroused by the prayer among the subscribers to the King's Theatre was such that the most influential of them offered, as a mark of his gratitude, to propose the manager for membership of White's Club! In the circumstances it is satisfactory to know that *Mosè* was the first composition for which Rossini received anything like adequate remuneration: he was paid 4,200 francs, exactly seven times as much as for *Tancredi*.

He spent a considerable portion of the summer at Pesaro. A new theatre had been built there, which the inhabitants had set their hearts on opening with an opera by their famous fellow citizen. Rossini entered into the project with enthusiasm, promising himself to produce the opera and to accompany the recitatives. The choice had fallen on *La Gazza Ladra*, and Rossini took infinite trouble to secure the best possible performance. He wished to bring with him from Naples Colbran and the admirable tenor, Nozzari, but funds did not permit of this. In the end, however, he himself secured not only an adequate cast of singers and an excellent orchestra and chorus, but a well-known choreographist, a corps de ballet, a scene-designer and the necessary artificial magpie!—a fact worth recording in view of the charge of laziness and indifference so often brought against him.

The production, which took place on the 10th of June, 1818, was, needless to say, a spectacular success. In addition to *La Gazza Ladra* there was an important ballet, *The Return of Ulysses*. Rossini's appearance in the orchestra pit was greeted with prolonged applause, and the performance, we are told, did not end much before daybreak, when a crowd of admirers escorted the composer in triumph to the house where he was staying.

One of the most enthusiastic members of his audience was no less a person than Caroline of Brunswick, Princess of Wales, then established with her motley retinue of parasites and adventurers at Pesaro. She had at first been received with open arms by the local nobility but the ubiquitous presence of the unsavoury Bartolomeo Bergami (he with whom, at her subsequent trial before the House of Lords, she was accused of "sleeping on deck under an awning") soon put an end to their assiduity. Rossini, prompted by his friends or by his unerring instinct for mundane values, seems to have sized up the situation accurately, for, when the Princess invited him to her house, he excused himself on the ground that "certain rheumatic affections in his back prevented him from performing the bows prescribed by court etiquette." Not a very convincing excuse from an active young man!

It is clear that the insult was duly noted and resented, for, when Rossini returned to Pesaro the next year, Bergami organised a hostile reception to accompany his entrance into the theatre. Much to the indignation of the inhabitants, who were beginning to make a veritable cult of their illustrious fellow citizen, there were hisses and opprobrious shouts. Apparently there was a danger that this hostile demonstration might pass from words to deeds, for the bravoes in the service of the exiled Princess of Wales, already notorious in the city for their truculence, were armed. The management, therefore, smuggled Rossini out of a side door so as to avoid any collision between Bergami's ruffians and the crowd of admirers who were waiting with torches to escort the composer to his hotel. The Pesarese, however, were not wholly disappointed. Rossini was leaving the city that very night, and on this fact, as well as the incident at the theatre, becoming known with the incredible rapidity typical of an Italian town, they decided, if they could not escort him from the theatre to the hotel, that they could at least escort him from the hotel to the gates of the city.

Immediately after his departure the local Academy, to show where their sympathies lay, decided to order a marble bust of Rossini and place it in their assembly hall, proposing further that the town council should associate itself with some public manifestation in his honour. But the Papal administration took alarm. Some of Rossini's more exuberant adherents had already been arrested for threats against Bergami and the Princess; vicious libels were current everywhere in the city. They prohibited, therefore, any kind of official action, and Rossini's admirers had to rest content with the distribution of a pompous Latin decree to accompany the erection of the marble bust in the house of his birth.

If Rossini's rheumatism was diplomatic, the throat trouble which attacked him soon after the production of *La Gazza Ladra* was genuine enough. In fact, it nearly killed him, and for two days Naples actually believed that he was dead, until the composer himself, anticipating Mark Twain, wrote to say that the report had been exaggerated. By the end of July he was well enough to attend the magnificent banquet given in his honour by his host, Count Perticari. Soon after, he went to Bologna to see his parents and incidentally to write an entirely worthless comic opera for Lisbon called *Adina*, which was only performed once, and should, apparently, neither have been written nor performed at all.

Little need be said about the two operas written by
Rossini for Colbran after his return to Naples at the
beginning of September, of which the first, *Ricciardo e
Zoraide*, was produced on the 3rd of December, 1818.
The libretto, which tells the usual story of the strife
between two incredible potentates for the hand of an
equally incredible princess, reflects even less credit on
the talents of the Marchese Berio than his handling of
Otello. The music represents a definite concession on the
part of Rossini to the tastes of the conservative faction.
Here the singers reign in undisputed pre-eminence, the
orchestra being relegated to a position of insignificance;
boldness of harmony and modulation is rigorously
eschewed. The result did more honour to Rossini's
perspicacity than to his artistic conscientiousness. Admirers and detractors, public and press, joined in
acclaiming *Ricciardo*. Yet it never attained either a long
life or wide popularity. Largely, no doubt, this must be
ascribed to the idiocy of the libretto and to the accident
that the opera demands two first-class tenors; but the
music, if not exactly worthless, is exceedingly unequal.
Hérold, who heard the opera in Florence three years
later, noted in his diary that two-thirds of it were very
effective, that there were three charming duets, a
delightful quartet and some energetic and melodious
choruses. Which, on an optimistic view, sums up
admirably the merits of *Ricciardo*, such as they are.

The second opera, produced on the 27th of March,
1819, was *Ermione*, a bungled version of Racine's
Andromaque, for which Tottola was responsible. Most of
the biographers, following Stendhal, have represented
Ermione as being a definite attempt on Rossini's part to
write an opera in the manner of Gluck. Radiciotti

85

insists that this is not so, and that even the description of the opera given by the composer himself to Hiller as being "all recitative and declamation," is quite unjustified. The recitatives, he says, are long and slovenly, the chief object of the composer's solicitude having been rather to provide Colbran with two elaborate and well-contrasted essays in pathos and brilliance, as well as to give the tenor, David, a highly effective *cavatina* suitable for insertion in any opera in which he might be appearing anywhere, at any time. Probably the association with Gluck was suggested by the comparative austerity of the second finale, which contains a fine duet and a few pages of declamatory music for Ermione absolutely of the first order; alike as regards vigour and plasticity the composer of *Orphée* need not have felt ashamed of them. But one scene does not make an opera, and, except for a novel use of the chorus, which is heard singing before the rise of the curtain, there is little else of interest in *Ermione*. At any rate it was a failure, being almost the only *opera seria* by Rossini which failed to survive its first season.

Between the composition of these two operas, Rossini occupied his time in reducing *Armida* to two acts, in writing a cantata to celebrate the recovery of King Ferdinand from a serious illness, and, as we have already seen, in retouching the final act of *Mosè*. Immediately after the production of *Ermione*, however, he left for Venice where he had been commissioned to write a new *opera seria* for the San Benedetto Theatre. In the strict sense of the term he cannot be said to have fulfilled his contract, for of the twenty-six numbers of which the opera is composed nineteen were extracted from other operas, mainly *Adelaide* and *Ricciardo*—a fact of which the

Venetians, when they went on the 24th of April, 1819, to hear the "new" opera, *Edoardo e Cristina*, were fortunately unaware. It is said, however, that a Neapolitan merchant let the cat out of the bag by innocently asking his neighbour in the stalls why the libretto had been changed! There was no question of dishonesty; the impresario knew the facts, and such a proceeding was by no means uncommon, though rarely, perhaps, on quite the same scale. At any rate, when the story became known, the Venetians, who professed none of the austerity of the Milanese in these matters, were amused rather than angry. Indeed, they voted the music delightful, and only regretted that the three gentlemen, to whose combined lack of imagination the unspeakable libretto was due, had not produced a result more worthy of Rossini's talent. In the circumstances *Edoardo e Cristina* is obviously not an opera that demands consideration, however slight. Its sole importance lies in the accident of it having been the means of introducing Rossini to Meyerbeer, who was also in Venice at the time for the production of an opera of his own, *Emma di Resburgo*.

Rossini's next opera, *La Donna del Lago*, an adaptation of Sir Walter Scott's *The Lady of the Lake*, produced at the San Carlo on the 24th of September, 1819, was of a very different calibre. It appears that Rossini first had his attention called to the poem by a young friend of his, a French student called Berton, who told him that he had found an admirable subject for an opera. Rossini then asked for a copy of the poem, and a couple of days later (rather like Beethoven in the case of Paer and *Fidelio*) told the inexplicably delighted Berton that the subject was so excellent that he would himself set it to music! The inevitable Tottola was then and there put to work.

He produced some execrable verses but a first act with several effective situations which much appealed to Rossini, and, as usual when this was the case, provided a definite stimulus to his musical imagination. Doubtless, the first act is the better, in that it includes not only the admirable finale containing the famous Chorus of Bards, but some delightful pastoral music for the heroine and chorus, to say nothing of a beautiful duet and, best of all, a graceful trio that is full of character as well as of charm. But Radiciotti has exaggerated somewhat in making such a sharp distinction between the merits of the first and second acts. The latter, too, has some good music, notably an excellent duet and trio with interspersed chorus. Still, generally speaking, the interest of *La Donna del Lago* remains primarily historical. Here we find for the first time traces of romanticism in Rossini: a real feeling for nature and for local colour, those qualities, in short, which were later to characterise his most admired masterpiece, *William Tell*.

The opera was not well received on the first night. The conservative faction, annoyed by the elaboration of the orchestral score and the concerted numbers, manifested in no uncertain manner their disapproval of what they considered to be Rossini's backsliding from the simplicity of *Ricciardo;* while the majority of the public, devoid, as always, of any fixed principle whatever, were only interested in the commonplace fireworks of Colbran's final rondo. Rossini was mortified, furious. At the end of the evening he went to Colbran's dressing-room to congratulate her on her fine performance and possibly to receive some consolation. When the management despatched somebody there to request his presence on the stage for a call, his sole answer was to deal the man a stunning blow; after which he immediately left the theatre for Milan. The incident is of importance as showing that the strain of his life had already begun to develop in Rossini that hypersensitiveness which was afterwards to become so characteristic. The sequel also was typical of the man. When he arrived in Milan, he conceived the odd idea of telling everybody that *La Donna del Lago* had been a triumphant success. But he had journeyed too slowly, for at all performances subsequent to the first the opera was extremely well received by the public, so that, by the time of his arrival, what he had intended as an ironical, self-protective joke was nothing but the sober truth. One would like to know the precise reactions of this strange man to such a strange coincidence.

In marked contrast with the hurry of his departure Rossini had proceeded in a very leisurely fashion to Milan, where he was under contract to write a new opera for La Scala, *Bianca e Falliero*. Though the libretto, based by the famous Felice Romani on a typical story of seventeenth-century Venetian intrigue, was above rather than below the average, and although he had nearly two months to write the music, the opera must be accounted one of Rossini's least creditable productions. *Bianca e Falliero*, produced on the 26th of December, 1819, shows all the marks of haste and carelessness. Considerable use is made of music from other operas; there is a return to *recitativo secco*, as well as much purely conventional writing. Few scores by Rossini are wholly devoid of redeeming features, and here, too, may be found one or two good numbers: an effective introductory chorus subsequently used in the revised version of *Mosè*, some charming music for Falliero, a quartet which so impressed its contemporaries that Pacini, who was writing an opera for La Scala during the same season, declared it alone to be worth the whole of his own score. *Bianca e Falliero* possesses two points of similarity with *La Donna del Lago*: in both the part of the hero is written for a contralto, and both achieved popularity after a disastrous first night. But unlike *La Donna del Lago*, which did in fact attain to considerable success abroad as well as in Italy, *Bianca e Falliero* never became firmly established in popular favour. The divergence of fortune accurately represents, and is, one hopes, explained by, the notable difference of merit in the two operas.

By the 12th of January, 1820, Rossini was back in Naples where his first charge was to produce Spontini's *Fernando Cortez*. Though he seems to have lavished every care on the production, Spontini's style was too severe for the Neapolitans, and the opera was a complete failure. In March, he devoted two, or even three, days to writing a Mass, in conjunction with one Raimondi, for the Feast of the Seven Dolors of the Virgin Mary. The music is lost, and the assessment of its value by contemporaries is amusingly conflicting. For instance, Stendhal and the local press exalted its beauties to the skies, while one of the priests is said to have declared that Rossini had only to knock on the gates of paradise with this Mass for St. Peter to open them, despite all his sins. On the other hand a German amateur, Von Miltitz, was disgusted by its levity and theatricalism. But then he was plainly shocked by the whole proceedings, of which he left a very revelatory account. Apparently they opened with an overture by Mayr containing a spirited dance theme, this being followed by the overture to *La Gazza Ladra*. Throughout the service the organ was disgracefully played; the orchestra tuned up as and when they fancied, and, from time to time, Rossini could be heard giving the players his instructions in a loud voice! Those familiar with the conditions that prevail in smaller Italian churches even to-day will find no reason to doubt the accuracy of this description, even if the writer's valuation of Rossini's music may have been coloured by Teutonic prejudice.

About the middle of May, when he received the libretto for the new opera at the San Carlo, Rossini embarked on more serious labours. The libretto in question, the work of a certain Duca di Ventignano, who for some inexplicable reason enjoyed a considerable reputation as a tragic poet, was called *Maometto II*, and the story, based on Voltaire, telling of the thwarted love of a Mohammedan conqueror for the Christian daughter of the Governor of Corinth, seems to us more or less indistinguishable from those of other contemporary *opere serie;* there are the usual misunderstandings and disguises, the usual poverty and improbability of plot. The Neapolitans, however, appear to have thought otherwise, for, when *Maometto II* was eventually produced on the 3rd of December, 1820, the libretto rather than the music found favour with the public. Since Rossini subsequently produced in Paris a revised version of this opera under the title of *Le Siège de Corinthe*, consideration of the music can with advantage be postponed. It must, however, be said at once that the charge of negligence and haste brought by some biographers against the composition is unfounded. The comparatively long time that elapsed between the receipt of the libretto and the date of production means little, because in July of that year there was a kind of miniature civil war in Naples, in which Rossini himself played a no doubt inglorious part as a member of the National Guard. The refutation of the charge is rather to be sought in the signs of care obvious in the score itself. There is a distinct development in the style, which has a wider sweep altogether and a certain rather sombre dignity; dramatic verities are more scrupulously observed; harmony and orchestration show signs of unusual care and thought. The contemporary public seem to have taken a dislike to the opera for these very merits, as well as for its defect of excessive length. *Maometto II* was never a success either in Naples or elsewhere. The Milanese definitely preferred Winter's setting of the same subject, and a new and happy ending had to be inserted to make it palatable to the Venetians.

Little need be said about *Matilde di Shabran,* produced on the 24th of February, 1821, at the Apollo Theatre, Rome. Almost everything connected with it seems to have gone wrong. The original librettist, a Neapolitan, had been so slow and incompetent that Rossini on his arrival in Rome was forced to have recourse to Ferretti, the author of *Cenerentola,* who obligingly provided an entirely new libretto, retaining, however, a variant of the original title so as not to invalidate the announcements already made by the management! This muddle, not Rossini's carelessness, as has often been alleged, was responsible for the delay in the production, and, moreover, gave the composer so little time to write the music that he had to make use of certain numbers out of other operas, besides calling in Pacini as a collaborator. Pacini seems to have done his work well enough, but upon the facts becoming known to the impresario of the theatre, he refused to pay the final instalment of the money due to

Rossini, who had to lay his case before the Governor of Rome in order to get it. The performance was distinctly mediocre, and on the day fixed for the dress rehearsal the conductor had an apoplectic fit. This disaster led in fact to the most interesting thing about *Matilde di Shabran*, for Paganini, who was in Rome giving concerts and had amused himself by playing each number as Rossini wrote it, came to the rescue with an offer to conduct the opera. And not only did he conduct, but, when a horn player fell ill, he played his solos on the viola as well. In view of all the circumstances, we can scarcely be surprised that *Matilde* turned out badly, though as a matter of fact the score is not without merit, particularly in the lighter parts, and subsequently achieved considerable popularity both in Italy and abroad. Incidentally, Paganini seems to have been Rossini's mainstay in Rome from every point of view. During the Carnival, for instance, the two musicians and a couple of friends decided to dress up as blind street-singers. Rossini improvised some music, and he and Paganini, disguised as women, played the accompaniment on two guitars. They must have been an odd-looking pair, for Paganini was very cadaverous and tall while Rossini was already beginning to put on flesh. Needless to say, the performance, which was given in several places, both private and public, on Shrove Tuesday, was a huge success.

The end of Rossini's sojourn in Naples was now drawing rapidly near. When he returned from Rome, Barbaia was just on the point of transferring his activities from the San Carlo to the Kärnthnerthor Theatre in Vienna; his own contract was well-nigh due to expire. Except for negotiations with Hérold for a visit to London, the rehearsal and production of Haydn's *Creation* and the composition of a cantata called *La Riconoscenza**** for his own benefit performance on the 27th of December, he seems to have done little during the remainder of the year, 1821. Possibly coming events, presently to be related, cast their shadows before. On the 16th of February, 1822, however, appeared the last of the series of his Neapolitan operas. This was *Zelmira*, based on a monotonous and wordy French tragedy which Tottola succeeded in making still more wordy, still more monotonous. But, whether from genuine liking for the music or regret at the composer's impending departure, the Neapolitan public decided to acclaim it as Rossini's masterpiece, better than *Elisabetta*, better than *Mosè*. Even if the preposterousness of the libretto did not put *Zelmira* out of court in any event, the score is far from deserving such superlative praise. From the dramatic point of view it registers a certain progress; the cut of some of the arias is new and foreshadows later developments in Rossini's style; there are two charming duets and a fine finale to the first act, to say nothing of a quintet in the second where the greatly daring composer made a bold experiment in consecutive fifths. But the care shown in harmony, counterpoint and orchestration are perhaps the outstanding characteristics of *Zelmira*, which Rossini knew would certainly be produced by Barbaia in Vienna. This much was patent even to contemporaries. Indeed, Stendhal, who flayed the libretto for its dull absurdity, declared that, whereas Mozart, had he lived, would have ended by becoming wholly Italian, Rossini might perhaps finish by being more German than Beethoven himself!

*"Gratitude."

On the day after the last performance Rossini, all his enemies silenced, left Naples for Bologna in a blaze of glory . . . and the company of Isabella Colbran. From a letter of the previous year it is clear that Rossini had for some time decided, probably at his mother's behest rather than from any urgent desire of his own, to legalise his relations with the lady. They were married on the 16th of March in a little church just outside Bologna. Interest, as well as affection and filial piety, may well have contributed to the decision, for Isabella Colbran was rich and courageously assigned half her capital and all her income to a husband seven years younger than herself. One would like to know what Barbaia, who had lost in the same year a theatre, a composer and a mistress, thought of it all. Perhaps he was rather relieved than otherwise. The Kärnthnerthor may have been well worth the San Carlo; the mistress, whose exacting whims had been the talk of Naples, had obligingly married the composer, and both were apparently not only willing but anxious to work for him in Vienna. At any rate, all three remained, except for a passing disagreement later over a matter of business, on very friendly terms. The world of opera, now as then, is not exactly one in which the more robust virtues, the nicer feelings, can be said to enjoy pre-eminence.

CHAPTER VII

END OF AN ACT

THE Rossinis, judging, perhaps not altogether without reason, a protracted honeymoon to be unnecessary, arrived in Vienna on the 23rd of March, accompanied by several members of the Neapolitan company, who had been engaged by Barbaia to appear at the Kärnthnerthor Theatre. That ex-waiter of genius had found the theatre in very low water after several years of governmental administration. His first, highly characteristic act had been to dismiss a large number of the personnel. He then introduced the Italian fashion of regular subscriptions and imported from Italy the newest operas and the best singers. Though these activities of Barbaia indubitably tended to encourage a predominant taste for Italian music in Vienna, he was far too shrewd to put all his eggs in one basket. One of his first acts had been to invite Weber, who, two years previously, had won a spectacular success in Berlin with *Freischütz*, not only to come and conduct that opera in Vienna, but to write a new one, *Euryanthe*. Indeed, *Freischütz* was the first opera seen by Rossini in Vienna, where it received its initial performance four days after his arrival. It was something of a master stroke on Barbaia's part to have thus attracted to his theatre the two outstanding personalities of Italian and German Opera respectively.

Nothing could have well been more striking than the contrast between the two men. Weber, small, sickly, averse from society of every kind, by nature bitter and envious, nourished a passion for German Opera, which, as Wagner observed to Rossini in later years, was positively fanatical. Rossini, gay, witty, still in the enjoyment of perfect health, going everywhere, knowing everybody, possessed all the sceptical tolerance of the successful man of the world. At the time the two men did not meet, but both then and later Weber pursued Rossini and his music with something very like hatred. He barely tolerated *The Barber;* he dismissed *Tancredi* as worthless; he was so annoyed by the success of *Cenerentola* and his own friends' enthusiasm for it that on one occasion he left the theatre in a rage. As Radiciotti truly remarks, Rossini was to Weber the Lucifer of music. After having heard the second act of *Mosè* he once exclaimed: "Satan can do everything, even good; but he does not often want to." As a matter of fact, it is clear that it was Rossini's success rather than Rossini's music which really irritated Weber. He could not forgive his greater popularity, the possession of a facility denied to himself.

Rossini on the other hand, whether or no, as Berlioz affirms, he ever really said that Weber's music gave him the colic, undoubtedly much admired the orchestration and originality of his overtures, and spoke to Wagner of the great creative power of his genius.

The feud between the two men had a curious ending. Four years later, when Weber was in Paris on his way to London for the production of *Oberon*, he wished to go and call upon Rossini but not unnaturally felt that his visit might be unwelcome. Rossini, hearing of this, sent word that, on the contrary, his visit would be most acceptable, later describing it in some detail to Wagner: "Immediately the poor man saw me," Rossini said, "he

thought himself obliged to confess, with an embarrass-
ment intensified by his halting French, that in some of
his criticisms he had been too severe on my music. But I
did not let him finish. 'Don't let's speak of it,' I interrupted; 'I did not read your articles and I don't know
German. The only words of your language (which is the
very devil for us Italians) that I ever managed to remember or pronounce after a heroic effort are *Ich bin
zufrieden.** I was very proud of them, and at Vienna I
used them indiscriminately on every occasion, public or
private. . . . Moreover, in discussing my operas at all
you only did too much honour to one who is of so little
account in comparison with the great geniuses of your
own country. Allow me to embrace you. If my friendship can be of any value to you, I offer it with all my
heart.' Whereupon, I embraced him warmly.

"He was in a pitiable state: livid in the face, emaciated,
with a terrible, dry cough—a heartrending sight A few
days later, he returned to ask me for a few letters of
introduction in London. Aghast at the thought of
seeing him undertake such a journey in such a state, I
tried to dissuade him, telling him that he was committing
suicide, nothing less. In vain, however. 'I know', he
answered, 'I shall die there; but I must go. I have got to
produce *Oberon* in accordance with the contract I have
signed; I must go.' "

Rossini duly gave him the letters, including one to no
less a person than George IV, and Weber, as we know,
duly died. Whatever may have been Rossini's precise
motives, he must be allowed to have won the final and
deciding trick of the rubber. His gesture may have been
prompted by courtesy and tact as much as by un-

*"I am well pleased."

adulterated kindness, but it was a singularly graceful gesture, not easy to parallel in the somewhat boorish annals of musical history.

If Weber's attitude towards Rossini was extreme, his point of view in general was by no means uncommon. Rossini had never in person previously visited Vienna, or, for the matter of that, left Italy at all; but several of his operas, including *The Barber*, *L'Italiana in Algeri*, *Tancredi* and *La Gazza Ladra* had already been performed there. Indeed, it was the triumphant success of the last-named, a year or so before, which first split Vienna into pro- and anti-Rossini factions. The extravagant claims of his admirers not unnaturally provoked the resentment of a certain section of the press, as well as of some musicians jealous for the honour of Mozart and Haydn, not to mention their own. The production of *Zelmira*, then, which took place on the 13th of April, 1822, acted as a kind of trumpet call to two armies already drawn up in battle array. There can be no doubt whatever as to how the battle went. Though Madame Rossini was indisposed and did not sing as well as usual, though the other members of the company found some difficulty, apparently, in adapting their voices to a theatre so much smaller than the San Carlo, the first night proved a great success; Rossini, who had refused to displace the exceedingly conscientious Weigl at the conductor's chair, was called before the curtain again and again. On this occasion it was the music rather than the performance which aroused the admiration of the Viennese, for Rossini, with his usual shrewdness, had gauged the effects of his "Germanism" to a nicety. After the first night, as the standard of performance improved, admiration turned to enthusiasm;

the theatre was crowded night after night. Presently, when Rossini produced opera after opera, *Ricciardo*, *Elisabetta*, *La Gazza Ladra*, enthusiasm became something very like fanaticism; the public hardly knew which to admire the more, the genius of the composer or the excellence of the singers. Nor was the success transitory. The philosopher Hegel, writing to his wife two years later, said that as long as he had enough money to go to the Italian Opera and pay his return fare, he intended to stay in Vienna. "Now I understand why Rossini's music is cursed in Germany, especially in Berlin. The reason is that it is music made for Italian throats, just as velvets and satins are made for ladies of fashion and *pâtés de foie gras* for gourmets. This music demands to be sung by Italians in the Italian manner; then there is none better."*

Nor must it be imagined that all the German musicians were against Rossini, though they might deplore the stupid excesses of his admirers. Schubert sharply differentiated his operas from the rest of the trash heard in Vienna. Beethoven himself (who so admired Barbaia's company that he told a friend he would write an opera for them) said that Rossini would have been a great composer had his teacher only given him a good licking, and surprised a certain organist and composer called Freudenberg by declaring that Rossini, though his music was the embodiment of the frivolous spirit of the times, was a man of talent and an excellent melodist, whose facility was such that he could write an opera in as many weeks as a German would take years. His own

*Rossini's music seems to have made an especial appeal to the more gloomy philosophers. Schopenhauer, it is well known, found his chief relaxation in playing arias from the operas on the flute! What the composer of *Tristan* thought of this diversion on the part of the man responsible for the philosophic concepts of his libretto has unfortunately not been recorded.

ardent supporter, the composer Kanne, wrote a detailed and laudatory analysis of *Zelmira*, while Carpani, another of Beethoven's friends, produced a pæan of praise on the subject so fulsome that one understands only too easily the irritation of Weber and those who thought like him.

Not only, according to Carpani, had Rossini shown himself in *Zelmira* to be a musician on an entirely different plane from the composer of *Otello*, *Tancredi*, *La Gazza Ladra* and all the preceding operas, but he had incorporated in it the typical characteristics of the best masters, "so that at times you seem to hear Gluck, at others, Mozart and Handel; the gravity, the learning, the naturalness and the suavity of their conceptions live and blossom again in the score of *Zelmira*. The transitions, learned in themselves, are inspired more by considerations of poetry and sense than by caprice or a mania for innovation. The vocal line, always natural, never trivial, though it expresses the words to perfection, never ceases to be melodious. . . . The instrumentation is absolutely incomparable in its vivacity and freedom, in the variety and felicity of its colouring." In brief, according to Carpani, there was enough music in *Zelmira* to make four operas. Yet Carpani, whose *Letters to Haydn* was a book much esteemed among musical people, seems to have been by no means a fool. True, he was librettist to the Imperial theatres and had himself written the verses for an extra number inserted in *Zelmira* for the benefit of a German contralto. There is no reason, however, to doubt the genuine nature of his enthusiasm.

If musical opinion was divided in its admiration of Rossini, popular opinion was unanimous. He was the hero of the day. His wit, his good temper, his beautiful manners opened to him every door in Vienna. Crowds followed him wherever he went. Partly, no doubt, owing to the considerable Italian element in Vienna, the city was introduced for the first time to demonstrations in his honour *à l'Italienne*. Thus, after Rossini's benefit night, when the composer was giving a supper to the principal members of the company, an enormous crowd assembled in front of his house, apparently in the expectation that the artists of the Vienna Opera were going to serenade the composer. In this they were mistaken but Rossini, on learning the reason of the huge concourse outside, determined that they should not be wholly disappointed. Placing himself at the piano he improvised a concert. Colbran sang an aria from *Elisabetta;* Nozzari, the last tenor aria from *Zelmira;* there were even two duets. The enthusiasm of the crowd knew no bounds. So much so, that they began to call upon Rossini himself for a song; to which he obligingly responded with a performance of Figaro's "Largo al Factotum" from *The Barber.* By this time it was two in the morning, and Rossini and his guests not unnaturally wanted to go to bed. The crowd, however, had other views, asking clamorously for more and becoming quite angry when it was clear that no more was forthcoming, so that eventually they had to be dispersed by the police.

If Rossini gave much to Vienna he received from it much in return. Previously, he can have known little of Beethoven's music except a few early quartets and piano sonatas. During his stay there he was introduced for the first time to several new quartets and, above all, to the *Eroica* Symphony This seems to have made such a deep impression on him that he ardently desired to pay the composer a visit, an ambition by no means easy of accomplishment, for Beethoven remained notoriously unapproachable. The publisher, Artaria, was first tried as an intermediary without success; next Salieri. It was Carpani, whom Beethoven much liked, who eventually procured for Rossini the desired interview.

A strange meeting! On the one hand, the thirty-year-old Rossini, elegant, popular, successful, bubbling over with the joy of living; on the other hand, the prematurely aged, Titan-like Beethoven, dishevelled and dirty, racked with care and disease. In any case, the interview must have been difficult, for Beethoven was totally deaf, and Carpani had to write down everything Rossini said. Rossini later gave Wagner an extremely vivid account of the visit, describing with much feeling how deeply he had been affected by the squalor of Beethoven's lodgings, so filthy and untidy, with large holes in the ceiling. The story is best related in his own words:

"The familiar portraits of Beethoven give a good general idea of what he looked like but no picture could express the indefinable sadness apparent in his every feature. Under the thick eyebrows his eyes shone as if from the back of a cavern; they were small but they seemed to pierce. His voice was soft and rather veiled.

"When we entered he at first paid no attention but continued to correct some proofs. Then suddenly, raising his head, he said in fairly good Italian: 'Ah, Rossini, so you're the composer of *The Barber of Seville*. I congratulate you; it is an excellent *opera buffa* which I have read with great pleasure. It will be played as long as Italian Opera exists. Never try to write anything else but *opera buffa;* any attempt to succeed in another style would be to do violence to your nature.'

" 'But,' interrupted Carpani, 'Rossini has already composed a large number of *opere serie—Tancredi, Otello, Mosè*. I sent you the scores a little while back to look at.'

" 'Yes, and I looked at them,' answered Beethoven, 'but, believe me, *opera seria* is ill suited to the Italians. You do not possess sufficient musical knowledge to deal with real drama, and how, in Italy, should you acquire it? Nobody can touch you Italians in *opera buffa*, a style ideally fitted to your language and your temperament. Look at Cimarosa; how much better is the comic part of his operas than all the rest! And the same is true of Pergolesi. You Italians have a high opinion of his religious music, and I grant that there is much feeling in the *Stabat;* but as regards form it is deficient in variety, and the effect is monotonous. Now *La Serva Padrona . . .!*'

"I then expressed my profound admiration for his genius and my great gratitude for having been allowed to voice it in person. He answered with a deep sigh: 'O un infelice!' "*

After a pause Beethoven asked for certain details about theatres and singers in Italy, whether Mozart's operas were frequently performed, and so on. Finally, with an expression of good wishes for the success of *Zelmira*, he led Rossini and Carpani to the door, his last words being: "Remember, give us plenty of *Barbers*."

Rossini told Wagner how, going down the dilapidated stairs and thinking of Beethoven's isolation and destitution, he could not restrain his tears. Carpani remarked that it was Beethoven's own fault; he was a morose old

---

*The necessary paraphrase, "O, unhappy I!" gives perhaps some idea of the dramatic misery of Beethoven's original Italian.

misanthrope incapable of keeping any friends. Rossini, however, could not drive the impression of sadness out of his mind; the sigh of "infelice" haunted his ears. That evening there was a dinner party at Prince Metternich's house. Conscious of a feeling almost of resentment against the consideration shown to himself by the brilliant society of Vienna, he tried to persuade several of the people he met to subscribe towards a permanent income for Beethoven. Nobody, however, would have anything to do with the scheme, assuring him that, even if Beethoven were provided with a house, he would very soon sell it, for it was his habit to change his abode every six months and his servant every six weeks.

After dinner there was a reception at which the whole of Viennese society was present. Among the music performed was one of Beethoven's trios, rapturously applauded. The contrast between the squalor in which the composer lived and the elegance of the surroundings in which his work was given, again struck Rossini with a sense of tragic incongruity. Later, he tried once more to do something for Beethoven, himself heading a subscription list. To no purpose, however. The answer was always the same: "Beethoven is impossible."

Rossini stayed altogether some four months in Vienna. Just before his departure, on the 22nd of July, a grand banquet was given in his honour whereat he was presented, as a token of Viennese esteem and gratitude, with 3,500 ducats in a silver vase. He gracefully acknowledged the gift by an aria in two sections entitled: *Addio ai Viennesi*. More interesting, perhaps, than this exchange of courtesies, is Radiciotti's statement that during the last few days of his stay he wrote a quick step for military band, which, seven years later, in a more elaborate form, was destined to become the famous march at the end of the *William Tell* overture.

After a quiet summer at Colbran's villa at Castenaso, which he devoted to finishing a book of singing exercises, Rossini was called in October to Verona for the opening of the famous Congress. The invitation emanated from Metternich himself, who wrote that, since Rossini was the god of Harmony, he certainly ought to come to a place where harmony was of such vital importance. It was duly accepted, and Rossini undertook to provide the music for four or five cantatas in honour of the manifold glories of the Holy Alliance. "Provide the music", is the only accurate expression that can be used, for he had no time to compose anything new. The music consisted of various pieces from his operas dished up in a form more or less adapted to cantata requirements. For one of these, *La Santa Alleanza*, an unfortunate poet called Rossi had, at express speed, to provide the words, rewriting them, moreover, three times because the censorship would tolerate no allusion to politics and no mention of either war or peace! And, as if that were not enough, the Podestà of Verona, to make assurance doubly sure, forbade the printing of them on the only too solid ground that in that case nobody would be able to understand anything, anyhow! This cantata, performed with an orchestra of 125 players, a choir of twenty-four picked voices, and a ballet, was the outstanding feature of the festival in the famous Roman arena on the 22nd of December, 1822. The proceedings (which opened with a lottery) seem to have been highly successful, though Rossini went in terror of his life at being obliged to conduct the music immediately under a huge statue of Concord, so inadequately fixed to its pedestal that it threatened to fall over at any minute. Another cantata, *Il Vero Omaggio*, was given ten days later in the theatre, where Rossini further supervised the production of two of his operas. All the chief personalities of the Holy Alliance were, of course, in attendance at these various festivities. Rossini was presented to the Czar of Russia, and sang at private parties given by Metternich and the Duke of Wellington.

By the middle of December the Rossinis were in Venice, where he had been offered the then unprecedented sum of 5,000 francs to write an opera for the Fenice. Before the new opera, however, he was under contract to produce *Maometto* suitably adapted to the characteristics of the Venetian company. To put it bluntly, *Maometto* was a disastrous failure. Owing to his unexpected activities at Verona, as well as the obligation to direct two court concerts at Venice, when the Czar of Russia and the Emperor of Austria passed through the city on their way back from the Congress, Rossini had not the time to carry out the promised alterations. The tenor, a young Englishman called Sinclair, was handicapped by insufficient familiarity with the Italian language; Colbran, who seems to have been having continual trouble with her throat about this time, had the unwonted experience of being soundly hissed. All this unfavourably predisposed the public towards the composer, and his enemies in the press openly hinted that he could not possibly find the time to write an important new opera before the end of the season. Rossini, thoroughly on his mettle, confounded all prognostications by composing in thirty-three days an extremely long and complicated opera which the whole of Europe during the next six years agreed in regarding as his masterpiece—a feat as incredible in its way as the composition of *The Barber* itself.*

The opera was the famous *Semiramide*, produced on the 3rd of February, 1823, with a libretto adapted from Voltaire's well-known tragedy of the same name by Gaetano Rossi, the author of *Cambiale di Matrimonio* and *Tancredi*. The story is in essence that of Hamlet and Orestes, with the additional complication that the guilty Queen-mother falls in love with her avenging son before she discovers his identity, and that he kills her in mistake for her lover. It is exceedingly ponderous but possesses at least the unaccustomed merits of intelligibility and sufficiency of action. The music alternately rises to the heights and descends to the depths. Nothing, for instance, could be better than the overture, which, when properly played, sounds as effective to-day as ever it did. Unlike most of Rossini's overtures, it is mainly built on themes from the opera itself; the andantino is the tune to which an oath of loyalty is taken to Queen Semiramis, and the first theme of the allegro is associated with the awe that invests King Ninus's mausoleum—which, in view of the charming naïveté of the music, might, with greater appropriateness on this occasion, be designated "Ninny's tomb." It is a splendid composition alike as regards thematic material, form, treatment and scoring, but there are at least two important scenes in the opera worthy to stand beside it. For instance, the whole of the very lengthy finale of Act I is excellent from

*Radiciotti thinks that he used some of his leisure at Castenaso to sketch out a preliminary plan of the opera, apparently basing his statement on the fact that Rossini subsequently guaranteed to a purchaser the piano at Castenaso as being the one used in the composition of *Semiramide*. Radiciotti may be right, but the evidence is not conclusive. The piano might have been moved from Venice to Castenaso later. And why, if the opera had already been put on the stocks, should Rossini have made such a point of telling Michotte, as he did, that he had written it in thirty-three days?

every point of view. This contains the famous "Qual mesto gemito" ensemble from which Verdi undoubtedly derived the idea of the "Miserere" in *Trovatore*, both the tune itself and its treatment in canon being wholly admirable. But there is more than this. The utterances of the regal ghost are most impressive in what may be termed the *Don Giovanni* "Commendatore" convention, and as for the final vivace, it provides about the best example extant of the Rossini crescendo, for the effect of excitement produced by the rushing three-four rhythm could not well be surpassed.

The scene towards the end of the second act, where the Queen's lover lies in wait to kill her son, is also of the first order. Here is a most effective and appropriate orchestral introduction, succeeded by a splendid male chorus and one of the most beautiful and expressive arias for solo bass that Rossini ever wrote. Nor do the merits of *Semiramide* end here. There is a duet between the Queen and her son in the second act that could scarcely be more effective, introduced, too, by some orchestral writing which seems to suggest that Rossini had by no means forgotten his visit to Beethoven. At least two of the arias are very pretty; several choruses are fine, and the recitatives show real power.

On the other hand, much of the music is exceedingly poor, typical instances being the opening and final choruses. In the former the entrance of the "Babylonians and strangers of both sexes" into the Temple of Baal suggests that the cult of that god was a far more frivolous and syncopated affair than is usually supposed. As for the last chorus, it is frankly absurd in its summary cheerfulness, as if intended to suggest to the audience that the gloomy end of the opera is not really a matter for them to worry about. Generally speaking, moreover, the music is too often inappropriate to the situation, the "horror" and "terror" in which the libretto abounds being frequently associated with the most trivial musical phrases. The elaboration of the vocal writing, too, is excessive throughout the opera.

Inevitably, the defects of *Semiramide* were less obvious to a public that troubled little about dramatic verities than they are to us, who have come to take a certain measure of such verities for granted. Indeed, it looks very much as if what are in fact the best portions of *Semiramide* were those that appealed least to the first-night audience, at any rate. It is not true, as has often been stated, that the opera was unfavourably received. But the audience, though they went into raptures over the overture, did not like the first act, which, as a whole, is undoubtedly superior to the second, and contains, moreover, the magnificent finale already alluded to. The opera was redeemed for them in all probability by the prettiness of the tunes and the showy brilliance of all the vocal writing —not to mention the presence of a military band on the stage, a Rossinian innovation much discussed at the time. It is only fair to add that contemporary criticism, though exaggerated in its enthusiasm, did not fail to emphasise the best features of the work, while after the first few performances the public also began to appreciate the superior beauties of the first act. *Semiramide* ran for twenty-eight consecutive nights, in fact to the end of the season, and Rossini was once more the hero of the hour. Illuminated gondolas, with an Austrian military band playing a selection of tunes from his most popular operas, accompanied him to his house. Nor was his success confined to Venice. During the next few years *Semiramide* was destined to arouse the enthusiasm not only of Italy but of France, England and Germany. Already the popularity of Rossini's music was unparalleled. In this year, 1823, Radiciotti tells us, at least twenty-three of his operas were being performed in various countries. In Spain and Portugal people would scarcely listen to any other music. In Russia, South America and Mexico he was easily the favourite composer of the day. Even the Sultan of Turkey liked his military band to play marches and arias from Rossini's operas.

And now *Semiramide* came to sum up and crown the galaxy of successes, being in fact to Rossini very much what Austerlitz had been to Napoleon The comparison is not merely fanciful. With *Semiramide* Rossini had definitely ceased to be an Italian composer and became a world figure. His astonishing and rapid triumphs in that role can only be compared with those of the great Emperor. There has never been anything quite like them in the history of music. Stendhal, writing in this very year, summarised the facts accurately enough when he said of Rossini: "The glory of this man is only limited by the limits of civilisation itself; and he is not yet thirty-two."

CHAPTER VIII

AN ENGLISH INTERLUDE

AFTER a quiet summer Rossini set out on the 20th of October for London, where he and his wife had been engaged by the impresario of the King's Theatre On the way they made a stay of nearly a month in Paris. This was the first occasion on which Rossini visited the French capital, but his music was already well known and had, in fact, provoked the usual polemics in the press. Speaking generally, it may be said that the public and the more independent musicians were for, the Conservatoire entourage against, him. Indeed it was one of the professors at this august institution, Berton, who gave him the nickname of Signor Crescendo, which subsequently became world famous and is not forgotten even to-day. On the other hand, the austere Cherubini, at this time director of the Conservatoire, does not seem to have committed himself one way or the other.

Rossini's social gifts very soon placed his personal popularity, at any rate, beyond discussion. He immediately paid to his most distinguished colleagues, Lesueur, Cherubini and so on, all the visits then prescribed by etiquette. By associating himself with a special concert, he helped his old friend Panseron to raise the money necessary to free his brother from military service—a generous gesture which Panseron never forgot. He was asked to every kind of party both in artistic and social circles; the newspapers chronicled his every movement and witticism; when he appeared at the Opera during a performance of *The Barber of Seville* he was acclaimed by the entire audience, and at the end of the performance the band of the Garde Nationale serenaded him at his house His triumph may be said to have culminated in a brilliant dinner given in his honour at the Restaurant du Veau-qui-Tette, for which the most distinguished personalities of artistic Paris had sub-scribed. Boïeldieu, Auber and Hérold represented the composers; Pasta and Garcia the singers; Mademoiselle Mars and Talma the stage; Vernet, painting. An orchestra under the direction of the famous clarinettist, Gambaro, played selections from his music with such effect, a contemporary assures us, that the guests scarcely talked at all and even paid but scant attention to the food for which the restaurant was justly famous. At the end of the dinner there were the usual speeches. Lesueur proposed the health of Rossini, to which the composer responded with the health of the French school in general and the Conservatoire in particular. Lesueur, not to be outdone, gave the toast of Gluck, who, "rich in all the resources of German learning, grasped the spirit of French tragedy and faithfully followed his model." This gave rise to a regular competition of tributes. Garcia drank to Grétry, "the most witty and one of the most melodious of French musicians," Rossini countering with "Mozart," plain and unadorned. Hérold then gave the toast of "the ingenious and pathetic Paisiello, who made the Italian school popular throughout Europe." Even Auber, though himself too shy to speak in public, felt constrained to ask Panseron to salute on his behalf the memory of Cimarosa, "the forerunner of Rossini." All the while the orchestra made heroic efforts to accompany each toast with appropriate music, and finally, at an exceedingly late hour, terminated the proceedings by speeding the guests on their way with the well-known "Buona Sera" from *The Barber*.

The banquet made a considerable stir in Paris; so much so, that a fortnight afterwards there appeared a vaudeville, of which Scribe was part author, entitled *Rossini à Paris; ou Le Grand Dîner*. An amusing commentary on the feud between the supporters and adversaries of Rossini may be found in the fact that they could not even agree about the vaudeville. The former said that it was an entire failure; the second claimed that it had achieved a great and well-deserved success. One critic found that the whole fun of the thing lay in the ridicule poured on the professors at the Conservatoire; another praised it for its just exposure of the exaggerated enthusiasm shown by Paris for a foreign composer. All of which seems to suggest that Scribe's satire was, at any rate, remarkably impartial.

On the 7th of December the Rossinis, armed with several letters of introduction given them at Milan by the Duke of Devonshire, left Paris for London. The journey, which seems to have taken six days, reduced the composer to a state of nervous collapse. A bad traveller in the best of circumstances, he not only caught a chill, but had to endure the unaccustomed rigours of a rough Channel crossing. He was still suffering from the effects when, a day or two after his arrival, the Russian Ambassador, Count Lieven, whose wife had known Rossini at Verona, came to his lodgings at No. 90 Regent Street to tell him that George IV would gladly receive him at Court; but for some time Rossini was unable to take advantage of the invitation. When his nerves did not confine him to bed, he, apparently, took a pet parrot and sat on the top of the colonnade, which then adorned Nash's fine new street, watching the traffic below. It was not until the 29th of December that he was able to go to Brighton, where the King was in residence at the Pavilion.

His Majesty, who was playing at cards with a lady when Rossini was introduced by Count Lieven, received the composer very cordially and invited him to take a hand at écarté, an invitation which Rossini prudently declined, saying he would rather not have so powerful an opponent. After a few minutes' conversation, which left such an agreeable impression on Rossini that he later told Hiller that "it was scarcely possible to form an idea of the charm of George IV's personal appearance and demeanour," the King asked if he would like to hear his band and, taking him by the arm, conducted him to the concert-room. Under the heading of "The King's Grand Music Party" the *Morning Post* of the 1st of January, 1824, gives a typical description of what subsequently occurred:

"His Majesty, with that discrimination and fine taste which so eminently characterise all his actions, in introducing Rossini into the music-room and to the principal professional Gentlemen there, commanded his inimitable band to play the Overture to the Opera of *La Gazza Ladra*, and also the beautiful concerted piece "Buona Sera," from his popular Opera, *Il Barbiere di Siviglia*. Both these pieces were performed in such a stile of superior excellence as to obtain the most unqualified approbation of the composer, who expressed to his Majesty his astonishment that such powerful effects could have been produced by wind instruments alone. At the conclusion he went to Mr. C. Kramer, the Conductor and Master of the Royal Band, bestowed upon him the highest encomiums for the masterly manner in which he arranged his music, and declared that he never on any occasion felt more gratified.

"Rossini was seated at the pianoforte and accompanied himself in two songs, one of which, an *Aria Buffa*, he gave with true comic spirit and humour; the other, Desdemona's beautiful Romance, from his own *Othello*, he sang most divinely, with exquisite pathos and expression of voice and countenance: his voice is a good clear tenor. His Majesty honoured him several times with marks of his royal approbation."

The honour shown to Rossini excited jealousy in various quarters, and many stories were circulated as to his incorrect, or actually impertinent, behaviour. The only basis for these seems to have been that Rossini begged to be excused from giving a third encore asked for by the King, and that some people were shocked because in the "Salce" song he was supposed to be suggesting the soprano voice of "one of those singers of the old Italian school, now banished for many years from the stage owing to the offence they caused to the English feelings of humanity and modesty".

That the modesty of the King, at any rate, received no mortal wound is proved by the fact that during Rossini's subsequent stay in London he delighted in singing duets with him. George had a flabby bass voice (rather like his person), and Rossini, whose natural quality was that of a light high baritone, used to sing tenor and, of course, to play the piano. It is said that on one occasion His Majesty interrupted the performance, saying that he had made a mistake in the time; to which Rossini replied with courtly irony: "Sire, you have every right to do exactly as you please; I will follow you to the grave." The spectacle of these two fat gentlemen—for Rossini by this time had already begun to put on flesh— singing *buffo* duets from *Cenerentola* and suchlike operas must have been highly diverting. It provided material for the caricaturists of the time, one of whom had a thrust at the now crystallised Toryism of the King by suggesting that he would be better employed in raising his voice on behalf of the people of England.

Small wonder, with this lead from the Court, that Rossini rapidly became the favourite of London society. His music had been immensely popular for several years, but it was rather his personal gifts which captivated fashionable London at this time. No smart musical party was complete without him. He had fixed as his fee for the appearance of himself and his wife the then extravagant sum of £50, which was gladly paid over and over again. Occasionally he received much more. A certain member of the peerage paid him £200 for two evenings, and a rich Jew, for one only, presented him with shares which he subsequently sold for £300. Sometimes he, as well as she, sang, but as a rule he only acted as accompanist. Further, he appeared with some regularity at the musical matinées which took place every Thursday at the house of Prince Leopold of Saxe-Coburg, where the future King of the Belgians and the Duchess of Kent, both excellent amateur singers, used to sing duets. This, in fact, was the scene of the exploits with George IV already described. He even gave singing lessons; they were few but exceedingly well paid.

It may well be asked where the more serious musical objects of his visit to London came in; to which the reply must be that they scarcely came in at all. He was to have composed an opera, and did, in fact, write the first act, but, owing to the bankruptcy of the management of the King's Theatre, or for some other reason, the score was never completed. The whole incident is very obscure, for nobody seems certain even of the title of the opera in question, which is variously designated as *Ugo, Re d'Italia* and *La Figlia dell'Aria*. It gave rise to a certain amount of rather bitter comment in the press, which pointed out with perfect justice that Rossini's professional activities in London appeared to be limited to a few formal appearances at the piano in the orchestra pit on the occasion of productions of *The Barber, Zelmira, Semiramide* and other operas. He did, however, honour London by one composition, an octet for voices entitled *Il Pianto delle Muse in Morte di Lord Byron.** Even here one of the most important movements was extracted from *Maometto*, and the *Morning Post* and the musical periodical, *Harmonicon*, do not seem to have been so far wrong in their unfavourable judgment of the music as Radiciotti would like us to believe. It was given at the second of two concerts organised at Almack's for Rossini's benefit during the second week in June. The tickets cost £2; the principal Italian artists then in London gave their services; the hall was packed, not improbably owing to the fact that Rossini himself sang the part of Apollo, so that the results must have been extremely profitable.

Which, to be frank, was the whole aim and object of all Rossini's activities in London. He was singularly

*"The Lament of the Muses for the death of Lord Byron."

successful, for he went away after six months the richer by about 175,000 francs, a phenomenal sum for that time. He should not be charged with exceptional cupidity. London was then the milch-cow of every foreign musician, regarded, not without reason, as a source of income rather than as a musical centre. English music had in truth sunk to about the lowest depths of its too often depressed history. The fashionables of London would certainly have been indifferent to the fact, even had they known it, that Samuel Wesley, the only English musician of genius, had sufficiently recovered from his mental derangement to undertake the duties of organist at Camden Town They were more likely to have heard that a composer, devoid of genius but not of charm, called Henry Bishop, had, a year previously, written an opera containing a pretty tune entitled "Home, Sweet Home." There was nothing else for them to know, for even Balfe was still a mere lad playing in the orchestra at Drury Lane. Not that they would have known anything in any case, for their ignorance seems to have been positively sublime. They were the prey of every quack and charlatan, a fact on which Rossini himself commented, citing the instances of a second-rate flautist who earned quite a good living as a teacher of the piano and of singing, and of another highly successful *maestro* so musically illiterate that, before giving a lesson on a song, he had himself to be taught the notes by his accompanist!

In the circumstances it can scarcely be a matter of surprise that concerts, whether public or private, were regarded primarily as encouragements to conversation, the only exception being when the performer was too famous to be ignored. In short, names counted for everything, excellence of performance for nothing. Rossini told Hiller an amusing story as evidence of this: "I made a lot of money in London, not so much as a composer as an accompanist. To tell the truth, when I was in Italy I would never accept money for accompanying; it went against the grain. But in London it was the custom, so I followed it like everybody else. . . . Besides, musicians over there have no other object except to make money, and I saw some fine instances of this. The first time I took part in a soirée I found there the celebrated horn player, Buzzi, and the famous double-bass player, Dragonetti. I naturally thought that they had been engaged to play solos Not a bit of it; all they had to do was to help me accompany. 'Have you got your parts?' I asked them. 'No,' they answered, 'we improvise!' Yet they were being very highly paid. As these tentative attempts at instrumentation seemed to me rather dangerous, I suggested that Dragonetti should do a pizzicato or two when I winked at him, and Buzzi fill up the final cadenzas with a few notes. So the whole thing went off without any mishap, and the audience was completely satisfied."

Rossini would have been more than human had he failed to take advantage of conditions like these; and he was very human indeed, especially where money was concerned. However, one of his experiences in England may at least have interested him for its own sake. This was his visit to Cambridge for the annual musical festival during the first week in July, 1824. He played the organ in Great St. Mary's, and in the Senate House he not only sang a duet from *Il Matrimonio Segreto* with the well-known soprano, Catalani, but accompanied himself in "Largo al Factotum " His success as a comic singer was extraordinary. Also, we are told, he took a noticeably enthusiastic part in the chorus of "God Save the King" which terminated the proceedings.

On the 26th of July the Rossinis left London. As a final mark of his esteem King George asked the Duke of Wellington to give an evening party so that he might hear Rossini once more before bidding him farewell. It is pleasant to know that the composer quitted our shores, if with no very high opinion of English musical capacity, at least with a real liking for London (except on Sundays, when he found it very boring), and with a genuine appreciation of English hospitality and generosity. "During my stay in England," he told Hiller, "I received attentions which it would be difficult to parallel elsewhere." In retrospect he may well have looked back on his visit as the climax of a period when he enjoyed continuous health and happiness almost for the last time in his life.

CHAPTER IX

WHILE still in London, Rossini had been called to the French Embassy to sign a contract that ensured a year's residence in Paris as a composer. During his previous stay in the French capital he had been asked to assume the direction of the Théâtre Italien, but had refused the offer in order to avoid wounding the susceptibilities of Paer, at that time the director. Then he himself suggested an alternative scheme, rejected by the Minister of Fine Arts as too expensive. But Rossini's success in London, and rumours of tempting offers to induce him to stay there, frightened the French Ambassador (who, unlike our own diplomatic representatives, then as now, did not consider artistic matters unworthy of his notice), and he warned his Government that they had better take some definite step unless they wanted to lose Rossini altogether. The result was an embodiment of his original proposals in contract form.

When, however, he returned to Paris in August, 1824, he found the Court in general and the Minister of Fine Arts in particular so anxious to see him at the Théâtre Italien that he was induced to tear up the London contract and take command. With rare generosity or remarkable acumen he stipulated that Paer, who had always worked against him in Paris, should retain his salary and functions, he himself assuming general control at a yearly salary of 20,000 francs, with free quarters

and remuneration on a fixed, and by no means un-
generous, scale for operas to be written either in French
or Italian. Though the terms of the London contract
were, if anything, more advantageous from the purely
financial point of view, there were several inducements
for the change. First, the prestige of the Théâtre Italien,
which, unlike the Italian Theatre in London, was an
official institution linked with, though subordinate to,
the Opera itself. Ever since the days of the great
Napoleon it had been the main vehicle for bringing
Italian music to France. Indeed, Napoleon, who always
remained a thorough Italian in musical matters, founded
it with that very object.

Further, it seems as if Paer's administration had left
a good deal to be desired in the matter of performances,
and Rossini's operas were not likely to have received any
especial consideration from a rival composer who so
cordially disliked their begetter. The best of the French
biographers is indeed emphatic in stating that, till
Rossini took control, none of his operas, despite the huge
success of *The Barber* in 1820, of *Otello*, *La Gazza Ladra*
and *Cenerentola* in the following years, had ever been
properly given, and that one of Rossini's main objects
was to let the Parisians know how they should sound.
He certainly made some important changes, appointing
Hérold chorus-master and recruiting from Italy new
singers on whom he could rely. It may have been partly
with this object, as well as from a desire to see old Vivazza
and the adored Anna, that he paid a short visit to
Bologna in September before definitely taking up his new
duties on December 1st.

It cannot be said that his administration was wholly
successful. True, the standard of performances improved

notably, but the public complained, not without reason, of the lack of novelties. The sole opera that Rossini actually wrote for the Théâtre Italien was *Il Viaggio a Reims o l'Albergo del Giglio d'Oro*,* a kind of cantata-opera in one act rather hastily improvised in honour of the coronation of Charles X. Produced on the 19th of June, 1825, it was withdrawn by the composer himself after three performances. In view of the fact that he subsequently used the best of the music in *Le Comte Ory*, nothing need be said about the score, some of which was not even new. The most striking thing about it was the incorporation in a banquet scene of no less than seven national tunes, including "God Save the King" and the Austrian National Anthem; which, as a contemporary critic acidly observed, seemed a heavy kind of accompaniment for dessert, especially after such a long dinner. For everything in *Il Viaggio* is long, and appeared even more so owing to the lack of action in the libretto. Not improbably it holds the record for length among one-act operas; the performance, we are told, lasted three hours. Nevertheless, *Il Viaggio* cannot be written off as a total failure. Twenty-three years later, an enterprising impresario disinterred it and changed the title and the story to fit the circumstances of the 1848 revolution, the journey to Rheims to see Charles's coronation becoming a trip to Paris to visit the proletarian barricades!

Undoubtedly the most notable event of Rossini's reign at the Théâtre Italien was the first production in September, 1825, of Meyerbeer's *Il Crociato*, on which he lavished great care. Immediately after *Il Viaggio* he had fallen seriously ill—the first symptom, perhaps, of that trouble which was soon to ruin both his health and

*"The Journey to Rheims or The Inn of the Golden Lily."

happiness—but nothing could have surpassed the conscientious care that he lavished on the production. Meyerbeer was asked to take the final rehearsals, and nothing that could be done to ensure the opera's success was overlooked. The fact is worth stressing, for it explains the gratitude and admiration that Meyerbeer always professed to feel for Rossini It also shows the baselessness of the charge, so often brought against him, of utter indifference to the interests of others.

Nevertheless, we can hardly be surprised that accusations of laziness and cynicism became rife in Paris. After a year an insignificant trifle like *Il Viaggio* was little enough for such a famous and highly paid composer to show; for *Ivanhoe*, a so-called opera produced at the Odéon, was in reality only a collection of favourite numbers from other Rossinian operas, to the fashioning of which Rossini himself contributed nothing except a permission that had in fact better not have been given. The truth of the matter was that Rossini never intended to stay at the Théâtre Italien for more than a year or two, proposing rather to consolidate his position in Paris as a composer of French, rather than Italian, operas.

To realise such an ambition an intensive study of the very different conditions was necessary. An expert in matters of this kind, as we have already noticed on more than one occasion, Rossini devoted himself with ardour to the task, all the more assiduously, perhaps, owing to certain unflattering comparisons that had been instituted between his brilliant improvisations and the solid integrity of Weber and Spontini.

First and foremost, he had to master the niceties of the French language, in which he was so successful that Saint-Saëns, writing many years later, bestowed on him special praise for his treatment of French prosody, favourably contrasting his skill in this respect with the clumsiness of Meyerbeer. Next, he had to give serious consideration to the modification of his musical style. In the matter of general taste the French differed considerably from the Italians; they may have been less musical, as Stendhal roundly insists, but they certainly possessed a better literary sense and were by no means so ready to overlook absurdities and incongruities. Nor did they attach the same importance to vocal *fioritura*, which, indeed, is not particularly well suited to the characteristics of the language.

Moreover, in writing for the Opera, Rossini had at his disposal a far more competent orchestra and, generally, an apparatus superior in every way to that of any Italian theatre, even the best. Except, of course, in the domain of solo-singing, where the Italians still enjoyed an undisputed primacy. Lastly, he was able to take advantage of the comparative leisure available for composition as contrasted with the feverish haste that characterised most Italian productions. As regards many of these points, Rossini was greatly helped by his friendship and collaboration with Adolphe Nourrit, a tenor of exceptional intelligence, who, in return for some valuable hints as to the management of his voice, gave the composer much useful information about French idiosyncrasies in general and French singing in particular.

The results of all this were first patent to the world on the 9th of October, 1826, when *Le Siège de Corinthe* was given at the Opera. This was, in fact, a French version of *Maometto II*, considerably revised. The librettists, Soumet and Balocchi, preserved the main outlines of the original story but, by changing the names, by making the psychology of the characters, notably the heroine, well-nigh credible, by giving an ingenious twist to the ideas of patriotism and self-sacrifice inherent in the plot, they succeeded in fashioning a libretto that was not only effective but topical. For just at this time the struggle of the Greeks for independence was the fashionable cult of European Romanticism. And what could be more symbolic than this story of a Greek girl who, though she had known and loved, in ignorance of his true identity, the Turkish Sultan in earlier days, prefers to die with her outraged father and valiant compatriots amidst the ruins of Corinth, rather than share the glories of a throne with a lover who is the oppressor of her country and her religion?

All concerned were well rewarded for their perspicacity, in that *Le Siège de Corinthe*, apart from its musical attributes, aroused the enthusiasm of all the supporters of the Greek cause. They staged a great demonstration in the theatre, and Rossini himself, well aware of the extent to which politics were responsible for the triumphant success of the first night, discreetly refused to take the call so insistently demanded by the audience, lest he should appear thereby to be taking also an undue share of the credit.

Nevertheless, there can be no doubt that the music did make a great impression on its own account. Nothing quite like it had been heard at the Opera before; in particular the dramatic vigour of the finales and the emotional excitement of the last-act chorus, in which the Greeks vow to die on the battlefield, drove the audience wild with enthusiasm. Though they did not know it, they were assisting at the first opening of the path that was subsequently to lead, through Auber and Meyerbeer, to Verdi and Wagner. Grand Opera had, in fact, been born.

Even to-day we can feel the dramatic intensity of the best of the music. There are some dreary pages in the first two acts, but the last act is splendid. It begins with an orchestral introduction, most expressive in the bold clashes of its harmony, followed by a chorus for female voices that is truly poignant. All the music for the tenor, especially in his recitatives, is of the first order. There is a lovely aria for the heroine (transposed from the first act of the original *Maometto*) breathing a truly Mozartian pathos, a delicious trio and a final orchestral climax of great power, during which Corinth is seen burning in the distance. The excellence of the choruses has already been mentioned, but it cannot be exaggerated; whether sombre or vivid, the writing is a model of dramatic expression.

Nearly all the good music of the first two acts, except a charming bridal chorus in the second, is to be found in the two finales; but, in view of the fact that they are very long and consist of several distinct numbers, this means more than would appear at first sight. Perhaps the high lights are the beautiful scene in the first where Pamina discovers to her horror that her erstwhile lover is none other than the Turkish Sultan, and, in the second, the vigorous orchestral *fugato* accompanying the Mohammedans' cry of surprise at the unexpected resistance of Corinth; which, incidentally, would sound strangely familiar to admirers of *La Boutique Fantasque*. All through both acts the recitatives are uncommonly expressive and apposite, on a very different plane from the conventional rigidity of *Semiramide*. As a matter of fact, these and the simplification of the vocal line, particularly noticeable in the tenor part (Nourrit was the tenor), were the main objects of Rossini's revision, which, though it produced three or four of the best numbers, consisted in the main of omission rather than addition.

Some biographers have written as if the overture had been composed for *Le Siège de Corinthe*. This is not so; it was composed for a Venetian performance of *Maometto*, already referred to. In many ways it is an admirable composition. The themes themselves, perhaps, are not so immediately attractive as usual, but they are better adapted to symphonic development. Indeed, solid workmanship and excellent scoring rather than charm and brilliance are the outstanding characteristics of an overture which is, in a sense, unique in Rossini's output.* Perhaps, with the reservations inherent in any generalisation, the same may truly be said of *Le Siège de Corinthe* as a whole. Incidentally, too, it was the first score that Rossini sold to a publisher.

In less than six months he had another opera ready, *Moïse*, an adaptation of *Mosè in Egitto*, produced on the 26th of March, 1827. Harder work—almost two months of it—had been entailed than in the case of *Le Siège de Corinthe*, for, if he omitted no less, he added considerably more, music; even if portions of it, notably the introduction and the ballets, were based on numbers from *Armida*. The French adapters, Jouy and Balocchi, while

---

*The so-called "Greek Funeral March" that follows the opening allegro has been cited as an instance of flagrant plagiarism, for Rossini was accused of stealing the subject from Mayr. Radiciotti, however, has now shown that, if Rossini stole from Mayr, Mayr stole from Marcello, who wrote the tune for one of his paraphrases of the Psalms! The whole proceeding, whatever the explanation, shows a Handelian laxity that is usually supposed to have ceased with the 18th century.

leaving the main story untouched except as regards
certain changes of nomenclature, had added an act and
transposed the order of various scenes in order to
heighten the dramatic effect; Pharaoh hardens his heart
more often; Moses is more lavish with his plagues.
On the whole they did their work competently enough,
though the monotony of so many apostrophes to the
Heavenly Powers cannot be denied. Fortunately, however, these were precisely what inspired Rossini to the
writing of his best music.

People who think of him primarily, or even exclusively, as a writer of brilliant solos must have overlooked
Moïse, whereof the most happy characteristics are the
dignified utterances of Moses himself and the grandeur
of the choruses. There are other beauties, notably
a delicious duet between Miriam and Anaide, the
Jewish girl who remains in the French, as in the
Italian, version, the main cause of the trouble between
Pharaoh and the Jews; a quintet in the second act, and
a quartet in the third, that are as remarkable for the
excellence of their treatment as for the beauty of their
themes; admirable writing for the orchestra in many
passages, not least at the end where, as in *Le Siège de
Corinthe*, Rossini exceptionally concluded his score with
an orchestral movement depicting, on this occasion, the
overwhelming of Pharaoh and his host in the Red Sea.

But, generally speaking, it is Moses and the Jews who
hold our attention. Moses is perhaps serene rather than
austere, a little too much inclined to perpetual and
conventional dignity *à la* Sarrastro, but most of the music
allotted to him, alike in ensemble, recitative or aria,
possesses real grandeur. It is in his delineation, it has
been said, that the new version shows the greatest

improvement on the old. As for the Jews, nearly all
their music, minatory, exultant, or supplicatory, except
for a disastrous march, remains truly expressive, contrasting most markedly in this respect with the music of
the Egyptians, who, Pharaoh included, show a regrettable tendency to the showy and the flippant. Fortunately, when the Jews and Egyptians sing together (as,
for instance, in the splendid finale of Act I, so justly
praised by Fétis, and in the almost equally fine finale of
Act III, so reminiscent of the trial of strength between
Elijah and the Priests of Baal in Mendelssohn's oratorio),
the Jews keep the upper hand, not only as regards the
outcome of the drama, but the spirit of the music as well.
As a result *Moïse*, as an entity, possesses a style and distinction wanting in *Le Siège de Corinthe;* it is disfigured
by a certain amount of trivialities, but the blemishes do
not spoil the loftiness of the conception as a whole.

Apparently the Paris public were not slow to appreciate this difference between the two operas. Though
Moïse had none of the political advantages of its predecessors, its success was far greater, far more enduring.
A contemporary journalist, by no means a partisan of
the composer, neatly summed up the situation when he
wrote that the public applauded *Le Siège de Corinthe*
because of the high esteem in which they held Rossini,
but that they applauded *Moïse* because of *Moïse* itself.
Balzac may be regarded as their mouthpiece. He
described *Moïse* as "an immense musical poem."
Praising the famous prayer, he seemed, he said, to be
watching (a little prematurely!) the liberation of Italy;
he justified the repetition, as opposed to the development, of the principal theme, which is so noticeable in the
poignant opening number of the second act, on the very

literary ground that "grief is always one, whatever its manifestations." The professional musicians, headed by Cherubini himself, were surprised and impressed; the well-known critic Fétis wrote an eulogy rather than a criticism; even Rossini's old enemy, the correspondent of the *Allgemeine Musikalische Zeitung*, could scarce forbear to cheer.

For the first time in his life, perhaps, Rossini was unable to enjoy his triumph. During the rehearsals of *Moïse* he had heard that his adored mother was very ill. His first impulse had been to rush to Bologna but he was dissuaded by a doctor friend, who, knowing Anna's nervous and excitable temperament, pointed out that the joy of seeing him might well prove fatal. Had she not been so overcome two years previously, when he went home, that she had to take to her bed for a fortnight?

On the 20th of February she died, apparently from an aneurism. Poor old Vivazza scarcely knew what to do. He had nothing with which to reproach his conscience. With typical and rather lovable pride he wrote to a relation that he had called in "four doctors each more illustrious than the other," but that he could not bring himself to break the news to his son. Knowing his extreme, not to say pathological, sensitiveness, he preferred to let him be told by somebody else. Later, when Rossini had heard the news and wrote inviting his father to Paris, Vivazza took pains to dilate on the fine funeral he had given Anna, "quite on the scale you would have approved of". Clearly he felt a little afraid of the reactions that the mother's death might provoke in the breast of such an abnormally devoted son. Besides, prudent even in the midst of his grief, he wished to assure himself that his meteor-like Gioacchino really intended to stay in Paris; the journey was, he wrote, arduous, the weather bad; he himself incapacitated by old age in general and a chill in particular. Nevertheless, these fears or disabilities allayed, he finally, on the 28th of March, set out for Paris, where his son's affectionate welcome banished any nervousness he might have felt. Anna's death had tightened, not loosened, the bonds between them.

Beyond the bare fact of his great sorrow we know nothing as to how Rossini was affected by his mother's death, except that two of the singers in *Moïse* used to relate that, when taking his call after the triumph of the first night, he murmured to himself: "Ah, but she is dead!" It is sufficiently revelatory. *Moïse*, which definitely turned the tide of fortune for the Opera, as definitely marked the beginning of the ebb of his own lighthearted exuberance.

There was enough left, however, to inspire one of the most original and delightful works that he ever penned: *Le Comte Ory*, produced on August 20th, 1828. But even here there is not the irresistible vitality, the uncontrollable flow of music characteristic of *L'Italiana* or *The Barber*. The charms of *Le Comte Ory* may be scarcely less, but they are different. Possibly, the comparatively long interval that elapsed after the production of *Moïse* indicates that Rossini needed time to recover from the shock of his mother's death. He seems to have done little or no work during the winter. When, however, he did begin to compose, all his old facility seems to have returned to him. He had made great friends with the banker, Aguado (for whom, incidentally, he wrote about this time some vocal quartets and a cantata in honour of his son's baptism, receiving in return a magnificent Sèvres dinner service), and at Aguado's country house, during the early summer of 1828, he wrote the music. He accomplished the task, some say, in less than a month. At any rate, as is attested by contemporary satirical comment, he completely outstripped his librettist, who was none other than the famous Scribe.

Scribe, however, had a particularly tiresome task. In its original form *Le Comte Ory*, written twelve years previously, was a one-act vaudeville based on a well-known Picardy legend. A new act (the first) had to be provided and French words to be fitted to the four last numbers from *Il Viaggio*, which Rossini decided to incorporate in the score. Once again the invaluable Nourrit was pressed into service, Scribe, apparently, as well as Rossini profiting from his ingenious advice. Few tenors in the history of opera have made themselves as useful as Nourrit.

Without pretending that Scribe's libretto is a worthy specimen of his great talent, it certainly is among the better specimens handled by Rossini. Count Ory, a regular medieval Don Juan, disguises himself as a hermit in order to further his amorous purposes, receiving in this capacity the confidences of the Countess Adèle, whose husband, accompanied by all the other husbands of the district, has gone on a Crusade. Ory and his boon companions dress up as nuns and thus gain admittance to the castle where the Countess and her husbandless friends are trying to console themselves. The inevitable is about to happen when the return of the husbands is announced. The Countess decides to forgive Ory; he and his companions are smuggled out of a side door; that is all. The thinness of plot, the absence of cumulative interest are obvious, but some of the situations are in themselves amusing, and there is a genuine sense of style.

Rossini's music is of the first order. No score of his shows such elegance, such piquancy, such grace. The delicacy of the orchestral writing, the ingenuity of modulation and rhythm, are remarkable. There are a few instances of excessive *fioritura*, notably in the numbers imported from *Il Viaggio*, but no number in the opera is wholly without merit, and many are altogether delightful. The first act contains at least four such: an allegretto in Spanish rhythm, perhaps a subtle tribute to Aguado; a delicious duet between the Count and his page, who is certainly the spiritual prototype of Oscar in *Ballo in Maschera;* an example of unaccompanied vocal writing, which, though a relic of *Il Viaggio*, is for charm and skill one of the best things in the opera; a final allegro spiritoso that concludes the act in a spirit of irresistible gaiety. There are also good songs for the Countess and the unfortunate tutor of the Count.

The second act is scarcely less good. It opens with an orchestral introduction that suggests Rossini's familiarity with the eighth symphony of Beethoven, the subsequent duet based upon it being in every way worthy. There is a typical, highly effective "storm," most ingeniously handled so as to frame the sham placidity of the supposed nuns; there are excellent things in the duet between the Count and Countess, and in the final section of the aria sung by the former's friend, Robert. But the high light of the act, indeed of the whole opera, is the trio "A la faveur de cette nuit obscure". For loveliness of melody, originality of harmony, charm of part-writing, it is beyond praise, worthy of Mozart at his best. Berlioz, who cannot be suspected of undue tenderness towards Rossini, wrote, on the occasion of a revival eleven years later, that *Le Comte Ory* had enough stuff in it to make the fortunes of two or three ordinary operas, and that this particular trio was, in his opinion, the composer's absolute masterpiece.

The music of *Le Comte Ory* has been treated in such comparative detail, firstly, because of all the lighter operas by Rossini this might be revived with the greatest chance of success; secondly, because no English musicologist has fully appreciated its historical importance. Rossini, with his uncanny flair, seems to have absorbed the general characteristics of the French style before composing it; that is to say, it might not have been written as it was, had there been no Grétry, Boïeldieu or Hérold. But *Le Comte Ory* influenced even this last composer, whose best works, generally speaking, came before, not after, it. It fixed the characteristics of French Light Opera for the best part of a hundred years. Without it the products of Auber, Lecocq, Offenbach and Messager could scarcely have been what they were. For *Le Comte Ory* is essentially an operetta, albeit an operetta of outstanding genius. All the high spirits of Offenbach, the grace of Messager, the tunefulness of Lecocq and Planquette, are united and surpassed in this delightful score. Here Rossini remained himself, it is true, but he remained himself with a difference. For this very reason, perhaps, *Le Comte Ory* never achieved in Italy the success it immediately won, and retained, in the French capital. But it is not without significance that the same fate befell *Le Siège de Corinthe* and *Moïse*. They were not, it is true, so thoroughly Gallicised as *Le Comte Ory*, but the Gallic flavour remained unmistakable, and, of all the great musical nations, the French and the Italians are often the least compatible in matters of taste.

CHAPTER X

ROSSINI was now the most popular figure in Paris. His triumphs had silenced the last remnants of nationalist or academic opposition among the musicians; in society invitations and private engagements rained upon him. Old Vivazza wrote proudly to a crony that "Paris had finally crowned the Rossinian glory," adding that, if his correspondent did not believe this account of his son's popularity and grand friends, he had only to seek confirmation from any French gentleman who might be passing through Bologna. Not all Rossini's activities, however, were frivolous. He used his influence with the Court to obtain support for Habeneck and his new Conservatoire concerts, and is said himself to have given that talented conductor many hints as to how Beethoven's symphonies should be played. Which, in view of the fact that the performances by Habeneck and his orchestra were later considered by competent judges (including Richard Wagner) to be the first that did real justice to Beethoven, must be reckoned a service of primary importance to music.

Such distractions, however, were not favourable to composition, so, after the second performance of *Le Comte Ory*, Rossini withdrew to the country house of his friend Aguado at Petit Bourg to grapple with his new opera. He had decided on the subject some time previously, in fact before the composition of *Le Comte Ory*,

when Jouy, one of his collaborators in *Moïse*, had presented him with a version of Schiller's *William Tell*.
Even Rossini's scanty literary sense sufficed to convince
him that the libretto in its original state would not do; it
was too cold and pompous altogether. But, not improbably, recollections of the appeal of *Le Siège de
Corinthe* induced him to look on the subject with a
favourable eye. Patriotic fervour and the spectacle of
small nations struggling to be free possessed as potent a
charm in 1828 as self-determination and a world safe for
democracy were to acquire in 1919. It may be doubted
whether Rossini in reality troubled his head more about
the one than he would have about the other, but he
possessed something of a Noel Coward's sensitiveness to
the swing of public taste; so Jouy was preferred to
Scribe, who had offered him the choice of two excellent
librettos.* A promising young poet called Bis was
entrusted with the delicate task of rendering Jouy's
verses more suitable for musical purposes without
unduly wounding that gentleman's academic susceptibilities. Rossini himself made some suggestions; later,
even Aguado's secretary took a hand—and by no means
the least skilful—in the game. Such was the genesis of
the exceedingly stiff and dull production that is the
libretto of *William Tell*.

Exactly how long Rossini took to write the music is
uncertain; he himself said variously five and six months.
Too much value should not be attached to his own story
that he evolved the whole idea of the great conspiracy
scene while out fishing—to the great gain of the fish who
took advantage of his preoccupation by making off with

Gustave III, subsequently set by Auber and, travestied as *Un Ballo in
Maschera*, by Verdi; *La Juive*, for which Halévy wrote the music.

138

the bait! Rossini loved to exaggerate his casualness in such matters, and we know from other sources that he did in fact work at the opera with exceptional care and assiduity. He undoubtedly came back to Paris in the middle of October with most of the music written but the scoring was done in his flat in the Boulevard Montmartre, not at Aguado's house. Moreover, it seems certain that some of the music was, at any rate, sketched before he went to the country at all. Even if, however, by adding together all the possible periods of time, we arrive at a total of some nine months for composition and scoring, it is difficult to understand how he accomplished such a feat. *William Tell* is exceedingly long and complicated; the scoring is rich, the writing impeccable. We are faced once again with the miracle of *The Barber* in another, and only less striking, guise.

Paris was all agog for the new opera, the first, be it remembered, that Rossini had written wholly and exclusively for the French stage. Every month, beginning in the summer of 1828, the newspapers gave more or less accurate accounts of its progress and of the movements of its distinguished composer. It was in rehearsal; it was not in rehearsal but soon would be. It was to be produced at the end of the year, in the spring or summer of 1829. For each successive postponement various reasons were found, notably the interesting but exasperating condition of the leading lady, who had, most inconsiderately, got married. Her substitute, specially imported from Germany, had proved a failure; later, when she herself had recovered from the effects of matrimony, an attack of hoarseness unfortunately prevented her singing.

There was a certain amount of truth in some of these stories, but the real reason for the repeated postponement of *William Tell* was quite different. It may be summarised as more or less legitimate blackmail on Rossini's part. For some time past he had been engaged in negotiations with La Rochefoucauld as regards his position in France. When, just before the production of *Moïse*, his Théâtre Italien contract had come to an end, a special post had been invented for him: Composer to His Majesty and Inspector General of Singing, at a yearly salary of 20,000 francs. Inevitably this strange appointment, which was in reality only an excuse to keep Rossini in touch with the Opera and secure the benefit of his advice, gave rise to a good deal of ill-natured comment. Rossini, first and foremost, saw the humour of it, and on occasions, after listening with the utmost gravity to the performances of street singers on the boulevards, informed enquiring friends that he was merely carrying out his official duties! As a matter of fact, the money was not ill spent or the post ill named, for everyone was agreed that Rossini did more than any other man to raise the standard of singing in France.

Nevertheless, from an official point of view the position was not satisfactory. To begin with, he did not wish to be tied in perpetuity to residence in Paris; like Verdi later, he sometimes sighed for the comparative tranquillity of Italian life, and, as early as 1827, he was asking a friend in Bologna to have his house put in order, because "I shall be back there sooner than you think". Secondly, he felt that his appointment was too dependent on the goodwill of the minister who happened to be responsible for the Civil List; not to mention, perhaps, the permanence of the monarchy itself. For some years he had been trying to get the whole matter regularised in a proper contract. At last, in February, 1829, he decided to bring matters to a head, writing in this sense both to La Rochefoucauld and the minister. He wanted a yearly salary in perpetuity of 6,000 francs, in exchange for which he promised to write five operas during the next ten years, *William Tell* ranking as the first, and to remain in Paris for nine months each year; for every opera he was to receive 15,000 francs and a benefit performance.

It was not, he wrote, a mere question of self-interest; as La Rochefoucauld knew, he had had better offers from England, Germany, Austria. Did he not desire to show his gratitude to a sovereign who had treated him with such marked consideration, and to work for a theatre that was admittedly the best in the world, he would prefer to go home to enjoy a nice long rest; and so on. In all of which there was some truth and a considerable amount of diplomacy. Charles X considered Rossini to be one of the principal ornaments of his Court and capital; both La Rochefoucauld and the minister, La Bouillerie, were well disposed. Nevertheless, the desired contract failed to materialise. So, in March, Rossini let the director of the Opera understand that, unless it did, he might have to suspend the rehearsals of *William Tell* and refuse permission for the last two acts to be copied. A little later, he put his threat into execution, bringing everything at the Opera to a standstill for a fortnight. The director wrote despairing letters to La Rochefoucauld. Scenery and costumes, all were ready; only Rossini refused to move and would quite possibly withdraw the opera altogether unless his demands were satisfied; it might be unreasonable of him but there it was. Even then, despite the insistence of La Rochefoucauld, certain influences at Court hostile to Rossini delayed matters till April 18th, when he finally received

the contract. It bore the signature of the King himself, a
point which may or may not have seemed of importance
to Rossini at the time. Rehearsals began again and
William Tell was saved for Paris.

On August 3rd, 1829, it was finally produced before an
audience bursting with curiosity. Every seat had been
sold for a long time past; boxes were said to have changed
hands for as much as five hundred francs. The interest
of both the public and the press had been stimulated by
rumours about the opera. Rossini, they whispered, had
sworn not to indulge in a single crescendo, in any of the
familiar devices associated with his name; this was to be
an entirely new kind of music. And so it was, a great
deal of it, but by no means entirely to their liking.
Though *William Tell* was hailed with a salvo of applause
by every musician and critic of note, the public remained
comparatively indifferent, judging the opera as a whole
to be long, cold and boring.

Doubtless much of the responsibility should be laid on
the libretto. Schiller's play, if not calculated to appeal to
the tastes of the present day, possesses certain redeeming
features of sincerity and genuine characterisation. The
adaptation of it by Jouy and Bis is at least as
unpalatable as an entity without being redeemed by
anything at all. The main lines of the story (fortunately
so familiar that it need not be retold) are much the same
in both. Perhaps the substitution for Ulric and Berta of
Mathilde, a Hapsburg princess, and Arnold, the son of a
martyred Swiss patriot, Melchtal, as the necessary
lovers, is a theatrical improvement; which, incidentally, is said to have been suggested by Rossini himself.
Beyond question, the deliberate disclosure to Arnold of
his father's cruel execution instead of his accidental

discovery of the fact, as in Schiller, is more effective from the dramatic point of view. That, however, is the sum total of any merit that can be claimed for Messrs. Jouy and Bis. Everything else that they touched they worsened, so that their libretto remains little more than a travesty of the original play. Radiciotti is quite right in describing the last two acts as devoid of action and, worse still, of interest. It may be added that the characterisation is equally at fault. Tell himself is rather a series of attitudes than a human being; Gessler a mere ogre; Melchtal a lay figure. Mathilde and Arnold show some signs of life, but it never rises above the life of conventional stage lovers.

To these defects must be added the accidental handicap of locale and nomenclature. Even the most fervent lover of liberty and patriotism finds some difficulty in being inspired by the Swiss, who, whatever their other virtues, remain the least exciting people in the world. The Englishman in particular, owing to his natural humour and a succession of parodies, finds it not so much difficult as impossible to take the familiar episode of the apple seriously as the climax of a drama; the more so when he discovers that William Tell has christened his son Jemmy, repeatedly addressing him by that depressing name at the most poignant moment in the opera! None of which has in reality anything whatever to do with the merits of *William Tell*, but cannot wholly be overlooked in any consideration of its chequered fortunes.

It is something of a tragedy that a better canvas was not provided for Rossini's genius to work upon, for the excellence of the best music in *William Tell* can scarcely be exaggerated. But how could any man deal satisfactorily with those two last acts, so cold, so unimaginative? As a matter of fact, Rossini did pretty well with the fourth act. The prelude and Arnold's aria possess an admirable vigour, and the general contours of the music, though now familiar enough, must have seemed decidedly original to contemporaries; both the trio and the scena that precedes it are effective, the prayer is not only in itself a lovely and original tune; but ends with a charming harmonic cadence in the orchestra. Best of all, however, is the final "apotheosis" built on the well-known Ranz des Vaches; it shows a real spirit of exaltation, and foreshadows, in its general line and progression of tonality, Wagner's Entrance of the Gods into Valhalla.

The third act, on the other hand, is a well-nigh complete failure. There is a fine, robust scene between Mathilde and Gessler, a pretty number, familiar to everybody, for unaccompanied chorus and four solo female voices. Some of the music wherein Tell prepares his son for the apple ordeal, which, incidentally, earned the special praises of Wagner and Berlioz, is very beautiful and pathetic in itself, but it is ruined for us, as already hinted, by the bathos of such words as "Jemmy, Jemmy, think of your mother". There is nothing worthy of remark in the rest of the act, a considerable portion of it being taken up by ballet music, mostly dull and uninspired. One might be tempted to consider this a reflection of the sullen mood of the Swiss, compelled to dance for the delectation of the tyrant Gessler, except that his own soldiers dance to a number no whit more distinguished—save by the accident that it contains the sole example of a Rossini crescendo in the entire opera.

The first two acts are on a different plane altogether. The pastoral mood characteristic of much of the first act becomes perhaps a little monotonous, but there is some delicious music in this vein, notably the opening chorus and the quintet and chorus, "Ciel, qui du monde," while the use of various Ranz motifs is often highly ingenious. Wholly charming, too, are the bridal chorus and the allegretto dance number that follows it, a notable contrast to the ballet music in the next act. The classical feeling obvious in Melchtal's powerful exhortation and in Arnold's expressive thoughts of Mathilde, is very pleasant, but the best thing in the act is the finale, which is dramatically most effective, though some of the effects, having since been repeatedly stolen by other composers, have lost a little of their bite. This, however, does not apply to the final 3/4 veloce, a style of writing which nobody has ever been able to handle quite so well as Rossini, its bustle and vigour remaining to-day as fresh as ever.

As for the second act, it is, with the possible exception of two choruses, a masterpiece from beginning to end. Nobody, not even Wagner or Verdi, has written anything more effective for the stage. Indeed, both those great masters owe much to this magnificent music, witness the Verdian vigour and the Wagnerian contours of Tell's address. Meyerbeer never achieved the grandeur of the final chorus, and the influence of one passage may be traced even in *The Ring*. Enumeration of the merits of the act in detail would be wearisome, but one must emphasise the ravishing beauty of the introduction and aria in Mathilde's "Sombre Forêt," as well as the only inferior excellence of the scena, duet and trio that immediately follow them. Even the conventional concluding allegro in the duet is superior to Verdi's earlier essays in that style, while the orchestration possesses a richness unknown to Donizetti and Bellini. All the recitatives throughout are remarkable both for power and plasticity; the instances of bold harmonic innovation are most striking; the writing for the voices alike in solos and ensemble is of the first order. It can scarcely be mere coincidence that this act, which is by far the best in the libretto and, moreover, the most closely related to Schiller's original, inspired Rossini to compose music not only splendid in itself, but exceptionally true to the psychology of the action. In short, once again we see of what this man was capable when his imagination really caught fire.

Presumably a word must be said about that little symphony in miniature which is the overture, however familiar it may be. None of the subjects has any connection with the opera, though, as a matter of fact, the final quick-step, in essence, as we have seen, an importation, was originally sung in unison at the end of the second act but subsequently (and fortunately) removed. In recent years one or two excellent orchestral performances have gone far to reveal to the English musical public the overture's great merit, so long obscured in moribund interpretations by military bands. The sombre romanticism of the opening, the pastoral feeling of the second section, the martial vigour of the third, the storm: all these, admirable in themselves, are worked by a master hand into a whole that, for sheer brilliance, has rarely been equalled and does in fact harmonise uncommonly well with the various moods of the opera. Its very popularity, perhaps, has done much to obscure its greatness.

The importance of *William Tell* is best attested by the enthusiasm of contemporary musicians. Fétis wrote that

Rossini had achieved the apparently impossible in registering a further advance on what was best in his previous operas; the most hostile of French critics, Ortigue, added a postscript to his book on Rossini and French Opera, emphasising the unexpected beauties and originality of "this sublime music"; the German critics pointed out the veritable revolution that had taken place in Rossini's conception of dramatic writing. Nor did the composers lag behind the critics. Mendelssohn expressed to Chorley his unstinted admiration; Bellini said that *William Tell* made all contemporary music, including his own, seem like the work of pygmies; Verdi railed against the mutilations subsequently inflicted on such a great masterpiece, and soundly rated the Paris public for gaping at Meyerbeer before they had begun even to understand *William Tell;* Wagner, in his famous interview, told Rossini that, doubtless unwittingly, he had in the best moments of *William Tell* anticipated his own theories.

Most significant of all, however, was the attitude of Berlioz, who had little love for Rossini's music in general and, even after the first performance of *William Tell,* refused to believe that the enthusiasm of the musicians and the critics was really justifiable. But five years later he changed his mind, writing a detailed analysis of the opera that amounts, a few minor criticisms apart, to a veritable pæan of praise. Radiciotti reprints the article in full on the excellent ground that it does not figure in the usual collection of Berlioz's prose writings. Such a luxury is, rather unfortunately, impossible here. Suffice it to say that, except for its length, which with perfect justice he described as excessive, Berlioz expressed not so much admiration as wild enthusiasm for the opera as a whole. Though he much admired the overture, he was, needless to say, principally impressed by the second act, of which the following are typical criticisms:

"Here," he writes of the trio, "we must own that, despite our role of critic and the obligations that devolve from it, we find it impossible to apply a cold dissecting knife to the heart of this sublime creation . . . oh, no; let others do so if they possess sufficient courage . . . I can only shout with the crowd: 'Beautiful! Superb! Admirable! Heartrending!' "

Then, after a warning that he must keep some of his superlatives in reserve, he thus describes the finale: "Here we have all the characters, the chorus, the orchestra and the instruments of percussion which have not been heard since the beginning of the act. 'Aux armes!' And lo! all that instrumental mass rushes like an avalanche into an impetuous allegro with a last, terrible war-cry uttered by hearts a-quiver in the dawn of a first day of liberty.

"Ah! It is sublime! Let us take breath."

It is also very characteristic of Berlioz, whose transports, whether of disgust or admiration, were always couched in such terms of hyperbole.

The inclusion of *William Tell* in the repertory of the leading European opera houses followed as a matter of course during the next few years. Needless to say, in Italy there was trouble with the Austrian censorship, which, in Milan, insisted on the hero becoming William Wallace; the Swiss, the Scotch, and the Austrians, the English! All references to patriotism, liberty or tyranny were suppressed, and the scene of the apple was omitted altogether. In Rome the Papal censorship discovered another innocuous patriot for the title role in the person of Rudolf of Sterling; they also thought it well to sprinkle the opera with pious references to God, Heaven and the saints! In Prussia William Tell was replaced by Andreas Hofer; in Russia by Charles the Bold. In Vienna, of all unlikely places, the libretto was allowed to stand, but the public took care to shout "Long live the Hapsburgs" at the end of every performance, lest the authorities should think their loyalty had been undermined!

None of this would have been of vital importance had the opera achieved anywhere a really popular success. But it did not. The Italians are said, for many years, to have preferred *Semiramide*, and the receipts of the first twelve performances at the Paris Opera, so notably inferior to those for a similar number of performances of *Les Huguenots* and *Robert le Diable*, or even of *La Juive* and *I Vespri Siciliani*, provide the best possible evidence of its comparatively small hold on the public. Doubtless, the excessive length was largely responsible. Rossini himself made some drastic cuts almost at once, and three years later authorised a version in three acts which was produced at Bordeaux and Prague. Even such drastic operations failed to save the life of *William Tell* as an entity; the Opera began giving performances of isolated acts; finally of the second act alone. Years later, the Director, meeting Rossini in the street, thought to please him by relating that the second act was being given on that night at the Opera. "What! the whole of it?" came the caustic reply. He had a bitter tongue when the occasion so demanded.

All the biographers unite in stating that the public failed to appreciate *William Tell* because its style was so elevated, its intellectual quality so superior to that of any other Rossini opera. To some extent this is true; but is it wholly true? To begin with, there has always been a tendency to exaggerate somewhat the lack of appreciation. *William Tell* secured for the composer the Legion of Honour and a serenade from Habeneck and his orchestra which filled the Boulevard Montmartre with such a crowd of enthusiastic admirers that Rossini, who had been dining out, was forced to appeal to the police to open a passage to his own house. It seems slightly absurd to talk of failure, however comparative, in face of honours like these, calculated to turn the ordinary composer green with envy. Still, *William Tell* was not, and never has been, a popular success in the sense that *Tancredi* and *The Barber* and *La Cenerentola*, or even *Moïse*, were popular successes. Why?

If the orthodox judgment of musical historians be accepted, that *William Tell* is pre-eminently Rossini's greatest achievement, then the public must shoulder the responsibility. It is possible, however, that orthodox judgment has gone astray. No doubt *William Tell* remains on every analysable ground the most *remarkable* product of Rossini's genius; in every attribute of the kind on which musicians and musicologists like to expatiate, it is superior to all his other operas. Nay, more, it does in fact contain the most striking and beautiful music that he ever wrote. None of this, however, necessarily implies that *William Tell* as an entity is the high-water mark of Rossini's accomplishment.

Apart from questions of libretto, length, technique and so on, it does not so appear to me. Rossini undoubtedly strained every nerve to do the very best he could with *William Tell*, and his purely musical gifts were so great that he accomplished something very fine, something that was of great importance in the history of music. But there are artists, despite our Puritans, who cannot, when effort is too conscious, attain to the greatest vitality of which their personality is capable; and Rossini was such an artist. I believe that this is the explanation of what happened in the case of *William Tell*. It is a monument, a splendid monument, to Rossini's musicianship . . . but it is not Rossini himself, as the lighter operas are, because it does not truly reflect his personality. Rossini had nothing of the heroic in his nature, and a subject like that of *William Tell*, to come wholly to life, demands such a quality. Thus, in trying to rise above himself he ceased to be wholly himself, with a consequent loss of vitality which the public, however ignorant, is never slow to realise.* In short, *William Tell* may be written down as providing yet another justification of that most acute of all aphorisms: *Le mieux est l'ennemi du bien.*

*Not improbably Rossini realised it also, for, when he was asked as an old man which of all his output was likely to survive, he answered: "The last act of *Otello*, the second act of *William Tell* and *The Barber of Seville.*" Only one act, be it noted, as compared with the whole of *The Barber!*

CHAPTER XI

ENTR'ACTE

TEN days after the production of *William Tell*, Rossini, accompanied by his wife, set out for Bologna, whither old Vivazza, who seems soon to have had enough of Paris life, had preceded him. On the day of his departure he wrote a *Song of Farewell* to the Parisians. He was grateful to Paris, as well he might be, with its plaudits ringing in his ears and Charles X's contract in his pocket; but he was delighted to be going home. He undoubtedly felt tired, for him exceptionally tired, and he had been suffering from insomnia; a few months' rest would put all that right. No one would have been more surprised than he if he had been told that he would never again write an opera.

On their way the Rossinis stopped at Milan, attending a performance of *Il Pirata*, whereat young Bellini was first introduced to the composer. During the first week in September they arrived at Bologna, going immediately to Castenaso where Rossini loved to play at being the country gentleman.* An exceptionally early and severe winter, however, soon drove them back to the fine new town house which Rossini had acquired seven years previously, now restored, redecorated and enriched with two Latin inscriptions that certainly neither of them could have translated. He gave parties,

---

*Rossini's occasional expression of longing for, and delight in, the country should not lead the reader to imagine any similarity in this respect between himself and Verdi, who really remained a farmer at heart.

comparatively modest forerunners of the "Saturday Evenings" that were later to be so famous in Paris, whereat he and Isabella sang and the best local instrumentalists played to his accompaniment. All Bologna wanted to obtain invitations, and the nobility in their turn assiduously courted Rossini. One of them, the Marchese Francesco Sampieri, honoured the composer's Name Day* by a particularly brilliant garden-fête which was the talk of the neighbourhood. Nevertheless, Rossini did not wholly neglect music, for during the autumn of 1829 he helped to produce *Otello*, *Semiramide* and *Tancredi* at the Teatro Comunale† in Bologna, besides keeping himself informed of what was happening at the Théâtre Italien. Indeed, by the summer of 1830, when he had again retired to Castenaso, he was becoming seriously worried at not having received his new libretto. "How," he wrote to La Rochefoucauld on the 4th of May, "can I work without a libretto? It is now nine months overdue and I should so much have liked to take advantage of the fine weather and country life to get on with my opera." On the 7th of July he wrote again to the director of the Théâtre Italien in the same sense. Rossini later told Hiller that the expected libretto was to have been based on Goethe's *Faust;* which shows the direction and scope of his ambitions at the time. But the mere fact of his insistence is what remains of real importance, in that it proves conclusively that he had as yet no idea of giving up composition.

Almost immediately, however, there occurred the

*In Catholic countries it is not the Birthday, as with us, but the Name Day—that is to say, the day associated with the saint after whom a person is called—which is usually celebrated.

†So called because various members of the local nobility had clubbed together to build it, reserving for themselves certain boxes in perpetuity.

first and perhaps the most important of the series of circumstances which were to lead to that much discussed renunciation. At the end of July there was a revolution in Paris, and Charles X abdicated in favour of Louis-Philippe. It was a grievous blow to Rossini, who saw his contract imperilled and his whole future in jeopardy. How well justified his anxiety was, is attested by the fact that, when he arrived in Paris in September, expecting to stay only a few weeks, he found that the contract had been cancelled and that he would have to take legal proceedings to prevent the pension being cancelled also. We need not pursue the matter further. After six years of wearisome litigation Rossini won his case, apparently owing to the accident that the contract bore the late king's personal signature. Rossini's insistence on dealing direct with the Court instead of with the Opera was certainly justified. Is it fanciful to trace here the hand of the astute Aguado?

The services rendered by that financier to Rossini cannot be exaggerated. His country house had always been open to the composer, but now, in this crisis of his fortunes, when the lawsuit necessitated Paris being at any rate his headquarters, Aguado enabled him to live practically for nothing. True, when Rossini first came to Paris in the autumn of 1830, he was lent a modest apartment on the top storey of the Théâtre Italien itself, but in February Aguado took him as his guest to Madrid, entertained him as usual, no doubt, during the summer, and, when the cholera appeared in Paris in 1832, kept him from May till September in bored but safe seclusion at Bayonne, with occasional visits to Pau and other watering places.

During the visit to Madrid the usual honours were

showered upon Rossini; a special performance of *The Barber* was arranged, with King Ferdinand in the royal box; he was cheered to the echo in the theatre, serenaded in his hotel by all the Opera singers and the choir of the Chapel Royal. A few days later, he received a command to go to the palace where Ferdinand, an inveterate smoker, offered him a half-smoked cigar! He respectfully declined it; whereupon Queen Maria Cristina, who came from Naples, whispered in Neapolitan dialect that such an honour was quite unusual and that he ought to accept. To which Rossini replied in the same dialect that he really must refuse because he happened not to smoke. So, what might have been an awkward incident ended in a laugh. Later, he was summoned to visit the King's brother who begged as a special favour to be accompanied in an aria from *Semiramide*. The royal amateur then proceeded not only to sing but to act the number with appropriate gestures, to the great amusement of his wife and the considerable astonishment of the composer. George IV of England had never gone quite so far as that!

More important than these royal eccentricities was the request of an eminent prelate, a friend of Aguado, that Rossini should write for him an autographed *Stabat Mater*. Now this was about the last thing Rossini wished to do, for, as he told Hiller, his admiration for Pergolesi's *Stabat Mater* was such that he had vowed long ago not to invite odious comparisons by setting the same words. He could not, however, very well refuse the urgent request of the friend of a man to whom he owed so much; so he consented, on the express condition that the manuscript should not leave the possession of its owner. On returning to Paris he kept his promise but, being

seized with a severe attack of lumbago after the composition of the first six numbers, and being continually
pestered by the insistent cleric, he entrusted the remainder to Tadolini, the conductor of the Théâtre
Italien. Finally, on the 26th of March, 1832, the
manuscript was sent to Madrid, duly autographed and
with a dedication in which the various titles of the
recipient are punctiliously enumerated. The fortunes
and merits of the *Stabat Mater* will be considered presently; suffice it to say now that Rossini received in
exchange a gold snuffbox with eight large diamonds
worth at least 10,000 francs. One wonders what Tadolini
got!

The most important event of his various peregrina-
tions, however, was the meeting in 1832 at Aix-les-
Bains with a certain lady called Olympe Pélissier.
Olympe belonged to the same caste as Madame Du
Barry, Cora Pearl, Marguerite Duval and other ladies
famous in history or romance. She was in fact a genuine
demi-mondaine, a specimen of a class that has never been
so numerous as Anglo-Saxons imagine and is now
practically extinct. Contemporary gossip may have
exaggerated, but can scarcely have invented, the
sordidness of her origin. Sold by her mother as a mere
girl, first to a French duke, then to a rich Anglo-
American, her first voluntary act was to place herself
under the protection of the painter, Horace Vernet, who
has left a record of her dark, youthful beauty in his
famous picture, *Judith and Holofernes*. The pair seem to
have been genuinely fond of one another but Olympe, as
is the manner of her tribe, was capricious and explosive;
so after a few years Vernet tried to hand her over to a
banker-friend, desirous of entering into the succession.

Olympe, however, had other views and chose a wealthy stockbroker, who with the utmost consideration died almost immediately, leaving her an income for life of six thousand francs and the opportunity of a fashionable liaison with a young count.

It must have been soon after this that she met Rossini. The two got on well from the outset. Olympe's directness of speech made her amusing—a quality which, in Rossini's view, doubtless covered more sins than ever did charity—and her solicitude for his health, her practical good sense, made her reposeful. One wonders if they were frank enough to be amused by the coincidence of the six thousand francs, precisely the annual income for which Rossini was suing the French Government! At any rate Olympe, having experimented with the bourgeoisie, the nobility, and the art of painting, seems to have determined to try a permanent association with the art of music, this time without any mercenary motive. At heart, like so many French courtesans, extremely respectable, she asked nothing better than to settle down to the practice, if not the theory, of domesticity. She wanted to look after the already failing Rossini, to put a little order in his life, in short to "mother" him. And this during the next few years, whenever he was in Paris, she did, with a loving assiduity that earned his undying gratitude Olympe Pélissier, however murky her past, however equivocal her present, was a nice woman in the best, if least accurate, sense of that much-abused term.

Where, it may well be asked, was Isabella all this time? Isabella was in disgrace at Bologna. Even from the beginning the marriage does not seem to have gone too well. It is clear from one of Rossini's letters that some of his friends did not approve of Isabella; which may or

may not have mattered. What mattered very much was
that Isabella quarrelled with her mother-in-law, always
a dangerous thing for a wife to do in any Latin country,
but positively suicidal when the mother-in-law happened to be Anna Rossini. Still, it was not till the
Rossinis settled in Paris that there was a serious breach.
Isabella, always extravagant, took to gambling, and, to
pay her debts, gave singing lessons on the quiet, much to
Rossini's disgust. As a punishment, she was left at
Bologna in the charge of old Vivazza, who seems to have
come to dislike her as much on his own, as on his late
wife's, account. His letters to his son during these years
are so delicious in their typical illiteracy that it is a
thousand pities they cannot be quoted in full. In the
first year of Rossini's absence they began in comparatively mild fashion, being little more than suggestions
that Isabella spent too much money on parties. Gradually the complaints became more precise: Why did she
buy so many horses, only to sell them again and buy new
ones? Why did she have to have dogs, parrots, a whole
Noah's ark of animals? Why did she tell everybody that
he was keeping her short when she had everything, from
bread and wine to doctors and gardeners, that a reasonable woman could wish for?

In 1832 he refers to her more bitterly as "My lady, the
Duchess of Castenaso," whose caprices are such that she
is no longer able to find anyone (especially women) to
serve her, who "does things that are not done even in
Turkey". In 1833 he is positively venomous, writing that
she may have killed his poor wife but that he would be a
match for her. Then comes the climax. "How can
anybody get on with so vile and haughty a woman whose
one object is to make trouble? And all because one

refuses to give in to her extravagances and vagaries. And she does not remember, not she, that she too was the daughter of a poor trumpeter like me and has a sister in Midrit" (he meant Madrid!) "who bombards her with letters. And she does not remember the time when Crescentini gave her lessons out of charity at Midrit. And I might add many other things but I won't except one and that is 'Hurrah for the Venetians who damned her with hisses'. It would have been better if they had really got at her as they intended; then my poor wife would not have died of anger. What's more if things go on like this I shall die too or go crazy. You're lucky to be far away and may God keep you so! . . . She should thank Heaven that she's got you as a husband, for if she'd married somebody of her own kidney you'd both be in the workhouse by now."

Old Vivazza must have been an uncommonly tough nut even for Isabella, with all her experience of Barbaia, to crack. Needless to say, he exaggerated to a comic extent, outraged in all his natural frugality as an Italian, as well as in his jealous care for family interests. But there is no doubt that Isabella was wantonly extravagant, even allowing for the large dowry that she brought Rossini—a fact, incidentally, which she lost no opportunity of recalling to Vivazza's memory on every possible occasion—and again ran deeply into debt. A very foolish woman! Neither of the Rossinis, father or son, was the kind of person to treat laxity in money matters lightly And, though she did not yet know it, there was now Olympe Pélissier on the horizon.

Between his various sojourns with Aguado, Rossini, as we have seen, returned to Paris, where everybody of note seems to have climbed the long flight of stairs at the

Théâtre Italien to come and see him. Except for the six numbers of the *Stabat* and various small pieces destined for various concerts at private houses, he wrote no music. These concerts were, it seems, his main preoccupation, for they brought him a good deal of money. He confessed as much to Malibran, who seems to have been his principal stand-by as a singer on such occasions. Sometimes he had difficulty in getting her to rehearse, but he always returned valiantly to the attack. She commanded his unstinted admiration, and the two, reinforced on occasions by her lover and subsequent husband, the celebrated violinist de Beriot, were in great demand at parties.* But, despite the lectures and attentions of Olympe, his health gradually became worse, so that in the summer of 1834 the doctors advised him to go home and take a rest in the country outside Bologna. Though to all outward appearances he was still the picture of gaiety and robust health, he rarely felt well, and anything unpleasant or annoying so upset his nerves that he became as exhausted as if he had a serious illness.

Nevertheless, on this occasion two months' rest, however much the feud between Isabella and Vivazza may have disturbed it, sufficed to make a different man of him. Much to the surprise of the Parisians, many of whom seem to have thought he was dying if not dead, he returned about the end of August to Paris, where his case was still dragging out its interminable length. In 1835 he handed over to his publisher, Troupenas, twelve of the songs and duets he had written for various parties during

*Malibran, a Spaniard like Isabella, was an exceedingly talented person. Not only was she probably the best singer of her day, but she spoke four languages, wrote agreeable songs and, as her portrait of Bellini shows, had a real talent for painting. In addition she was a fine horsewoman, swimmer and fencer and a remarkably expert needlewoman. It seems a pity that she did not marry that other prodigy of versatility, Mendelssohn.

the last few years, which, under the title of *Soirées Musicales*, subsequently achieved great fame, Liszt transcribing several for the pianoforte and Wagner scoring one of the duets, *I Marinai*, for use at a concert in Riga. As a matter of fact, despite the apparently casual nature of their origin, they deserve to rank among Rossini's best compositions. Beautifully written for the voice, with accompaniments that are a model of delicacy and charm, they show unusual care in workmanship. *La Danza*, that intoxicating tarantella once so splendidly sung by Caruso, is deservedly the best known of them, for it is a little masterpiece; but some of the others are only less good, notably the delicious duet for soprano and tenor called *La Serenata*. Rossini, who was beginning more and more to assume a protective pose in such matters, doubtless professed to regard them as mere trifles, thrown off almost by accident. In fact, however, all the internal evidence goes to show that he took a great deal of trouble with them. Singers, gifted with sufficient taste and competence, will find them well worthy of attention.

A considerable proportion of Rossini's time during this period was devoted to helping young Bellini, to whom he had taken a great fancy. Perhaps the fact that he conceived the highest admiration for the "sweetest melancholy" characteristic of the *cantilena* of that unfortunate young man, so different from his own vivacious muse, is in itself significant. He was prodigal with advice in general, which always costs little; the proof of his genuine interest should be sought rather in the trouble he took to see that Bellini secured a proper contract for his new opera, *I Puritani*, and the practical hints he was always ready to give in the matter of theatrical effectiveness. Bellini repaid the kindness with something that eventually amounted to sheer devotion. It is clear, reading between the lines of his letters, that he was at first inclined to be suspicious. Could this be the cynical, mordant, avaricious Rossini of popular repute? But, as he brought the composer page after page of *I Puritani*, being received with invariable kindliness, his suspicions melted away, and he proclaimed to his family and friends unbounded trust in Rossini's loyalty. His judgment was soon proved right, for the triumphant success of *I Puritani*, the very thing most likely to make a lesser man envious, led to no change in Rossini's attitude.

Poor Bellini! He only lived a few months longer. When he died, at the age of thirty-three, Rossini, though far from well, insisted on attending his funeral in the pouring rain, immediately inaugurating a subscription list to pay for it. There was at the time, apparently, no money and no will, but he spared no effort to settle the young man's disordered affairs so that, eventually, the full financial benefit of the operas might be enjoyed by the family in Catania. Their gratitude is enshrined in a touching letter.

His last duty to his dead friend was a curious one. In Paris Bellini's premature death had given rise to the same legend of poisoning that followed Mozart's death in Vienna; so Rossini, unwilling, perhaps, to figure as a second Salieri, insisted on an autopsy, which put an end to the rumour once and for all. The whole story of this association with Bellini shows us a kind of man very different from him whom the public, not to mention himself, liked to set up as Rossini.

In 1836 the lawsuit with the French Government was

finally decided in Rossini's favour, so, there being no further reason or excuse for him to remain in Paris, he was about to set out for Bologna when another banker, one of the Rothschilds this time, invited him to come to Frankfurt. They went by way of Belgium and the Rhine, and Rossini thoroughly enjoyed himself, uncertain, it seems, which gave him the greater delight, the pictures of Rubens and Van Dyck or the natural beauties of the Rhine. He was fêted wherever he went. At Liège he received the customary serenade from the musicians of the city; at Brussels the inevitable king summoned him to the inevitable audience to receive the inevitable decoration. Weary of such publicity, he escaped one day, incognito, to Antwerp where, greatly daring, he thought he would patronise that remarkable modern invention, the railway. The experiment was not a success, his wretched nerves being so shaken that he was ill for days. Never again, so long as he lived, would he set foot in a train.

His own reputation, seconded no doubt by the paramount influence of the Rothschilds, assured his welcome in Frankfurt. There were banquets, receptions, concerts in his honour. It was here that he first met Hiller, who in his Reminiscences has left us a record of so many interesting talks with Rossini. And at Hiller's house he made the acquaintance of Mendelssohn, who does not seem quite to have known what to make of him. Mendelssohn did not altogether relish, it appears, being told that one of his sonatas had a distinct flavour of Scarlatti; he could not understand at all why Rossini begged him to arrange for a performance of the B. Minor Mass and sat for hours by his side at the piano asking him to play Bach fugues. Rossini a Bach enthusiast! It was incredible. True, he showed equal enthusiasm for Rhine wines, and, when he dined in a restaurant, would have carried off the wine-list unless the waiter had interfered. One could never be sure if the man was joking when he was serious or serious when he was joking. "The respect Rossini shows to everybody present is so profound that one might be tempted to believe in it altogether unless one had eyes to see the twinkle in his own! What wit, what vivacity and subtlety all the time! Anybody who does not recognise him as a genius has only to hear him talk and he will change his opinion at once."

Rossini on his side kept an equally flattering recollection of Mendelssohn. He told Wagner how much he had enjoyed his playing some of his own "delicious *Songs Without Words*," Weber, and, last and best of all, Bach; how stupefied Mendelssohn had been when he had proclaimed, "perhaps a little too casually" his passion for German music. What a charming person!

It is very difficult to realise that this Rossini was the same person who, as we know, was suffering at the time from disappointment, depression, nerves and the consciousness, in all probability, of a losing fight against disease. Was there ever a more impenetrable mask, a greater disharmony between appearance and reality? We come nearer to the real man in Bologna whither Rossini, after his journey with Rothschild, returned in October, 1836. He wanted quiet, quiet above all things; so one of his first acts was to settle up with Isabella. Their separation was not legally registered till a year later, but in practice it came into effect almost at once. The negotiations on both sides were wholly amicable. Rossini, apart from a desire not to prejudice public opinion by any unfairness, wished to do the right thing; Isabella, recognising her faults or the inevitability of circumstances, suddenly became so reasonable that she earned the praise even of her husband. She kept Castenaso, of course, and received an allowance sufficient not only to live in comfort but to rent an apartment in Bologna during the winter. Her relations with her husband, if not with her father-in-law, continued to be friendly till the day of her death. She even asked Olympe Pélissier to lunch when that lady, at Rossini's urgent request, came to settle in Bologna. Olympe was the one thing in Paris he had regretted, and during the negotiations for separation he often wrote to his friend Severini, the director of the Théâtre Italien, thanking him for the kindness he had shown her and sending her most affectionate messages.

Now at last she had come to give him the care and attention he so missed; Isabella seemed in a fair way to be making friends with her; dear old Vivazza, just entering on his seventy-eighth year, did not conceal his delight in having him home again; all Bologna was proud of his reputation; he had saved sufficient money to live comfortably. In short, Rossini thought he had at last found contentment if not happiness. On one thing his mind was made up: Never again would he write an opera for those scoundrels in Paris who had treated him in so scurvy a fashion; never again, so far as he could see, would he write an opera at all, though here there may have been a mental reservation, conscious or un-conscious. If it came to that, why write any music of any description? *Vanitas vanitatum!*

CHAPTER XII

THIS appears to be the psychological moment to consider the reasons which induced Rossini to retire from active musical life. It is perhaps unnecessary again to stress the fact that the phenomenon is unique in the history of music and difficult to parallel in the whole history of art. When Rossini wrote *William Tell* he was thirty-six years old; even at the time he settled down in Bologna, when his mind seems to have been definitely made up, he was only forty-four! Is there any other artist who thus deliberately, in the very prime of life, renounced that form of artistic production which had made him famous throughout the civilised world?

Though countless people endeavoured at one time or another to extract an explanation from Rossini himself, few ever succeeded in getting an answer at all. It was the subject above all others which he desired to avoid. For instance, when Aguado once wrote, begging him to compose another opera for Paris, he merely replied that he had just sent off the two finest sausages to be found in Bologna, accompanied by precise instructions to Aguado's cook how to prepare them! If this was all Aguado, to whom he owed so much, could get out of him, it may be imagined that there was little chance for the ordinary person. Most of the answers he did give were in fact given many years later, when time had cast a veil over some of the pain and the bitterness.

166

Thus, he wrote to Pacini in 1866: "This art (of music), which is based solely on sentiment and ideals, cannot escape the influence of the times we live in, and the sentiment and ideals of the present day are wholly concerned with steam, rapine and barricades. Remember my philosophical determination to give up my Italian career in 1822, my French career in 1829. Such foresight is not vouchsafed to everybody; God granted it to me, and I have been grateful for it ever since."

Thirteen years earlier, he had written in much the same vein to a young librettist, praising his work as being exactly suited to the spirit of the times but insisting that that spirit, alike in life and art, was wholly repugnant to him. A year later, in refusing the request of a correspondent, who had written to enquire whether he would accept a commission to compose some music, he definitely stated that his silence proceeded, partly from a dislike of having to follow the evil tendencies of the day, partly from a desire to give a good example.

So much for what may be called reasons of a political and æsthetic nature.

On other occasions he found other reasons equally cogent. Thus, he wrote in 1852 to the tenor, Donzelli, one of his dearest friends, emphasising his ever-increasing impotence of mind and utter incapacity to write any music even to oblige him. "Believe me, it was a sentiment of delicacy rather than vanity which led me to renounce money and fame; otherwise I should not so soon have hung up my lyre on the wall. Music needs freshness of ideas; I am conscious of nothing but lassitude and crabbedness." His answer to a direct question by Maffei is a variation on the same theme. "I wrote operas when melodies came in search of me, but, when I realised that the time had come for me to set out and look for them, I, in my well-known capacity as an idler, renounced the journey and ceased to write."

Then there are the miscellaneous reasons like those given to the painter De Sanctis and Richard Wagner. Rossini told De Sanctis that, had he had a son, he would have continued to compose despite his natural tendency to laziness. His answer to Wagner's courteous reproach is particularly interesting. After having remarked that the composition of nearly forty operas in less than twenty years surely gave him the right to feel tired, he added that, furthermore, there were no longer any singers capable of interpreting his music. And, on Wagner's expressing astonishment, he gave as a reason the disappearance of the *castrati*, who on their retirement used to teach singing with a competence never approached by the new-fangled methods at conservatoires.

To Hiller he gave most of the reasons already cited and, in addition, his dislike of the 1830 revolution in Paris and of the consequent changes in the administration of the Opera. He also stressed his desire to be with his old father during the last years of his life. Only on one occasion, apparently, did he make any direct reference to the cause which probably counted for more than any other. This was in a conversation with a certain Chevalier Neukomm recorded by the English biographer, Edwardes. Neukomm had said that life without work was inconceivable to him.

"You have a passion for industry; I always had a passion for idleness", exclaimed Rossini.

"The forty operas you have composed scarcely bear that out", answered Neukomm.

"That was a long time ago. We ought to come into the

world with a packthread instead of nerves . . . but let us drop the subject."

Such are, to the best of my belief, the sole important recorded pronouncements made by Rossini on a subject which has always intrigued the world. There are others, of course, often apocryphal. In this category, unfortunately, must be placed the story of Rossini's famous answer to the questioner who asked when he would write another opera: "When the Jews (Meyerbeer and Halévy) have finished their Sabbath." He may at times have felt something like this but he explicitly denied having said it.

The reader, now in possession of the facts revealed by these pronouncements or by incidents already related, can, at any rate, make up his mind as to the validity and the mutual compatibility of the pronouncements in particular, as well as to the credibility of the author's reconstruction of the psychological drama in general. Mainly, no doubt, the reconstruction must depend on deductions rather than stark facts. There are, however, a few such facts that should be isolated. For instance, we know that Rossini, though desirous of a rest even before *William Tell* and exhausted to a well-nigh pathological extent after it, definitely intended to write another opera in the following year, certainly up till the time of the 1830 revolution, which jarred his susceptibilities and invalidated his contract; perhaps till even a little later.

By 1836 at the latest he had resolved to sever his connection with the stage, but it seems possible that, had the right treatment of the right subject been found, and the right pressure applied at the right time, he might have changed his mind. As a matter of fact we even know what "the right subject" was: Joan of Arc, of all

unlikely people! She seems to have made a special
appeal to his imagination, and the fact that in 1832, in
the first flush of his passion, he wrote a cantata so
entitled for Olympe Pélissier, is not devoid of significance.

By 1848 he was incapable of serious effort and so
remained for many years. As we shall see, the political
troubles of the times came to aggravate his already
aggravated maladies. He was a nervous and physical
wreck. Had the dangerous benefits of psycho-analysis
been revealed to the world in the 'thirties, they might
have saved Rossini for music; in the 'forties it would have
been too late. Possibly, however, they would have
availed nothing unless the discoveries of Wassermann and
Ehrlich had also been anticipated by a century. It is
difficult not to think that some of Rossini's troubles were
of venereal origin; his later symptoms, disease of the
bladder and urinary tract, his premature baldness and
toothlessness, seem revelatory. His acute neurasthenia,
too, though inherent in his constitution, may well have
been intensified by the same cause.

Needless to say, these troubles were not so acute in the
'thirties and early 'forties as they became later, but the
seeds of them were present and explain much. Nobody,
except Radiciotti, has sufficiently emphasised Rossini's
poor health almost immediately after *William Tell*. His
nerves in particular were a torture to him. Even granted
that the first experience of a railway train may have
been terrifying and unpleasant, it is impossible to
imagine the journey from Antwerp to Brussels causing
anybody to faint! Which is what happened to Rossini in
1836. But the exceptional value he attached to the
ministrations of Olympe provides, perhaps, even better
evidence of the ravages of the various illnesses which she

helped to assuage. He simply could not do without her. One has a feeling that, had Isabella not obligingly provided real grounds for separation, they would, sooner or later, have been invented.

It is a fact, no doubt, that Rossini felt mortified by the cavalier treatment meted out to *William Tell* by the Opera authorites after the revolution, especially when contrasted with the lavishness shown in respect to Meyerbeer's operas. This, however, by no means justifies the assumption that the failure of *William Tell* and a dislike of Meyerbeer were responsible for his retirement. To begin with, it must again be emphasised, *William Tell* was not a failure. So to describe a work that earned for its composer the highest regard of the whole musical world, and achieved in his own lifetime five hundred performances at the Opera alone, is a sheer misuse of words. It was not even merely a *succès d'estime;* it failed to achieve a great popular success, that is all.

As regards Meyerbeer, the question is a little more complex. Radiciotti has tried to prove that the relations of the two men, far from being antagonistic, were something more than cordial. In my opinion he has failed to establish his case. No doubt Meyerbeer was at great pains to show Rossini every sign of affection and veneration on every possible occasion; but that was Meyerbeer's way. There is some reason indeed to think that Rossini saw through the manœuvre,* and the fact that he was genuinely moved by Meyerbeer's death and wrote a

*There is a well-authenticated story that Rossini, when out walking one day with a friend, happened to meet Meyerbeer, who asked anxiously after his health. Rossini replied with a recital of various distressing symptoms, so, when Meyerbeer had gone, the friend suggested an immediate return home. "Not at all," said Rossini, "I feel perfectly well, but dear Meyerbeer would be so delighted to hear of my death to-morrow that I hadn't the heart to deny him a little pleasure to-day."

little funeral ode to his memory implies little.* The two men had been in constant contact for many years, and the cessation of a long-established relationship means much to an old man. My own impression, for what it is worth, is that Rossini did not positively dislike Meyerbeer, indeed rather liked him than otherwise, but considered him a bit of a fraud as a man, and hateful, though greatly talented, as a composer.

Of Rossini's distaste for Meyerbeer's later music and all that it stood for, there can be no question. It is inherent in the scorn and disgust he poured on contemporary musical ideals, of which Meyerbeer's operas were the outstanding embodiment; in the adroitness he showed in parrying questions intended to elicit his opinion of *Les Huguenots*, *Le Prophète* and *L'Africaine*. Under a vow of secrecy he was quite explicit with Michotte, emphasising Meyerbeer's lack of confidence in himself, the brevity of his musical ideas, his preoccupation with mere effects intended to astonish the public, his excessive use of the pianoforte in composition, and so on.

Possibly this aspect of the case is best summed up by saying that it was the exclusiveness of the fashionable craze for Meyerbeer's music, rather than the success of the music as such, which discouraged Rossini. There should have been room for both of them, but, if these people wanted nothing else but Meyerbeer, he could and would not compete. He might, perforce, be "old-fashioned," as they said, but he need not become a bore. After all, he had his own glory, unparalleled in musical history, to live up to. Why imperil it for the sake of a

---

*The story, which Verdi liked so much, about Rossini and Meyerbeer seems appropriate here. When Meyerbeer died, his nephew wrote a funeral march and submitted it to Rossini for criticism. "Charming, charming, my dear fellow," said Rossini, "but frankly now, don't you think it would have been much better if you had died and your uncle had written the funeral march?"

casual opera or two? If Rossini had been a man of robust health and strong character, like Verdi; if, like Wagner, he had had a consuming passion, instead of a pronounced taste, for his art, such considerations could scarcely have weighed with him. Being the man he was and of the temperament we have observed, they almost certainly helped to turn the balance in favour of renunciation.

Besides, there is no reason to doubt that the modesty he showed in his conversations with Weber and Wagner was wholly genuine, and that, when he reproached his friend Pacini for having, in his *Memoirs*, "turned me into an exclamation mark in the history of music instead of a wretched comma," he meant what he wrote. It is generally advisable to take everything said by Rossini about himself with a pinch of salt, but nothing in his career encourages us to think that he had an unduly exalted opinion of his gifts. "Which of all your operas do you like the best?" once asked an admirer. "*Don Giovanni!*" came the rapier-like reply. His excellent common sense saved him from being deceived by the flattery so freely lavished on him by his worshippers. He never pretended that he did not write music to make money, so, when he had accumulated enough to live on, he felt at perfect liberty to retire, free from the illusion, entertained by so many lesser composers, that the world could not get on without him.

It is even possible that he acted wisely. Heine thought so and said that, in his retirement, Rossini once more showed genius as distinct from talent. "An artist who possesses only talent preserves to the last an impulse to make use of his gifts; he is stimulated by ambition, feels that he is approaching ever nearer perfection. . . . A genius, on the other hand, conscious of having already

produced his best work, is satisfied; despising the world
and its petty ambitions, he goes off to Stratford-on-Avon
like William Shakespeare, or, like Gioacchino Rossini,
strolls down the Boulevard des Italiens with a smiling
face and a caustic tongue "

A reader of this book is scarcely likely to need to be
warned against the facile assumption that Rossini
retired from sheer laziness. Yet this explanation is often
taken for granted. Indeed, an English critic once
summed up Rossini as a composer who was so lazy that
he wrote his music in bed and retired in early middle age
to enjoy social life and the pleasures of the table! Since
nearly all the fallacies current about Rossini are contained in this diverting piece of impertinence, it may be
as well to dispose of them severally.

Scarcely anything about Rossini has been more
maligned than the pleasure he took in food and drink.
Except in his early years, when, like most Italians, he ate
and drank with a copiousness unknown to the modern,
but not the contemporary, Englishman, he was essentially fastidious in these matters. He took trouble to
secure good wines from all over the world, including
those from Peru, of all unlikely countries; and in later
days he was unashamedly proud of his cellar. He delighted in certain Bolognese products. Nothing, for
instance, gave him greater pleasure than the various
cheeses, sausages and hams which friends sent to him in
Paris from time to time. He valued these more highly, he
wrote to one of them, than all the decorations, orders
and crosses in the world. He took considerable interest
in recipes, and his weakness for *pâté de foie gras* is enshrined in the still famous *tournedos Rossini*. Generally
speaking, however, rich food does not seem to have

appealed to him; which in view of the nature of his maladies is not surprising.* What he mainly cared about was that the simple products, like those mentioned above, should be genuine. In short, Rossini, like Debussy, was an epicure; not a glutton like Brahms—a distinction which a generation, increasingly content with tinned, standardised and generally commercialised foods, cannot, perhaps, be expected to appreciate. To be frank, the matter is of little importance. The artistic temperament inclines sometimes to austerity, more often to indulgence of the senses; never to that anæmic, inhibited compromise between the one and the other which finds favour in our middle-class civilisation.

With regard to society, he frequented it not more, but less, after his retirement, as we shall presently see; and, in any case, it was illustrious people who came to see him rather than he who sought them out. As a matter of fact, Rossini's social activities throughout his working life were, in general, eminently practical, a point which the attentive reader can scarcely have failed to notice for himself. With regard to the writing in bed, it is based, presumably, on the well-known story of the occasion when Rossini preferred to write a new number rather than to get out of bed to pick up one already half completed. As a generality it is not even worth discussing.

Remains the laziness. Rossini himself took great pleasure in emphasising it on every possible occasion, but that means precisely nothing. The world had decided to call him lazy; he would be the first to say how right the world was. Thus, attention would be

*A French friend gave me a letter from an old lady who was once taken to lunch with Rossini. In view of his reputation she was, she writes, surprised at the simplicity of the food.

diverted from his hidden inner secrets which he guarded so jealously. Such was the procedure adopted by Rossini in many matters, and it worked surprisingly well. No man has ever taken more pleasure in maligning himself. What did a reputation for idleness, cynicism and greed matter so long as the reality of suffering and decay remained unsuspected? "Lord, what fools these mortals be!" he might have chuckled to himself, had he been sufficiently familiar with Shakespeare.

The only real justification of the charge of laziness against Rossini lies in his excessive self-borrowings. He did undoubtedly make too frequent use of old material in his various operas. On the other hand, it is only fair to remember that the practice was traditional in his early days; even Gluck had adopted it, while no Italian composer would have dreamed of questioning its necessity. Rossini's fault lay in pushing it to an extreme. Even, however, if the amount of operas he wrote be discounted in proportion, there remains a sufficient quantity to absolve Rossini from anything that can possibly be called indolence. Rossini was not indolent; he was deficient in æsthetic con-scientiousness, too easy-going and inclined, certainly, to sluggishness. He needed, that is to say, to drive him into action, a definite stimulus like a contract or a desire to please some particular person, or even, occasionally, an enthusiasm for some particular subject. All these were lacking after *William Tell*.

No single reason, then, suffices to account for his "great renunciation"; several causes, as we have seen, combined to bring it about. Laziness, in the true sense of the term, was scarcely even one of them.

CHAPTER XIII

A LOSING BATTLE

In November, 1837, Rossini and Olympe Pélissier left Bologna to spend the winter in Milan. The reason why Rossini made this move is not certain; perhaps the situation between Olympe and Isabella became too delicate. Inevitably, the first friendliness of the relations between the two women did not last, and the curious spectacle of Rossini in one house, Isabella in another and Olympe in yet another, must have set many tongues wagging in Bologna. It was not as if people regarded Rossini as a mere Bohemian. One of old Vivazza's typical letters proves that he was very much in the social view. "He is very happy here among us," wrote Vivazza in February, 1837, "and has a fine time at all the most important social functions and is well thought of by all the powers-that-be, that is to say our two most eminent Cardinals as well as our most worthy Senator Guidotti and many others. At Carnival time he was asked to the grand ball given by our most worthy Austrian General" (oh, Vivazza!) "where he went all dressed up with six decorations on his coat, each one different from the other, and round his neck a ribbon bearing the order sent him by the King of Sweden." Rossini may well have felt that "the two most eminent Cardinals", whose influence in a clerical stronghold such as Bologna must have been paramount, if not the General and the Senator, would view his equivocal situation with some disfavour. A few months absence might serve to soften the shock.

One thing is certain: music was the least of the factors that took Rossini to Milan. He wished neither to write nor hear it. Except for three insignificant military marches, which he had composed during a brief visit to Paris on the occasion of the marriage of the Duke of Orleans in 1837, the whole of this period seems to have been utterly barren. He would not even go to hear the performances at La Scala, writing to his friend Severini that it was an intolerable place. His energies seem mainly to have been concentrated on arranging a series of Friday evening musical parties where all artistic Milan assembled to perform or hear his music. Rossini himself, not at all prone to blow his own trumpet in matters of this kind, was frankly delighted with their success. "My musical evenings", he wrote to a friend in Bologna, "are making quite a sensation here in Milan. All the distinguished amateurs, the artists and the musicians come and sing in the chorus, which numbers about forty excluding the soloists. Madame Pasta* will sing next Friday; which, as you may well believe, is an extraordinary novelty considering that she will not sing in any other private house. With all the opera singers vying with one another to be asked to sing, I find myself obliged to struggle all day to prevent the admission of new satellites. . . . Olimpia does the honours of the house with great success, and we have a fine time. Why have I not got you and your bassoon here? My little dinners are excellent; so are my wines, in which I

*Giuditta Pasta, for whom Rossini had written *Il Viaggio a Reims*, was one of the most remarkable singers of her day. Her voice is said to have combined the characteristics of a genuine soprano and a genuine contralto, and her artistry to have been such as to enable her to blend both qualities to perfection.

often drink the health of my Bologna friends."

Needless to say, admission to such functions was eagerly sought for. Liszt, who stayed in Milan during that winter and remarked on the enthusiasm for music characteristic of the city, wrote a glowing account of them, which entirely bears out Rossini's description of their brilliance and musical excellence.

Inevitably, too, by way of return, various festivities were organised in his honour, at one of which was revived, to everybody's delight, the quartet from *Demetrio e Polibio*, written when he was a boy of fourteen. There was even a vaudeville entitled *I Rossiniani a Parigi* performed at one of the theatres, but, unlike Scribe's Parisian essay in the same vein, there was no question of satire on this occasion. Altogether Rossini must have found life, if a little vapid, at any rate agreeable.

Fate, however, had no intention of leaving him in even the semblance of content for very long. In the middle of January, 1838, the Théâtre Italien was destroyed by fire, and the director, Severini, who lived in the building, perished. The news brought back all Rossini's nervous trouble. It is doubtful which affected him the more: the miserable fate of a valued friend, or the thought of what might have happened if the fire had taken place when he, too, lodged above the theatre. His morbid imagination, his hypersensitive nerves, gave him no rest; he was, one of his biographers tells us, prostrate for many days.

There was, however, something even worse in store when he returned to Bologna in March to join his father, who was beginning to fail. He seems to have led a comparatively quiet life and was sufficiently himself again by the early spring of 1839 to accept with enthusiasm the office of "Honorary President in Perpetuity" of the commission appointed to carry out some very necessary reforms at the Liceo Musicale. This, as we shall presently see, would have entailed a very real amount of work, invaluable as a sedative for his unquiet mind; but the very day after his acceptance of the office old Vivazza died at the age of eighty.

Once again Rossini was plunged into the depths of depression. He had loved his father only less than his mother. Feeling unable to remain in the house where they had lived together, he immediately put it on the market, himself moving into the comparative discomfort of furnished apartments. The effect on his physical health was such that the doctors would not even allow him to go to the house in Paris, which Aguado, invaluable and solicitous as ever, had placed at his disposal, ordering him instead to recuperate for a few months at Naples. While there, except for a more or less official visit to the Conservatoire, presumably to mark the inauguration of changed and now friendly relations, he did not go out at all, but spent his time at Posillipo in the villa of his former employer, Barbaia, whose guest he was. Naples does not seem to have done its work. As Radiciotti somewhat naively observes, "neither the affectionate solicitude of his old friend nor the delightful surroundings, recalling so many pleasant and joyful memories, sufficed to restore his lost tranquillity of mind, any more than the balmy air of the delicious Gulf sufficed to restore his physical strength." The picture of Barbaia, on the very scene of their previous joint exploits, endeavouring to restore tranquillity of mind to the ex-husband of his own ex-mistress strikes one as more than a little comic.

The Sala Rossini in the Liceo Musicale at Bologna. This room contains his piano, one of his wigs and many other relics. The portrait in the corner is of Isabella Colbran

Offert a mon [?]ne Collegue
Arthur S. Sullivan.   G. Rossini
Paris 12 9: 1862.

Though Rossini returned to Bologna in September, it was not till January, 1840, that his health allowed him to devote any serious attention to the Liceo Musicale. When, however, he did do so, his conscientiousness and zeal were beyond cavil. Apparently, like Ferruccio Busoni many years later, he entertained the impossible ambition of turning Bologna into a kind of musical Athens. He certainly did not spare himself, for he became in practice rather the actual director of the Liceo than an honorary president of a committee. He reformed the teaching staff, trying, though without success, to induce, first Mercadante, then Donizetti, to accept the post of Professor of Composition. He paid special care, needless to say, to the singing curriculum, and personally selected or wrote two standard exercises in vocalisation.* He instituted public auditions for the more advanced students and weekly practices for the orchestra, which he himself conducted. So occupied was he by all this, that he does not seem to have left Bologna at all except for a fortnight's visit to Venice to encourage by his presence a friend who was tempting fortune with a new opera.

The story of Rossini's association with the Liceo is one of the most creditable in his career. The famous Belgian

---

*It may be of interest, as evidence of the changed standard of vocal technique, to state that I have tried these exercises on several professional singers, and that one has proved too much for nearly all of them. Yet it was a standard exercise for all the singing pupils at Bologna!

The intrepid fledglings who hop on to our concert platforms after a couple of years casual study may like to know that in Rossini's day five years of hard work were considered the minimum period necessary to train a female singer, the five becoming seven years in the case of a male! During this time it was by no means unusual for a master to devote months at a time to what Rossini calls "the gymnastic of guttural contractions", no note whatever being emitted. Permission to sing any kind of song was exceptional and only given, in any case, when production, pronunciation of vowels and consonants, breathing and so on were absolutely correct.

And then we wonder at the decadence of our singing!

musicologist, Fétis, who visited him in the summer of 1841, was immensely struck by his activity as contrasted with the slackness that had often characterised his administrative duties in Paris. He was also struck by the physical change that had taken place in Rossini, who looked much older and considerably emaciated. During the summer, apparently, when he lived outside the city, he drove on most days to the Liceo, but had to rest for a while in his town apartment before he felt able to attend to his duties. For the first time, too, Fétis had a glimpse of the real man, so different, as he himself observes, from the apparent egotist who, partly to protect himself, partly to please the French, had built up in Paris a reputation for trenchant and cynical wit. Nothing that Rossini could do for his friends was too much trouble. He went to infinite pains to procure for Fétis admission to the jealously guarded libraries indispensable to his critical researches; he used all his influence and all his wisdom to assist the career of his young protégé, the tenor Ivanoff, who seems to have succeeded Bellini in his affections. The only thing that appeared to interest him not at all was the making of music on his own account. He even protested that the piano in his house was solely for the use of other people, and insisted that in no circumstances would he write any more music—an insistence, however, which did not wholly convince the musical critic.

Quite rightly so, because almost, if not exactly, at that very time, Rossini with typical secrecy had made up his mind to complete the *Stabat Mater*. The reader will remember how, to oblige his friend Aguado, Rossini had, nearly ten years before, composed and dedicated this work to the Spanish prelate Varela, but that owing to illness he had been obliged to leave the completion of the last four numbers to Tadolini. When Varela died (in 1837) his heirs decided to sell the publication rights to a French publisher, though, it may be remembered, Rossini had expressly stipulated that the *Stabat* should never be printed. Aulagnier, however, the publisher in question, on the ground that the acceptance by Rossini of Varela's handsome present constituted an act of sale, decided to proceed with the publication, and wrote to inform Rossini of the fact. Rossini answered with the utmost firmness that he would do everything in his power to prevent any such thing, that in any event only six numbers had been written by him. As a matter of fact, he had already been informed of what was in the wind by his own publisher, Troupenas, to whom he immediately sold the rights of the revised and completed *Stabat* for 6,000 francs in order that Troupenas might be in a position to represent his interests in Paris. Whether, as he gave Aulagnier to understand, he had written one or two of the missing numbers very soon after the original date of composition; whether, as appears more probable, he did this after first hearing from Troupenas, is not clear; but he certainly revised the whole work and wrote the final fugue some time in the summer or autumn of 1841.

The rival publishers then proceeded to indulge in a complicated lawsuit which Troupenas eventually won. Aulagnier was ordered to destroy the plates he had had made, but was acquitted of the rather absurd counter-charge of "counterfeiture and theft". Though in the circumstances he could not well have acted otherwise than he did, there is no doubt that Rossini remained in his heart averse as ever from having his music printed. He even wrote to Troupenas urging him "not to talk too much nonsense (*ne blaguez pas trop*) in the papers about the merits of my *Stabat*"; to which request the publisher seems not to have paid the slightest attention. The publicity of the lawsuit, which was the subject of much comment in Paris, probably made reserve impossible in any case, but he might have prevented a paper associated with his interests making the inane suggestion that the *Stabat*, written in a style entirely different from Rossini's usual dramatic manner, was the result of the profound impression made upon the composer by the mystical atmosphere of the convents in Spain. Pure moonshine, of course! Rossini had written the *Stabat* for the purely mundane reason that he felt he could not refuse Aguado's urgent request, and had not altered his style in any particular of importance.

Theorists have often discussed whether there exists in reality such a thing as a musical style which is definitely ecclesiastical, whether it is not a mere question of convention and association of ideas. Certainly Beethoven, Mozart and Haydn would have been reluctant to accept the tenets now insisted upon by musicians and churchmen alike. Pergolesi, on whose *Stabat* Rossini's is clearly, perhaps consciously, modelled, would very likely not even have understood what they were talking about. Anybody who approaches Rossini's score with preconceived ideas as to the exclusive rights of counterpoint in the domain of Church music will inevitably condemn it altogether. It is, with the exception of the final "Amen" fugue, more secular, more theatrical even than Verdi's *Requiem*, and the fault found by old Padre Martini with Pergolesi for writing in a similar style his *Stabat Mater* and *La Serva Padrona* applies, *mutatis mutandis*, equally as well here.

If the *Stabat Mater*, however, is viewed as music pure and simple, there is much that is very attractive about it. Speaking generally, it may be divided into two parts: the first six numbers, and the four numbers written later as substitutes for Tadolini's contribution—which are definitely superior. Yet there are some charming things in the first numbers also, notably the almost danceable quartet, "Sancta Mater", and the "Eja, Mater", which, except for an unfortunate passage in six-eight, is genuinely expressive. It is regrettable that one of the worst numbers of all, the facile if effective "Cujus Animam", should be, perhaps, the best known; while the succeeding duet is only a little better. There is something to be said for all the last four numbers, the "Fac ut Portem" being really tender, the "Inflammatus" very eloquent. As for "Quando Corpus Morietur", admired by Wagner and recognised by Rossini himself as one of his happiest inspirations, it is a fine example of unaccompanied four-part writing, delightfully harmonised, from which Verdi in his Mass had clearly learnt a good deal. Best of all, perhaps, is the final "Amen", for the fugue, though it may have offended the pedants, is very vigorous, the boldness of the ascending passage that sets the words "In Sempiterna" being most striking. In short the *Stabat Mater*, if uneven, is a very characteristic and agreeable work.

To its contemporaries, however, it appeared as an indisputable masterpiece. On the occasion of the first performance in the Salle Ventadour on the afternoon of the 7th of January, 1842, the enthusiasm of the public knew no bounds. The composer's long silence had whetted their curiosity, and two private performances, at which the astute Troupenas had enabled the leading

critics and a few distinguished amateurs to hear before-
hand a portion of the work, had already filled Paris with
rumours of the excellence of Rossini's score. Heine, who
proclaimed its superiority to Mendelssohn's *St. Paul* alike
on religious and musical grounds, only interpreted the
current cultured opinion of the day when he extolled
the "eternal suavity and the serene sweetness" of
Rossini's music. Critical opinion was no less favourable,
the *Débats*, for instance, declaring that since the first
performance of Haydn's *Creation* in Paris no musical
event had so impressed or moved the public. Perhaps a
portion of the success was due to the excellence of the
performance, for Grisi was the soprano; Albertazzi, the
contralto; Mario, the tenor and Tamburini, the bass.*
But the almost immediate triumph of the *Stabat* in every
country of the world proves that the music won its way
on its own merits. Its attraction has not waned entirely
even to-day.

The only discordant note in the chorus of praise came
from the musical papers inspired by Aulagnier and his
associate Schlesinger, who, not unnaturally, were loth
to praise a composition that had caused them so much
expense and annoyance. By a curious and rather unfortunate coincidence Schlesinger was the man who had
enabled young Richard Wagner to live in Paris by doling
out unpleasant if useful hack work; and it may have been
a recollection of this service that prompted Wagner to
write an extremely unpleasant article on the *Stabat*, which
was not so much an attack on the music as an excuse for
questionable jokes about Rossini's journey to Spain, the
country, as with typical Wagnerian taste he took care

*It is typical of the regard paid to singers in those days that the manage-
ment ventured to divide the *Stabat Mater* (which is extremely short) by an
entr'acte of half an hour in order to allow them time to recuperate.

to remind his readers, traditionally associated with the exploits of Don Juan.

Rossini had not gone to Paris for the *Stabat Mater* but, inevitably, the *Stabat Mater* came almost immediately to him at Bologna. Three performances were arranged, of which, at his own wish, all the proceeds were to be devoted to the foundation of a hostel for old and infirm musicians. The best professional and amateur talent in the neighbourhood volunteered for service, so that the occasion assumed the character of a local festival of first-class importance. Rossini spared no pains to secure a performance worthy of it. As Bologna seems to have been lacking in 'cellists, he begged his friend Vitali to come with his son to strengthen the 'cellos in the orchestra; for solo parts he personally selected two professionals, Clara Novello and his protégé, Ivanoff, and two thoroughly competent amateurs; he persuaded several singers of note to take part in the chorus. Not feeling able himself to conduct, he begged Donizetti to undertake the responsibility on his behalf; and Donizetti, who accepted with enthusiasm, threw himself into the task with a zeal and conscientiousness that not only won for him the affectionate gratitude of the composer, but secured, apparently, uncommonly good performances. These took place on the 18th, 19th and 20th of March, 1842. The city went wild with delight; there were the usual serenades and demonstrations; Rossini had to appear on the balcony of his apartment to acknowledge the applause of the huge crowd. Had he had his way, however, he would not have been present at any of the performances. Even when Donizetti with great difficulty prevailed on him to come to the third, he refused to sit in the hall itself but remained in a neighbouring room with one or two friends. At the end, however, in response to the plaudits of the audience, he reluctantly consented to take a call on the platform where he saluted the conductor with a warm embrace.

It is clear that during this time Rossini was in a highly emotional, hypersensitive state. At the conclusion of the final rehearsal he slipped away, fell into a chair and, gazing at his mother's picture on the wall, burst into tears. The shouts of applause still ringing in his ears reminded him, it seems, of the pleasure she would have taken in his triumph. Again, while he was listening to the last performance, one of his friends, by way of a joke, began to read out an unfavourable criticism of the very music that was at that moment sending the huge audience into transports of enthusiasm. All those present, Rossini included, began to laugh, but, on a sudden, they noticed that he began to tremble and break into a heavy sweat. In a man, hitherto so indifferent, nothing could be more indicative of abnormality of body and mind.

When all was over, gratitude to his interpreters, Donizetti especially, rather than pleasure in the success of his music, seems to have been his paramount feeling. The composer of *Lucia* has himself given us a very revelatory account of his parting with Rossini, who wept as he embraced him and repeatedly murmured: "Do not abandon me, dear friend."

To secure a wider appreciation of the conductor's and singers' merits, he persuaded a friend, the editor of an important Milanese paper, to reproduce a laudatory criticism that had appeared in a local journal, insisting only that all references to himself and his music should be omitted. It was a singularly graceful and charming gesture, but how far removed are we from the devil-may-care, exuberant, gay composer of *La Cenerentola* and *L'Italiana in Algeri!*

CHAPTER XIV

DE PROFUNDIS

THE reception of the *Stabat* provided yet another striking exception to the rule that a prophet is not without honour save in his own country. There were a few dissentients among the writers on music, it is true; but their comparatively mild protests were swallowed up in the general chorus of praise. Rossini's admirers and friends turned his Name Day (the 21st of August) into a regular local festival. On the 19th of March, 1843, there was a performance of *Otello* at which the whole theatre rose to acclaim their illustrious fellow citizen, the greatest enthusiast of all being Isabella Colbran. Not only that. Honours rained upon him from abroad; the Kings of Prussia and of Greece bestowed Orders; the formal notification of his election as Honorary Fellow of the Berlin Academy of Fine Arts was accompanied by a covering letter from Meyerbeer, couched in the most flattering terms.

Whatever satisfaction Rossini may have found in these tributes was more than counterbalanced by his increasing ill health. The death in June, 1842, of his friend Aguado, dramatically killed by a blizzard on the very road that he had himself caused to be constructed over the mountains of the Asturias, gave him yet another shock which his enfeebled nerves were in no condition to withstand. Rossini had been genuinely devoted to Aguado as a friend, as well as grateful to him as a patron. His grief was such that he had to apologise to his intimate crony, Vitali, for not having been in a condition to answer a letter, assuring him, however, that the present accompanying it had been a great consolation. Which, as Vitali's presents almost invariably consisted of white truffles or olives, seems something of an anticlimax! The only thing that appears to have roused him from his lethargy was his enthusiasm for the dancing of Taglioni, who appeared at Bologna during that year.

Then his urinary disease, already very troublesome, became decidedly worse; an operation appeared inevitable. In the hope of avoiding it he decided to go to Paris to consult the famous surgeon, Civiale. Since Rossini refused, as always, to make use of the railway, his journey to Paris took thirteen days, during which, on the pass over Mont Cenis, he came near to sharing the fate of his friend, Aguado. He had no cause to complain of his reception in Paris where he arrived on the 22nd of May, 1843. The press welcomed him with enthusiasm; the Opera authorities had planned a special performance of the best, or at any rate the most popular, scenes from *William Tell* and three other operas; his house was thronged by visitors who, in default of seeing the illustrious composer, left cards and wrote their names in a book, as at an embassy. Civiale, wiser than his Bolognese colleagues, insisted on absolute quiet for his patient. Excitement and emotion were to be avoided at all cost, Olympe, who of course accompanied him, being the most Draconian of guardians. It is clear from his letters that Rossini was much affected by the unaccustomed solitude; he was haunted by the fear of death; the treatment was painful. Though at first he responded very slowly to it, by the beginning of August his condition took a decided turn for the better. The morning was still devoted to the cure, but in the afternoon he was allowed to go out for a walk and, in the evening, to see his friends. They came in the customary numbers: diplomats, literary men, musicians and, above all, singers desirous of advice or help. The painter Scheffer did a portrait of him in oils; the sculptor Etex, a statue, subsequently completed and placed in the Opera.* By the 20th of September he was permitted to leave Paris, ostensibly cured.

On his return to Bologna, Rossini was able to resume his usual habit of life, except that he went out less. The Liceo, to which, on his departure, he had bidden a moving farewell, assuring the staff that the day of his return amongst them would be the happiest of his life, continued to be his main preoccupation. He seems to have had no desire at all to write any music either then or at any time during the next five years. When he did, it was only a question of some trifle, or of adapting music already written to contemporary circumstances. The famous Chorus of the Bards from *La Donna del Lago* was particularly useful in this respect, for, with certain amplifications, it was made to serve not only for an ode in honour of the third centenary of Tasso in 1844, but for a hymn in honour of the succession to the Pontificate of Pius IX in 1846. It was also handed over to the tender mercies of a composer by the name of Niedermeyer for inclusion in an opera called *Robert Bruce*, a kind of free adaptation of *La Donna del Lago* embellished by various

---

*The statue seems to have been a poor one, but the malicious Heine gives us to understand that it was not only its lack of artistic merit that aroused some people's dislike. Meyerbeer, he says, was always at some pains to avoid it, on the same principle that the Jews in ancient Rome used to avoid the Arch of Titus erected to commemorate the destruction of Jerusalem! It was destroyed by fire in 1873.

numbers from other operas, which was produced in Paris on the 30th of December, 1846. *Robert Bruce*, it may be added, achieved a greater success with the public than with the critics who, not unreasonably, blamed the director of the Opera for becoming sponsor to such a mosaic, and the composer for having permitted its fabrication. Berlioz was bitter; Stephen Heller positively venomous. Indeed, the latter's article in the *Musical World* roused Olympe, always ready to flare up in defence of the man she idolised, to such fury that she wrote a letter to the director of the Opera in which she expressed her opinion of Berlioz and Heller in no uncertain terms. She had, she told him, sent to the *Débats* (Berlioz's paper) a box containing two large donkey's ears carefully packed in hay, one for the editor, the other for "Mr. Hector Berlioz, celebrated composer, to hand to his illustrious friend, the modern Midas, otherwise known as Stephen Heller". Rossini, she insisted, knew nothing of her action—which may have been true—adding that he himself remained, as always, entirely indifferent to criticism—which certainly was not. The incident doubtless reflects greater credit on Olympe's heart than on her head, but it affords a striking proof, if proof were needed, of her boundless devotion to Rossini, who, as she said on another occasion, "has always been to me like a god; his immortal genius is such that everything and everybody should prostrate themselves before him".

The sole composition of any importance at all during this period belongs in reality to the same category: a collection of three choruses for female voices with piano accompaniment called *La Foi, L'Espérance, La Charité*, which must be ascribed to Rossini's kindness of heart rather than to any artistic impulse. His friend, Gabussi, had unearthed two youthful compositions and sold them to Troupenas, always on the look out for undiscovered Rossini. But Troupenas, mindful of his experiences with the *Stabat*, thought it wiser to consult the composer himself before publishing them, making a journey to Bologna for that very purpose. At first Rossini would have nothing to do with the project, telling Troupenas that the best thing he could do with such inferior music was to hide it. In the end, however, partly to avoid depriving the not over-prosperous Gabussi of any profit that might accrue, partly to compensate Troupenas for the trouble he had taken in coming to Bologna, he yielded to the publisher's solicitations, and not only gave permission for the reprinting of his two youthful indiscretions, but consented to compose a third number. This, though originally written to the words of a prayer to the Virgin Mary, which Troupenas, a composer himself in his spare moments,* had already set to music, eventually became *La Charité*.

Though *La Foi*, *L'Espérance*, *La Charité*, these three, were favourably received by the Parisians when first performed on the 20th of November, 1844, their sole interest to us lies in the witty epigram of Berlioz, who wrote: "This *Faith* will never move mountains; *Hope* mildly disappointed us; as for the *Charity* which M. Rossini has just bestowed upon us, it must be admitted that, amid the profusion of his musical treasures, such a dole will certainly not ruin him."

*Rossini told Michotte a delicious story in this connection. Troupenas, apparently on the occasion of this very visit, asked him what he should do to find inspiration. Rossini, with perfect gravity, advised him to go out for a daily walk and contemplate the glorious blue Italian sky. The publisher conscientiously followed the advice every morning, but on his return to lunch had always to confess that he had found nothing.

Other people's music appealed to Rossini scarcely more than his own, though he occasionally attended a musical party. His visits to the theatre became less and less frequent, being apparently confined in practice to occasions when there was an opera by some composer in whom he was personally interested. Thus, in October, 1843, he went to hear the first performance at Bologna of *Nabucco* by a remarkable young composer called Giuseppe Verdi, to whom he had been introduced a year before, when that uncouth, taciturn young man, fresh from his first triumph at Milan, had visited Bologna. The fact was that Rossini disapproved of the orientation taken by the musical theatre in Italy. When Etex came to Bologna to finish the statue already mentioned, he heartily endorsed the sculptor's unfavourable impression of the Italian theatre. "Nowadays," he said, "it is not a question of who sings best, but who shouts loudest." What would he have said in the twentieth century?

The outstanding events of this period were the death of Isabella Colbran and his marriage to Olympe. It was in the middle of August, 1845, that Rossini first learnt that Isabella was seriously ill. He had not seen her for many years, but when, a month later, he received a message that his wife much wished him to go to her at Castenaso, he set out at once. Olympe was sensible enough to raise no objection, and in Isabella's sick room husband and wife had a final interview. What they said to each other we shall never know, but we do know that Rossini left the room with the tears flowing down his cheeks, and that he was at pains to instruct those in charge to do everything possible to meet the wishes of the dying woman. Poor Isabella! There is little doubt that she remained in love with him till the very end, for when she died, just a month later, on the 7th of October, his name was on her lips. Her death, despite all the comfort that Olympe lavished upon him, seems to have brought back all his dejection; he would not visit the Villa at Castenaso, giving orders for it to be sold at once. Not quite a year later, on the 16th of August, 1846, he married Olympe in the private chapel of a friend, with only two intimates, a celebrated tenor and a renowned bassoonist, as witnesses. She was forty-seven; he fifty-four.

Political troubles came presently to aggravate his distress, all the worse, perhaps, because unexpected. In 1846 the accession of Pius IX to the Chair of St. Peter aroused the hopeful enthusiasm of the Italians. Italy was at last to become a nation under his sacred tutelage; every city was decorated with flags; every street was crowded with demonstrators. Rossini, though Conservative rather than Liberal by temperament, did not escape the general enthusiasm, and, as we have seen, provided the music for a Hymn to celebrate the happy inauguration of a new era. But the revolutionary ferment of 1848, which drove Richard Wagner to the barricades, and overthrew the monarchy in Paris, in Italy went far beyond anything envisaged by the mild Liberalism of the new Pope. Bands of volunteers from all over the peninsula, their bravery and ardour equalled only by their lack of discipline and equipment, enrolled themselves to fight against the hated Austrians. Windy demagogues or ardent patriots, according to the view taken, launched fervent appeals to the masses to make every sacrifice, possible or impossible, in the common cause.

In Bologna, at any rate, the masses appear to have responded with far greater alacrity than the classes, among whom Rossini, unfortunately, owing to his comparative wealth, found himself numbered. True, he had given a donation, as well as two of his four horses for service with the artillery, which seems to have been totally unprovided with that then indispensable animal. But the more ardent spirits thought he should have done more; accusations, open or whispered, of avarice and lukewarmness began to be heard in the city. The donation was trifling in comparison with his riches; the horses, however much his friends might protest that they had been chosen by the military authorities themselves, were old hacks.

The climax came on the 27th of April, 1848, when a band, that had gone out to play some newly arrived Sicilian volunteers to their quarters, stopped in front of his house to pay the illustrious composer the usual musical honours. When, however, Rossini made his customary appearance on the balcony by way of acknowledgment, some of the Sicilians, or, as seems more probable, certain local patriots who had mingled with them, began a hostile demonstration. Shouts of "rich reactionary", threatening cries and hoots made themselves heard. Rossini, much incensed, withdrew immediately, but the effect on a man of his nervous temperament need not be emphasised, especially as stories of the lawlessness prevalent in the city, and the inability or unwillingness of the authorities to deal with it, had already caused him considerable perturbation. Olympe, who was ill at the time, seems to have been even more frightened than he was. They decided to leave Bologna at once, refusing to see anybody, even their most intimate friends, before their departure for Florence the next day.

There is no need to deny or defend Rossini's pusillanimity. A man who could be thrown into a state of prostration by a journey in a railway train, by the mere thought of what might have happened had he been trapped in the Théâtre Italien fire, could scarcely be expected to maintain any kind of equanimity in the face of a demonstration by a hostile mob, probably the most nerve-shattering experience a human being can undergo. The spectacle of the distracted Olympe, on whom he was accustomed to rely for comfort and support, must have added to his terror. Clearly each aggravated the condition of the other, so that the impression made on both remained permanent. Olympe never forgave the Italians for this insult to her idol. The idol himself never forgave Bologna, "the home of aggression and sausages," as with persistent bitterness he called it thirteen years later, for the fright caused to his devoted worshipper. He would never live there again. When he had to return for a few months in 1850 to sell his house and pack up his most valued possessions, he asked for an escort of four mounted policemen and permission to carry a revolver! By that time the political hopes of Italy had been extinguished, but civil order and discipline had been re-established; Bologna was definitely eager to welcome him back. It made no difference.

As a matter of fact, even the most ardent Bolognese patriots were dismayed when they heard that Rossini had left the city. The most prominent leader of the National movement, Father Ugo Bassi, on the evening of the 29th of April, led a huge crowd to Rossini's house, and there, standing on the very balcony where the composer had been insulted, solemnly rebuked the licence of those who had disgraced the cause of Italian patriotism, insisting that Rossini, by making the

Austrians recognise the superiority of Italian musical genius, had already contributed more than his share to the common victory, asking how the author of *William Tell* could be other than an apostle of liberty.

Father Bassi even wrote in person to the composer at Florence informing him of what he had done and begging him to return to the city of his adoption. Rossini answered with a protestation of his gratitude and genuine regard for Bologna, but excused himself from returning on the ground that his wife was really very ill. He promised, however, to set some verses by Bassi to music as a National Hymn. This Hymn, dedicated to the Civil Guard of Bologna, he did in fact compose a week or so later, but not to Bassi's words. Either, as some say, the words proved to be unsettable, or Bassi, who was wounded almost immediately afterwards on active service, was prevented from writing them.

Had the situation not been so tragic, the patent insincerity of Rossini's protestations of forgiving and forgetting on the one hand, and the absurdity of Bassi's claims on the other, would make a first-class comedy. Rossini, as we have seen, never forgave, probably never intended to forgive, the Bolognese. For one thing, he considered that his public-spirited efforts on behalf of the Liceo had been rewarded with the most base ingratitude. But there was something more fundamental. Wounded in his most vulnerable spot, his abnormal timidity, he shrank like a terrified animal from contact with the city that had so hurt him. As for Bassi's remarks about Austrian music, Rossini, to whom Mozart was a god, and Haydn the object of deepest veneration, would, in normal circumstances, have been the first to laugh at them. The subject of *William Tell*, as already pointed out, should quite likely be regarded as a tribute to his acumen rather than to any political enthusiasm.

Here, however, Rossini would in all probability have protested. When patriotic sentiment was wanted, he, like the wandering minstrel in *The Mikado*, kept *William Tell* and a certain passage in *L'Italiana* cut and dried for defensive purposes. Possibly he convinced himself; he certainly convinced his most eminent biographer, who is at some pains to stress the patriotism latent in the latter passage, where the heroine, in a musical phrase of great spirit and force, adjures her timid lover to think of his country and be brave. Internal evidence, however, does not seem to bear out this interpretation. Another character, duly rebuked, it is true, makes fun of Isabella's outburst immediately afterwards; the pendent chorus on the same theme is certainly not serious. Most significant of all, perhaps, when Isabella, in the finale of the first act, attacks the infatuated Bey for proposing to divorce his wife, she does so in a very similar kind of phrase, equally spirited and forceful.

Liberty and Patriotism were about the last things to preoccupy Rossini in 1813, when he was still in the first flush of his musical and amorous successes. It seems very doubtful whether they ever at any time seemed to him of paramount importance. In that he always remained first and foremost a musician; a musician, too, who liked his life to be as easy and free from disturbance as possible, he was naturally inclined to favour the established order of things. Which is not to assume, as some have done, that he had no feeling for the legitimate aspirations of his native land. He had; but music and a tranquil existence came first, the fiery political ideals of a Verdi being wholly alien to his epicurean nature. It is absurd to blame him; it is even more absurd to try to make him appear as an ardent, misunderstood patriot.

During the first year of his residence in Florence Rossini seems in his heart to have preserved a certain affection and regret for Bologna. When, however, in the middle of September, 1850, he decided, as already stated, to return there for the winter in order to settle up his affairs, he found the tension between the populace and the now re-established Austrian authorities so unpleasant that he was only too delighted to leave again for Florence on the 2nd of May, 1851, the break this time being permanent and irreparable. He continued to miss acutely the companionship of his more intimate Bolognese friends, notably the tenor, Donzelli, but, the more he missed them, the greater was his resentment against the city responsible for their separation.

Florence did her best to make Rossini feel at home. All doors were open to him. The Grand Duke of Tuscany himself gladly received him at his palace; aristocrats like Poniatowski and the English Dante scholar, Lord Vernon, for whom he seems to have developed a genuine liking, became his intimates; he was one of the most honoured figures of a collection of literary men, artists and cultured members of various learned professions, who met regularly at a villa belonging to one of his Pesarese compatriots. At first, though very low in health and spirits, it seemed as if his existence might again become tolerable. He even wrote a little music, albeit of no importance: A *Hymn to Peace* for bass solo and chorus, of which the music is lost but which was performed with considerable success at Bologna, and several other trifles, including a song, *A Grenade*, in bolero rhythm, and a march dedicated to the Sultan of Turkey. He also set a few verses of Dante for the album of his friend, Lord Vernon. Since Rossini had expressed himself most forcibly on Donizetti's unfortunate attempt to set Dante to music, remarking that even God himself, were he a musician, would find the task impossible, the last mentioned, at any rate, must be considered as a purely social gesture.

By the end of the year 1852, however, the state of his health began to go from bad to worse, and the story of the next three years is little but a chronicle of suffering and decay. There are still sometimes flashes of the old wit or fantasy in an occasional letter, but, as a rule, the correspondence is only too obviously that of a disappointed, miserable man. Such, for instance, is the letter written in 1852 to his lawyer with instructions for his will, in which he refers to "the abode in which I lived happily up to *that* day," and in which, incidentally, there is a charming recommendation of his little godson, Donzelli's boy, to whom he bequeathed "the little piano which was the aid and companion of my first musical studies," as well as a magic lantern and a prie-dieu.

After 1852, however, his condition became steadily worse; one cannot help being reminded of the inevitable, irresistible crescendo so closely associated with his own music. It is possible that Lombroso exaggerated somewhat when he asserted that Rossini became definitely mad, that he suffered from the delusion of being completely ruined and used to beg for charity from his friends. Olympe herself always denied that things were ever as bad as this. But they were quite bad enough. Professor Mordani, who saw Rossini several times in 1854, that is to say at the time when his neurasthenia had reached its most acute stage, definitely states that he seemed to be almost out of his mind. His face was pale, his eyes tired and sunken, his head bent and his cheeks withered. He had lost the faculty of taste and was unable to assimilate food. Worst of all were the tortures caused by lack of sleep. For three and a half months, he told Mordani, he never closed an eyelid. Sometimes, standing before a mirror, he would upbraid himself for his lack of courage in not committing suicide. "To what am I come," he pitiably exclaimed, "and what am I doing in this world? And what will people say when they see me reduced, like a small child, to having to rely on a woman?"

He had long ceased to entertain in his house; those privileged few who secured admittance after dinner used to find him still at the table, noisily chewing a toothpick. Music could scarcely be mentioned. There is a pathetic story of how on one occasion Romani and his wife and a certain Juva and his wife entered into a conspiracy with Olympe to bring back a little music into Rossini's life. Exceptionally, all four had been invited to dinner, and the conversation was cleverly turned on to artists and operas of past days. Romani even succeeded in making Rossini laugh, to Olympe's great delight; whereupon Signora Juva, to whom Rossini was much attached and whose voice he much admired, dragged him to the piano, begging him to accompany her in Desdemona's aria from *Otello*—that *Otello* which, three years before, Rossini himself had described to a correspondent as just about as decrepit as its composer.

Many years previously, Rossini had taught Signora Juva this very song, and he consented to play on the condition that there was no light in the room. He began the prelude, which he embroidered and enlarged considerably. Finally he turned to the singer and said, "Now it is

your turn, dear Desdemona." His playing and her singing were so moving, it seems, that Olympe had the
greatest difficulty in restraining the applause of the half a
dozen guests who had been permitted to join the party
after dinner. Rossini himself was so affected that he
broke down completely, sobbing like a child. Presently,
however, pulling himself together, he began again to run
his fingers over the keys and suggested that Signora Juva,
who had not moved from his side, should sing the cavatina from *Semiramide*. At the end he was as delighted as
he had before been dejected. "Music and Rossini are
reconciled!" exclaimed his friends in chorus; and the
evening ended in an atmosphere of cheerfulness to which
the house had long been a stranger.

Nothing, however, seemed to afford any permanent
relief to Rossini's hypochondria and neurasthenia,
though, physically, there was little, if anything, amiss. He
went regularly in the spring and summer to the baths
at Montecatini and Lucca; he tried the so-called magnetic
cure. All in vain. Olympe was in despair. Her thoughts
gradually turned more and more to Paris. Where the
Italian doctors had failed, the French might succeed. In
any case, a complete change of surroundings could
scarcely prove anything but beneficial. It was not easy to
persuade Rossini in his present state of health to undertake such an arduous journey, but finally her devotion
and good sense won the day. The train was, of course, out
of the question; they would take a coach and proceed by
easy stages, stopping a few days at Nice and other places
en route. Thus, on the 26th of April, 1855, accompanied
by his wife, his doctor and two servants, poor shattered,
unhappy Rossini left Florence. Italy was never to see
him again.

CHAPTER XV

THE news of Rossini's return awakened the most lively curiosity and satisfaction in Paris. Once again the newspapers were filled with laudatory articles; once again visitors thronged to the flat in the Rue Basse du Rempart where he was staying. At first, however, he was allowed to see nobody. The various celebrated doctors whom Olympe consulted had come to a surprising unanimity as to the severe regime to be followed. Everybody in the house had received the strictest orders. Even if a visitor more resourceful than the rest managed to get past the porter, there was Tonino, the composer's body-servant, who never left his master by day or night. Last of all, there was Olympe herself, more inflexible, more dragon-like than ever, with only one idea in her head: the recovery of her patient. What Rossini himself, when he progressed sufficiently to make jokes, called this "triple line of fortifications" existed for a long time, but gradually exclusion became a little less drastic. After a week or two he was allowed to receive very short visits from half a dozen of his more intimate friends, Carafa, Pillet-Will, Méry, Auber, and so on. We know how shocked they were by his condition. He could hardly walk, his eyesight was impaired; alike in speaking and writing he found the greatest difficulty in correlating his ideas. We are told that he suffered acutely from one particularly curious disability: he could listen to no sound without hearing at the same time the major third. This caused him so much distress that Olympe had to provide the porter with a special fund to keep away barrel organs and other street musicians.

Gradually, however, the beneficent influence of his new surroundings began to make itself felt. He was able to receive more visitors, including Verdi, who was then in Paris for the production of *Les Vêpres Siciliennes.* Artistic and social Paris vied with one another in paying tribute to the afflicted composer; he and the Crimean War, it is said, divided equally the interest of the gossips. The obsession, which had so tortured him in Florence, of being forgotten and despised by the world, began to pass away. By the 19th of June he was able to enjoy a little private concert that some friends had improvised in his house; he was even permitted to drive to the Conservatoire to pay a short formal visit to Auber as head of that august institution.

In July the doctors ordered him to Trouville, where the benefits of the sea air were enhanced by the company of Hiller, with whom he passed the greater portion of his time playing dominoes and—significant change!— talking about music and musicians. These conversations, it seems, were the principal source of the interesting Reminiscences later written by Hiller and so often quoted in this book. After two months at Trouville Rossini returned to Paris for the winter, which was devoted in the main to a thorough pursuit of his treatment. By a fortunate coincidence revivals of *Moïse* and the *Stabat* at the Théâtre Italien met with the greatest possible success, than which nothing, though Rossini attended neither performance, could have been better calculated to assist him on the road to recovery.

Then, in the summer of 1856, the doctors ordered him to the baths of Wildbad, Kissingen and Baden, with results that were unexpectedly satisfactory. It may have been the cure; it may have been the lively interest shown in his personality by the local population, or the solicitous attention of King Ludwig of Bavaria, or the serenade improvised in his honour at Strasbourg, where the orchestra and chorus of the theatre performed the over-tures to *William Tell* and *The Barber* and the choruses from *Comte Ory* under the windows of his hotel—one thing is certain: he returned to Paris in September a wholly different man.

Perhaps it would be scarcely accurate to say that he was completely cured; for the rest of his life there per-sisted in him some curious kinks. For instance, he never wholly overcame his timidity. He was extremely nervous when driving in a carriage, and his refusal ever to allow any house in which he lived to be lighted by gas may well have been due as much to a fear of explosion as to the hatred of all modern innovations generally cited by the biographers. An assortment of wigs, selected in accordance with the occasion and the company, suggest the persistence of an abnormal sensitiveness about his baldness. His strange secretiveness certainly grew no less.

Still he was incomparably better, able again to enjoy life within the limits of a prescribed routine. He took a new and spacious apartment at the corner of the Rue de la Chaussée d'Antin and the Boulevard des Italiens, then the centre of fashion as well as of activity, the noise and bustle outside appearing to this late sufferer from insomnia an attraction rather than a disadvantage. The summer months were spent in what was then the country at Passy. For the first time in his life his habits became wholly regular. He got up at about eight o'clock, when his wife helped him to dress. After being shaved by the barber, he breakfasted in the usual Continental fashion, while she dealt with his correspondence. At 10.30, if the day was fine, he took his broad-brimmed hat, stuck a pin with a medallion of Handel into his tie and went out for an hour's walk on the boulevard. Later, he took a cab for purposes of shopping, always, however, returning home to lunch except on two occasions in each year: the first, when he went to his friend Bigotini on the eve of his departure to the country; the second, when he lunched with Pillet-Will on his return from the country to Paris in the autumn. At six he dined, retiring immediately after to the bedroom, which also served as his study, to rest and smoke a very light cigar, the first of the day, though he followed his mother's example in frequently taking snuff. When the cigar was finished, he returned to the dining-room, where his wife was waiting to read the papers to him. At 8.30, but not a minute before, visitors were admitted. At 10.0 he went to bed.

Saturdays were an exception. On that evening as many as sixteen people might be asked to dinner, and more came in afterwards. Every rank and category of society were represented, only three visas being necessary to the passport of admission: ability to interest or amuse Rossini; extreme deference to Madame Rossini (indispensable); distinction in some line or other. Everything seems to have been rather formal, for we know that some people preferred Offenbach's evenings on that very account. It is hardly necessary to say that invitations were sought after with the utmost eagerness. Naturally, there was a preponderance of musicians, singers in particular stopping at nothing to obtain an invitation which was in itself almost a hallmark of their competence, for Rossini was decidedly strict about his singer-guests. He showed considerable ingenuity in never bestowing on them undeserved praise while avoiding at the same time unnecessary hurt to their susceptibilities. Thus, at the end of a song by a certain lady endowed with more temperament than vocal technique, he said: "You sing with your soul, and your soul is a beautiful one." Which delighted the singer and her friends without compromising Rossini. With the men he was more downright. On one occasion the servant announced Tamberlick, the famous tenor, who had set all Europe talking of the power and marvellous brilliance of his top C sharp. "Say that I shall be delighted to see him," said Rossini, "but only on condition that he hangs up his C sharp with the hats and coats outside; he can take it away when he goes."

The 15th of April, 1857, Olympe's Name Day, was a notable date in Rossini's career, for on that day he made his wife a present of a composition called *Musique Anodine*, consisting of a prelude for piano, followed by six different settings, two for soprano, one for mezzo-soprano, two for baritone, of a poem by Metastasio. Accompanying it was a dedication: "I offer these little songs to my dear wife, Olympe, as a tribute of gratitude for the affectionate and intelligent care that she lavished upon me in my excessively long and terrible illness." It is easy to imagine her delight. Ever since their first association she had served him with all her heart, mind, soul and strength. During the last few years she had never shrunk from performing any service, sometimes the most repulsive, that might benefit him. Olympe may have begun life as a prostitute, but she proved herself a companion whom any man would count himself fortunate to possess. Without her Rossini would beyond question have ended his life long before this, probably in a lunatic asylum.

The mere fact of the music having been written at all must have pleased her at least as much as the dedication. It was the best possible evidence of restored vitality. Indeed, it marked the first occasion since the *Soirées Musicales*, perhaps one might even say since *William Tell*, when Rossini wrote music because he felt a genuine desire so to do. Twenty-two, possibly twenty-nine, years! It seems an incredibly long time. But, the spell once broken, Rossini took up his pen again with avidity. Music began to sprout like freshly sown seed after rain. True, except for three compositions, to be specified later, one of major, two of minor, importance, the music that he wrote during the last ten years of his life was essentially miniature, very special; a collection of trifles, if you will. Nevertheless, these trifles are equally remarkable for their quality as for their quantity. There are no less than 186 of them preserved in the Liceo Musicale of Pesaro under the general title of *Sins of My Old Age:* songs, duets, trios, quartets, pieces for piano alone and for piano and other instruments, parodies, eccentric oddments of all kinds. It is unfortunately impossible to ennumerate them all, though one would willingly do so if only for the sake of the titles, which are a sheer delight. A few, a very few, are serious, such as *A Funeral Ode for Meyerbeer, A Deep Sleep, A Caress for My Wife, A Word to Paganini.* Some are half serious, like the delicious *Regata Veneziana* songs, which have, exceptionally, been printed.

In the main, however, they are satirical or grotesque.

There is a whole series of pieces for piano with the titles of various desserts and hors-d'œuvre, all the hors-d'œuvre except *The Radishes* appropriately consisting of themes and variations. Radiciotti thinks that these prosaic titles were intended as a satire on the Romantics, and he may well be right. It is impossible not to believe that the piano piece, *A Little Pleasure Trip in the Train*, with its various sections entitled "The Devilish Whistle", "The Sweet Melody of the Brake", "The Terrible Derailment", "First Wounded Man", "Second Wounded Man", "Funeral Ode", "Amen", and so on, was not intended to caricature the programme music that was beginning to come into fashion. Then we pass into the realm of the purely grotesque such as *Tortured Waltz*, *Tartar Bolero*, *A Hygienic Prelude for Morning Use* and, best of all, *Miscarriage of a Polka Mazurka!* There is a song written on a so-called Chinese scale which is in reality nothing but the whole tone scale subsequently popularised by Debussy. There are parodies of Offenbach and Meyerbeer. Practically none of these compositions is published, and it seems a thousand pities that this should be so, because everybody is agreed that they are full of the most individual and ingenious melodic and harmonic ideas. Respighi made use of many of them in the music he arranged for the ballet called *La Boutique Fantasque*, when they once again delighted and enlivened the world.*

*The Rossini purists seem to unite in a chorus of disapproval of what they presumably consider Respighi's sacrilege. I should like to indulge in a dissentient solo. It seems to me that Respighi performed a great service to the old master whom he notoriously loves so well. If he had performed his task with less sense of style, there might be cause for complaint, but, thanks to his technical skill and fine scholarship, he succeeded in preserving admirably the basic flavour of Rossini's music, thus making for the composer many new friends to whom he would otherwise have been known only as the composer of *The Barber of Seville*. Rossini, who too readily permitted far less skilled hands to turn isolated pieces of his music into one *pasticcio* after another, would, I am confident, have been the first to applaud. If it be not impertinent, I would like also to recommend *Le Comte Ory* to Respighi's notice.

They also possess considerable historical importance, for the whimsical humour that prompted them eventually led, via Chabrier and Erik Satie, to the drollery now associated with some of the young French composers, not to mention certain compositions by Lord Berners and William Walton. Thus, it is no exaggeration to say that Rossini in his old age came nearer to one of the aspects of modern music than any other of the great masters.

Just as Rossini adopted the pose of having thought of the best part of *William Tell* while out fishing; just as he pretended to a friend, while actually engaged in the composition of the final numbers of the *Stabat*, that his mind was entirely preoccupied with the qualities of certain new cheeses, so he was fond of asserting that all these trifles were tossed off for his own amusement, with scarcely a moment's reflection. It seems to have been quite untrue. The critic Filippi surprised him on several occasions making erasions and alterations, while the painter, De Sanctis, definitely asserts that he was at considerable pains to put the maximum amount of polish on them, and always made fair copies. Here, in short, we have yet another instance of that strange secretiveness so typical of the man.

When the report of Rossini's having again taken up composition was bruited in Paris, publishers besieged Olympe for permission to print the pieces, offering the most advantageous terms. In vain, however. Not one of them, least of all the one dedicated to her, would she part with at any price. As they were finished, she took them and locked them up in a cupboard, refusing even to show them to anybody except at Rossini's definite request.

They figured prominently in the famous Saturday Evenings, which, largely on that account became more and more sought after, more and more brilliant. Bologna had to pay an increasingly heavy indemnity in *zamponi*, *cotecchini*, sausages and cheese; Rossini's banker friends, Pillet-Will and Rothschild, continued to stock his cellar with their finest claret. These Evenings were eventually reduced to some eight or ten during the winter, and so continued until the eve of the composer's death. At one time or another almost every musician of note in Europe attended them. Among the composers were Meyerbeer, Auber, Gounod, Saint-Saëns and Verdi, who on one occasion was honoured by a special performance of the Quartet from *Rigoletto;* among the pianists, Liszt, Rubinstein and Thalberg. There came Servais, the 'cellist, and every singer of international reputation from Patti and Grisi to Faure and Mario. Sometimes, when a visitor was particularly distinguished, he returned the next morning to make more music. Liszt, for instance, who is said first to have played *St. François de Paul marchant sur les Flots* at one of the Evenings, did this on at least one occasion; so did Servais, whom Rossini thought to be the greatest virtuoso on any string instrument since Paganini. The Evenings reckoned the best of all were those when Rossini himself played. In his way he seems to have been a very remarkable pianist. Though he always referred to, and often signed, himself as "pianist of the fourth class," his playing was much admired by the most competent judges, notably Saint-Saëns. His touch was delightful, and he hardly ever used the pedals. Where he excelled particularly was in accompanying, for here, according to Liszt, nobody could touch him. Needless to say there was no question of virtuosity; his technique seems to have been all his own. It was essentially the playing of a musician of genius with an exceptionally sensitive feeling for the instrument.

A curious feature of these Saturday Evenings was that Rossini himself, unless he was taking part in the performance, never entered the drawing-room. He remained in the dining-room with his crony Carafa, and the door open. There anybody who wished to speak with him had to go. Probably he found the crowd and the heat too much for him. From an account given by the celebrated critic Hanslick, who attended one of the Evenings, he would seem to have acted wisely. "The house of Rossini," Hanslick writes, "is far from possessing the amenities necessary to such an innumerable quantity of guests. The heat is sometimes intolerable and the crowd so thick that when a fair singer (especially a singer of the bulk of Madame Sax) has to approach the piano to sing, she is forced literally to fight her way to it.

"Rows of ladies glittering with jewels occupy the whole of the music room; the men stand, so jammed against one another that they cannot move. The doors remain open, and from time to time a servant with refreshments pushes his way through the dense mass, though it is well known that very few people (and those for the most part strangers) take advantage of them; the lady of the house is said not to approve! I have nothing to say about the present Madame Rossini except that she is well off and once was beautiful. A haughty Roman nose, like some tower that has escaped the ravages of time, rises from the ruins of her former beauty. The rest is covered with diamonds."

Though one sympathises with Professor Hanslick's feeling of being honoured rather than amused by a function of this kind, his description of his hostess suggests that Wagner's caricature of his maliciousness in Beckmesser was not wholly undeserved.

Ricordi's account entirely bears out Hanslick's. When he went, the room was packed with duchesses, marchionesses, baronesses, ministers and ambassadors, not to mention a Papal nuncio; there were thirty people sitting on the stairs. But for the personal intervention of Madame Rossini, neither Ricordi nor his father would ever have got into the room at all. Had she been as tactful with Hanslick, he might have omitted to give us his views on her personal appearance.

As Saint-Saëns observed, the Saturday Evenings represented only one aspect of Rossini, not, perhaps, the most attractive. There was another aspect which is often overlooked; he remained, as always, ready to do everything in his power for those who aroused his interest or affection. He was kindness personified to Faccio and Boito when, still quite unknown, they visited Paris. He did not disdain to play duets with a young, struggling composer of twenty called Arthur Sullivan, who was quite fascinated by his kindly courtesy. He gave another young composer, a certain Georges Bizet, who had just won the Prix de Rome, a charming letter of introduction to Romani. In 1859, to please Auber, despite his great dislike of going out in the evening, he went to a Conservatoire concert. He attended an evening rehearsal of an opera by his beloved Carafa; he went twice to the Opera to hear an opera of Poniatowski and a ballet by Gabrieli. This may seem trifling enough, but nobody else, however important, ever succeeded in making him move out in the evening at all. The strongest evidence he could produce of his enthusiasm for Bach was to say that, even at midnight, he would have gone to hear the B Minor Mass. It was this disparity between the two Rossinis which so surprised Wagner when he paid him his celebrated visit in March, 1860.

Wagner had come to Paris to try to arrange for the production of *Tannhäuser* at the Opera, and, as was the custom in those days, paid visits of courtesy to every musical personality of importance. He felt especially nervous in the case of Rossini, for a story had gone the round of the drawing-rooms and the press that Rossini had shown his opinion of Wagner's music by asking an admirer of it to lunch, and then serving him with a dish called "Turbot à l'allemande," which consisted of sauce and no fish, the lack of the principal ingredient being intended to suggest that Wagner's music lacked the most vital thing of all: melody. But this wholly apocryphal story much annoyed Rossini, who had grown very tired of every cynical witticism in Paris being fathered on himself. He took the trouble to deny it publicly, and caused Wagner to be informed by Michotte that he would be more than delighted to receive him. The resultant interview, which took place, of course, in French and of which Michotte wrote down an account immediately afterwards, is not only of great interest, but shows both men in the most agreeable light. The exquisite urbanity of Rossini on the one hand, and the obvious desire of Wagner on the other to be as courteous and sympathetic as possible, make very pleasant reading. Many points raised during this interview have already been noted but a good deal of interest still remains.

Rossini's first care was to put his visitor at ease, saying that, though he knew he was neither a Mozart nor a Beethoven and made no pretence to be a very learned person, he did claim to have some manners. The last thing in the world he would do was to say rude things about a musician who, as he had been told, was trying to extend the limits of their common art. Before condemning Wagner's music he would first have to know it, and for that "I should have to hear it in the theatre, because only in the theatre, not by reading the score, is it possible to pass fair judgment on music destined for the theatre."* He advised Wagner not to be excessively discouraged by cabals directed against the production of *Tannhäuser*. Every composer, beginning with "the great Gluck himself," had suffered in the same way. Then in his typical racy, rather coarse idiom, which seems much to have amused Wagner, he described his own arrival in Paris in 1824, when a regular campaign of musicians and critics was launched against him, and he was nicknamed "Monsieur Vacarmini."†

After the accounts of his meetings with Weber and Beethoven already recorded, the conversation next drifted on to Rossini's early career, Wagner expressing his admiration for a man who, in the midst of such a Bohemian, wandering life, had been able to write so many noble pages in *Otello* and *Mosè*. It was in answer to this compliment that Rossini made the famous remark quoted (as a rule erroneously) in many musical histories. He did not say, "I too had talent". What he did say was: "O! I had facility and much instinct"—which is not at all the same thing, and, incidentally, disposes once and for all of the suggestion, sometimes made, that Rossini was merely being sarcastic.

Despite Wagner's polite protests Rossini then proceeded to insist that, had he been able to study in

---

*It would seem that the sole Wagnerian composition actually familiar to Rossini at that time was the March from *Tannhäuser*, which he had heard at Kissingen and much enjoyed.

†*Vacarme* means a noise.

Germany, he would assuredly have produced something better; that his most happy inspirations were very small beer in comparison with the work of a Mozart or a Haydn. How he envied their supple technique and their certain touch in the art of composition! How above all he admired Bach! "If Beethoven is a prodigy among men, Bach is a miracle of God." He then pointed out to Wagner the last volume of the complete edition of Bach to which he had subscribed, saying that the day on which the next volume arrived would be one of incomparable delight for him.

Finally, with infinite tact and a protest that they had talked far too much about himself and others, Rossini turned the conversation on to Wagner and the Music of the Future. Why did not Wagner write a French opera? Wagner replied that this was impossible owing to the development of his literary and musical style. He would now have to write, not a French *Tannhäuser*, but a French *Tristan*, which would inevitably fail to please the taste of the Parisian public. He then began to expose his theories, enlarging on his objection to the conventional operatic forms, especially the ensembles "indispensable in every self-respecting opera". Rossini agreed that sometimes these ensembles were ridiculous, and that the singers lined up in front of the footlights reminded him of a lot of porters come to sing for a tip; in Italy they used to be called "the row of artichokes!" Then, returning to Wagner's theories, he said that they were unanswerable so far as the literary side was concerned; the difficulty began when words had to be allied with some musical form, which must, in any event, always remain a convention. After all, in real life, with the possible exception of lovers who might be said to coo, nobody either lived or died in terms of song. Even in the most turbulent orchestral passages who could distinguish between a storm, a riot or a fire? All this was convention. Wagner admitted the necessary existence of convention but protested that he was opposing only its abuse. For this reason his enemies had maliciously invented the fable that, with the exception of Gluck and Weber, he was hostile to all previous operas, even those of Mozart. Rossini interposed with horror that that would indeed be sacrilege: "Mozart, l'angelo della musica!"

With considerable ingenuity Wagner proceeded to cite Rossini's share in the fashioning of the libretto of *William Tell* as a justification of his own theories about the necessity of a composer being his own librettist. An extension of this principle would give him his point; just as Rossini's influence in Italy proved the possibility of the complete revolution in the conceptions of composers, singers and public that he had in mind. Rossini, while admitting that in the abstract Wagner's theories seemed attractive, objected that, as regards musical form and practice, they must lead exclusively to declamatory recitative: "C'est l'oraison funèbre de la mélodie que vous prononcez là."*

Wagner agreed that, pushed to a logical extreme, this might be so. He, too, wanted melody in a generous measure, but his conception of it was something far more plastic, more independent than what was generally understood by the term. And once again he instanced the "Sois immobile" scene in *William Tell* as a perfect example of musical expression, both as regards the accentuation of the words and the use of the 'cellos that accompanied them. Rossini answered that he seemed

---

*"What you are saying is the funeral oration of melody."

to have been writing the Music of the Future without knowing it. To which Wagner replied that, in this instance, Rossini had written music for all time, and that was the best kind of music of all.

The composers took leave of each other with the utmost cordiality. As Wagner went down the stairs with Michotte, he frankly avowed that he had found Rossini entirely different from what he expected. He was surprised by his naturalness, his simplicity and his seriousness. Had he been less sceptical, less cynical; had he, above all, found the right instead of the wrong atmosphere in his youth and general career, to what heights might he not have attained? "But I must say here and now that of all the musicians I have met in Paris he alone is truly great."*

To the end of his days Rossini maintained his interest in Wagner, always refusing to take any part in the various attacks launched upon him, never failing to inquire of German visitors what progress he and his theories were making in Germany. It seems unlikely that Wagner's music ever really appealed to him, and there is no doubt that in his heart he felt that Wagner, despite his protests, did not show sufficient appreciation of the genius of Mozart. When Naumann paid him a visit at the very end of his life he roundly said that, while not wishing to deny for one moment Wagner's genius and originality, he could not understand how a nation that had given birth to a Mozart could forget

*It should perhaps be noted that another account of this interview, different in several particulars, has been given by the 'cellist Braga. This seems to carry its own refutation with it, in that Wagner is presented as a cringing figure, utterly unable to defend himself, and Rossini as devoid alike of tact and good manners. Apart from the fact that Wagner's own recollection of the interview was extremely pleasant, such behaviour is in no wise consonant with the known characteristics of either composer. Besides Braga was certainly not present, and Michotte was.

him for a Wagner. "Monsieur Wagner a de beaux moments mais de mauvais quarts d'heures aussi."* It is clear that Wagner on his part was much impressed by Rossini. From the spiteful things he had written in the past, as well as from his own description of the low kind of company that, for some reason best known to himself, he imagined as frequenting Rossini's house, he had obviously expected to find a person very different from the jovial, courteous old man who in fact received him. It is also fairly clear that he always found greater pleasure in Rossini's music than is usually supposed or even than he himself cared to admit.†

The two men never met again. After the fiasco of *Tannhäuser* in 1861, Rossini went to some pains to let Wagner know that he would be very glad to receive him, and no less authoritative a person than Liszt urged him to go. Wagner, however, perhaps not altogether unwisely, preferred to stay away, thinking that such a visit might be misunderstood, if not by Rossini himself, at least by the Parisian public. But he preserved to the end of his days a warm appreciation of the kindly gesture made at the time of his great disappointment. In the light of Wagner's sublime self-confidence and Rossini's oft-emphasised view of himself, it is not too fanciful, perhaps, to imagine that both men were fully conscious of the drama of their meeting; it was a mutual salute, not of the future and the present, but of the future and the past.

---

*"Mr. Wagner has some fine moments but some bad quarters of an hour."

†There is a delightful story told in this connection, which seems to be well authenticated. Wagner once attended a performance of *The Barber of Seville* with an intimate friend. In the middle he turned and exclaimed: "O Rossini! Rossini! How I love him! But for goodness sake do not tell my Wagnerians; they would never forgive me."

CHAPTER XVI

IT had been Rossini's habit, ever since the successful outcome of his cure in Germany, to leave Paris in May for Passy where, year after year, he took the same furnished house in the Rue de la Pompe. Eventually, however, he decided to build himself a villa in that pleasant quarter of the suburb known as Beauséjour, which borders on the Bois de Boulogne. The municipality of Paris, becoming aware of this intention, offered to make him a present of the site on condition that it should be returned to them after his death—an offer which Rossini refused, realising that it meant that in the end the municipality would get his house for nothing. Finally, the inevitable compromise was reached and Rossini obtained the site on exceptionally favourable terms. On the 10th of March, 1859, he himself laid the foundation stone, while Olympe planted the first rose tree in the garden. Very typical of Rossini's whimsical humour was his first impulse to place in the traditional casket underneath the foundation stone a recently discovered coin of the Roman Emperor Caracalla, so that he might enjoy in anticipation the prospect of future archæologists arguing as to whether or no a composer called Rossini had really lived in that reign. He thought better of it, however, and substituted for the Roman coin a medal struck in honour of the first performance of the *Stabat Mater*.

Everything about the new villa seems to have been associated with music in some way or another. Rossini always said he had chosen the site for its resemblance to the shape of a grand piano; the flower beds were laid out in the forms of various musical instruments; the decorations of the interior, painted by two well-known Italian artists, were based on different musical emblems and allusions. Medallions containing portraits of Palestrina, Mozart, Cimarosa and Haydn, occupied the corners of the ceiling in the drawing-room. A less harmonious quartet, Beethoven, Grétry, Boïeldieu and, of all unlikely people in the world, old Father Mattei, found corresponding places in the dining-room. When Rossini arrived at Passy from Paris, there was placed on the entrance gate a gilt lyre, duly removed in the autumn when he returned to town.

His habits in the country were much the same as in Paris, but he walked a little more, in the Bois de Boulogne in the morning, in his garden in the afternoon. The painter, De Sanctis, who stayed with him, was much struck by the orderliness of everything in the house, especially in Rossini's own bedroom, which here, also, served as a study. He was impressed in particular by the three or four wigs so carefully laid out on the chimney-piece. Apparently, when Rossini returned from the Bois de Boulogne, his first action was to take off the wig he was wearing, wrap a towel round his head, and presently select whichever of the wigs he judged to be the most suitable to the occasion. De Sanctis, who seems to have been about the only visitor ever allowed to see him in the unwigged interval, has left on record his admiration for the natural shape of Rossini's completely bald head: it reminded him, he says, of Cicero or Scipio Africanus.

Internal evidence suggests that the Villa at Passy, quite apart from its musical decoration, was primarily associated with the return of music into Rossini's life. To the many trifles which undoubtedly originated there, must be added *Le Chant des Titans*, his contribution to the Conservatoire concert given to raise funds for a monument to Cherubini. Originally written as a song for his friend Count Pompeo Belgioioso, it was furnished with new words describing the assault by the Titans on Olympus, an important orchestral accompaniment and a revised vocal part for four basses in unison. When it was produced on the 22nd of December, 1861, the audience, though they seem to have been surprised by a wild, not to say explosive, quality very unlike that usually associated with Rossini's music, unanimously demanded an encore. Later the composer sent it, together with a little pastorale, entitled *La Nuit de Noël*, to Vienna to be performed at another benefit concert, this time for a monument to Mozart. In 1862 he wrote for the Baroness Rothschild a Hunting Chorus to be performed by male voices on the occasion of the visit of Napoleon III to her country house. But by far the most interesting and important of all the compositions of this period was the *Petite Messe Solennelle*, which he wrote in the summer of 1863.

According to Radiciotti the idea of this was not due, as usually stated, to the performance of Liszt's Mass in the Church of St. Eustache. Rossini had for some time been meditating such an undertaking, and, apparently, it made him very moody and irritable. It is certainly one of the most remarkable compositions that he ever produced, the very title being misleading, possibly with intention, because the Mass is not "little" at all but longer than most Masses. More strange still are the notes appended by Rossini to his original score, of which the first, in all its original illiteracy, runs as follows:

"*Petite Messe Solennelle* à quatre Parties avec accompagnament de 2 Pianos et Harmonium Composée pour ma Villégiature de Passy.—Douze Chanteurs de trois sexes, Hommes, Femmes et Castrats, seront suffisant pour son execution, Savoir huit pour le Chœur, quatre pour les Solos, total douze Chérubins.—Dieu pardonne moi le rapprochement suivant. Douze aussi sont les Apôtres dans le celebre coup de Machoir peint à Fresque par Leonard dit La Cene, qui le crôirait! il y a parmi tes disciples de ceux qui prennet de fausses notes! Seigneur, rassure toi, j'affirme qu'il n'y aura pas de Judas à mon Dejeuné et que les miens chanteront juste et con amore tes Louanges et cette petite composition qui est hélas le dernier Peché mortel de ma vieillesse.— Passy, 1863."*

Then there is the letter on the last page, of which, alas! the best sentence of all is untranslatable:

"Bon Dieu—La voilà terminée cette pauvre petite Messe. Est-ce bien de la musique Sacrée que je viens de faire ou bien de la Sacrée Musique? J'etais né pour l'Opera Buffa, tu le sais bien! Peu de science, un peu de

---

*"*Petite Messe Solennelle* in four parts, with accompaniment for two pianos and a harmonium, composed for my summer stay in Passy. Twelve singers of three sexes, men, women and *castrati*, will suffice for its performance, that is to say, eight for the chorus and four for the solos; twelve Cherubim in all. May God forgive me the following comparison. Twelve in number also are the Apostles in the celebrated fresco by Leonardo called *The Last Supper*. Who would believe it? Among Thy disciples there are some capable of singing wrong notes! Lord be reassured, I guarantee that there will be no Judas at my luncheon, and that all mine will sing accurately and *con amore* Thy praises, as well as this little composition, which is, alas! the last mortal sin of my old age. —Passy, 1863."

cœur tout est là. Sois donc Beni, et accorde moi le
Paradis.—G. Rossini—Passy, 1863."*

These extraordinary epistles should on no account be
taken as denoting mere facetiousness or irreverence.
Rossini, like his own Figaro, had long ago come to the
conclusion that laughter was the best preventive of tears.
Nothing seemed to him too serious for humour, not his
naïve but obviously sincere piety, not even his God Who
had made him thus. There is not a trace of flippancy in
the music of the Mass; he must have taken exceptional
trouble with it. Something irresistible, however,
prompted him to issue his last, and most serious, composition as a kind of challenge to God and man to
recognise his peculiar temperament for what it was, and
at that to take it or leave it.

The Mass was first performed on the afternoon of the
14th of March, 1864, at the house of the Countess
Pillet-Will who gave the composer a free hand and, in
return for her generosity, received the dedication. No
pains were spared to secure a good performance. Auber
himself selected the chorus from the best students of the
Conservatoire; the leading artists of the Théâtre Italien
sang the solo parts. Two performances on successive
days were arranged, but it was the first that was really
interesting, for the audience consisted only of Meyerbeer,
Auber, Ambroise Thomas, Rossini's intimate, Carafa,
and a very few other people distinguished either in
society or the arts. Rossini himself did not take part but
stood by one of the pianists to turn over and indicate the

*"Dear God. Well, this poor little Mass is completed. Have I for once
written real Sacred Music or merely damned bad music? I was born for Opera
Buffa, as Thou knowest! Little skill, but some heart; that about sums it up.
So blessed be Thou, and grant me Paradise."

tempi. The atmosphere seems to have been rather electric. As the last chord died away, Meyerbeer sprang to his feet, and, with eyes burning and face working, rushed to where the composer stood and embraced him so warmly that Rossini felt constrained to warn him that such agitation was dangerous for his health. But Meyerbeer, who was, in fact, far from well* and for once, it would seem, wholly sincere, was not to be stayed. Turning round to the other musicians, he paid tribute to Rossini's undimmed genius, praised the originality, the daring and the beauty of the music, proclaimed the fugue "Cum Sancto Spiritu" as the finest composition of its kind ever written. Then, becoming more and more excited, he exclaimed: "What can we do in comparison with him, we who are always searching and groping, who hesitate at every moment? If this man had continued to write after *William Tell*, the primacy of the theatre would have been his incontestably. . . . See! in two months he has created a whole world! He is the Jupiter of our time and holds us all in the hollow of his hand."

Rossini, though unquestionably moved by his triumph and the general atmosphere of excitement, appears, typically, to have said very little; but it is significant, perhaps, that he elected to walk home along the boulevards to his apartment in the Chaussée d'Antin. One would give a good deal to know what his thoughts were as, with stiff, rheumatic joints, he threaded his laborious way through the crowded streets.

Meyerbeer, despite his sickness and Rossini's warnings, insisted on attending also the second performance, which, unlike the first, was packed with people, and on

*He died two months later.

the same evening wrote to "Jupiter Rossini," as he called him, a letter that can only be described as a pæan of adulation. The critics privileged to hear the Mass showed an enthusiasm no whit less than Meyerbeer's. They judged its musical value to be at least equal to that of *William Tell;* they were particularly impressed by the success achieved in combining scholastic ingenuity with genuine expressiveness. Most of all, apparently, they admired, as he did, the beauty of the melodies, the originality and the daring of the harmony.

A study of the Mass after seventy years has left one musician, at any rate, convinced that all this enthusiasm, if exaggerated, was not undeserved. The Mass is an exceedingly fine work, in one sense the most successful of all Rossini's serious compositions. When he himself read the criticisms, he is said to have remarked that it was quite true that he had not been sparing of dissonances, but that he had coated them with sugar. We are at times a little too conscious, perhaps, of the sugar, but the real inventiveness of the harmonic scheme will be clear to anybody gifted with historical perspective. The beauty of melodies such as the bass solo "Quoniam" and the soprano solo "O Salutaris", the exquisite part-writing in the "Gratias" trio and the final ensemble of the "Agnus Dei", should be obvious to anybody, whether gifted with perspective or not. At the same time the remarks already made about the *Stabat* apply here also. The Mass is less operatic in style; there are passages in the opening "Kyrie", particularly in the "Christe Eleison" section, which are quite ecclesiastical, while the "Prélude Religieux" shows that Rossini's subscription to the complete works of Bach had been by no means without effect. Nevertheless, the character of the Mass as a whole remains what, nowadays, would undoubtedly be called secular, though that in no wise invalidates its sincerity. There are some fine things in the "Credo" (which Rossini headed with the delicious indication, "Allegro Cristiano"!) notably the "Et Resurrexit" and the "Et Vitam Venturi" fugue. But beyond question the gem of the whole work is the "Gloria". True, the "Domine Deus" section suggests, perhaps, that the tenor is addressing the lady of his heart rather than his Maker, but as an aria pure and simple it is admirable; the "Qui Tollis" duet for soprano and contralto, too, though rather operatic, is exceedingly pretty and in places genuinely moving; the "Et in Terra Pax," like the beginning and end of the number itself, could hardly be more effective. But Meyerbeer was unquestionably right in singling out the "Cum Sancto Spiritu" fugue as the outstanding example of Rossini's genius Not only is the subject itself full of vitality and character, but the treatment is admirable, the long diminuendo passage, in particular, being an example of first-class inspiration. To the writer at any rate this chorus still appears to be one of the most inspiriting pieces of music ever written, a very present help in trouble. On a general view the *Petite Messe* may be said to have something in common with the Cherubini Masses, though it shows throughout a humanity sometimes lacking in the music of that rather sour old gentleman. It is even nearer akin to Verdi's Requiem Mass, of which, indeed, it is the direct spiritual ancestor.

The subsequent fortunes of the Mass were somewhat chequered. After another performance at the Pillet-Will's house in 1865, equally select, equally enthusiastic, Rossini was urged to score the accompaniment for full orchestra. This he did rather unwillingly, having previously taken the trouble, we are told, to consult several recent scores in order to study the progress of orchestration. It is by no means certain, however, that the orchestral version is an improvement; some of the best contemporary critics did not think so, and Rossini himself admitted on one occasion that he preferred the Mass in its original form, saying that he had only consented to score it because, had he not, somebody else would be sure to do so after his death, probably in a manner displeasing to him; it might even be handed over to the tender mercies of Mr. Sax and his saxophones. He seems to have been anxious, however, to know how the music would sound in its new form if given in some great church or other. Here, however, was a difficulty. Male sopranos and contraltos had ceased to exist, and women were not allowed to sing in church together with men. Rossini, nothing daunted, determined himself to write to the Pope to try and get this disability removed for the sake of music in general and his Mass in particular. He was encouraged in his project by the fact that Pius IX, who was well known to be a great lover of his music, had even once been heard singing a tune from *Il Turco in Italia* in the gardens of the Vatican. So he asked his friend Professor Ferrucci to draw up a suitable memorial in Latin, which was duly despatched to Rome. After three months he received a reply, also in Latin, signed by the Pope himself, containing a blessing and many compliments but not one word about the subject of his letter!

As a matter of fact, the Mass was never performed in public during Rossini's lifetime though his friend Michael Costa seems to have announced it for performance at the Birmingham Festival of 1867, where however, it was replaced by another unimportant composition from his pen entitled a *National Hymn*. It was not till after his death that the Mass became known in Europe, when, like Verdi's Mass eight years later, it was toured by an impresario and rapidly acquired great popularity. Performances were organised in many important cities from Moscow to Brighton. It even reached Australia, but never achieved complete success either in Germany or Italy where the public continued, inexplicably, to prefer the *Stabat*.

One cannot help feeling that it would have been fitting had the Mass in fact been Rossini's last composition; but it was not. In addition to smaller works, he contributed to the Paris Exhibition of 1867 a mammoth composition for chorus and orchestra which has been immortalised less perhaps by its merits than by its famous sub-title, which is a masterpiece:

"A Napoleon III et à son vaillant Peuple. Hymne (avec accompagnement a Grand Orchestre et Musique Militaire) pour Baryton (solo), un Pontife; Chœur de Grandprêtres, Chœur de Vivandieres, de Soldats et de Peuple.—Danses, Cloches, Tambours et Canons. Excusez du peu! Passy, 1867."*

In the presence of the Emperor, the Empress and the Sultan it was duly performed with 400 choristers and an orchestra of 600 civilian and 200 military players on the 1st of July, when it seems to have been received with popular rather than critical favour. Yet there were not wanting critics to defend it, and

---

*"To Napoleon III and his valiant People. Hymn (with accompaniment for Grand Orchestra and Military Band) for Baritone (solo), a Pontiff, Chorus of High Priests, Chorus of Vivandières, Soldiers and People. Dances, Bells, Drums and Canons. With apologies for such meagreness!"

Olympe at any rate was convinced that justice had not been done to its real merits. Before its repetition on the 15th of August at the Opera, she wrote one of her scolding letters to the editor of a paper, in which she informed him that he should on no account send his regular critic for two reasons: "Firstly, because his knowledge is on a level with his trustworthiness; secondly, because I will not have a paper directed by you forgetting the respect due to my name. I desire an impartial judge, competent and unprejudiced, like, for example, Berlioz, with whom I have not the honour of being acquainted but whom I know to be capable of rating the opinions of an ignorant press at their true value." She must have forgotten *Robert Bruce*, not to mention *La Foi*, *L'Espérance*, *La Charité!*

Rossini, who, needless to say, knew nothing of all this, would probably have been on the side of the critics, for he firmly refused to publish the composition, which he protested had been written for private performance in his garden at Passy, and had only been adapted to circumstances of such pomp and solemnity owing to his inability to refuse a request conveyed to him from the highest quarters.*

During these labours, of course, Rossini's manner of life followed the routine already described, in the spring and summer at Passy, in the winter at the apartment in the Chaussée d'Antin, where the Saturday Evenings continued in all their glory. As we have seen, almost every musician of importance who visited Paris came to pay his respects to the old man. Among the most interesting of these was Moscheles, then in the height of his success, who came twice to Passy in 1860. Naturally,

*Nevertheless, Costa inflicted it on Birmingham in 1873.

Rossini, that keen "pianist of the fourth class," was much interested in the great master of the instrument. Moscheles played to him and they talked about many things, in particular the decadence of singing, the lamentable state of Church music in Italy, and the horrid noise made by some contemporary virtuosos who played as if they would like "to smash not only the piano but the piano stool and the floor as well." In answer to Moscheles's question as to his preference among the classical masters Rossini answered typically: "I take Beethoven twice a week; Haydn four times, Mozart every day. . . . Your Beethoven is a colossus who often gives one a mighty thump in the ribs, but Mozart is always adorable. He was lucky enough to go to Italy when he was very young, at a time, too, when they still knew how to sing."

His adoration of Mozart again manifested itself in a conversation with Naumann, who came to see him in Paris in 1867, for, after enquiries as to the progress of the interesting Mr. Wagner, Rossini said: "The Germans have always been at every time the greatest harmonists and the Italians the greatest melodists. But from the moment that the north produced a Mozart, we of the south were beaten on our own ground because this man rises above both nations, uniting in himself all the charm of Italian melody and all the profundity of German harmony. So, if this music is to cease being recognised as supremely beautiful, sublime, we old back-numbers can heartily bless our approaching demise, which will enable us to go and hear it in Paradise in the company of its author."

Weber's son, too, has told us how much he enjoyed, in 1865, his two visits to Rossini at the Chaussée d'Antin and at Passy. They talked much of the older Weber of course, and something of Schumann and Wagner. Two points about the visit to Passy left a particularly deep impression on young Weber. When, not knowing the number of the house, he asked his way and said that he was going to see Rossini, he was told that that name was far better than any number. Second, there was Rossini's reply to his condolence on the unpleasant noise made by the train whistles. Rossini protested that he liked them. "The sound reminds me," he said, "of the happy days of my youth when I heard it so often, in particular at the first performance of *La Cenerentola*."*

There is no doubt that these manifestations of esteem and veneration meant much to Rossini, one of whose most painful delusions at the time of his illness had been that he was forgotten and despised. Fortunately, the last months of his life were rich in these and similar tributes. To begin with, King Victor Emmanuel bestowed on him high rank in the newly instituted Order of the Corona d'Italia. On the night of the 10th of February, 1868, when *William Tell* was performed at the Opera for the 500th time, the orchestra, the chorus and some of the soloists went, after the performance, to serenade the old composer in the Chaussée d'Antin. The orchestra played the overture; the baritone, Faure, led the chorus in an excerpt from the first act. Rossini was not well enough to come down in person to thank them, sending Olympe in his stead, but he showed himself for a moment at the window, to the delight of the huge crowd which enthusiastically acclaimed him.

*Perhaps it should be explained that in an Italian theatre whistling takes the place of hissing.

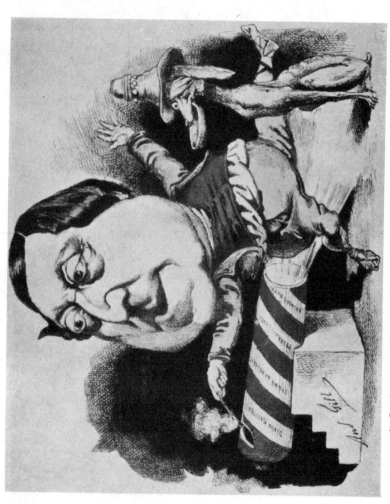

A Caricature of Rossini by André Gill published in 1867

Rossini. A woodcut engraved by Robert in 1867 from the
picture by Mouilleron

By a fortunate accident, too, the year 1868 being a leap year, he was able, exceptionally, to celebrate his birthday, when his friends and admirers took the opportunity to mark the occasion by great rejoicings. Telegrams and letters arrived from all parts of the world; there was a banquet and a grand concert in his house. Exactly a month later, the Italian Minister of Public Instruction honoured him by writing to crave his support for a singularly muddle-headed scheme for the reorganisation of Italian music, a support which Rossini accorded far too readily, apparently before he had understood the full implications of a project which in fact aroused the most bitter hostility in Italy, alike among public and musicians. The only practical suggestion of any real value that emerged from either the correspondence or the scheme itself was Rossini's proposal to establish a kind of small experimental theatre where young composers might have the opportunity to try out one-act operas. But subsequent events effectually prevented the matter being pursued any further.

Already at the end of November, 1867, Rossini's health had given rise to some anxiety; his chronic catarrh became worse; he was ordered complete quiet; the Saturday Evenings were suspended until further notice. By taking the most drastic precautions, sitting in his room with his neck wrapped in a thick woollen scarf and refusing to converse even with his intimate friends except by signs, he recovered fairly quickly. But, even when he recovered, his physical strength was obviously impaired; he could no longer go for his walks on the boulevards with the same frequency as before. Then, in the autumn of 1868, the bronchial catarrh returned in such an aggravated form that the doctors would not allow him to leave Passy, and there, on the 26th of September, took place what proved to be the last of the Saturday Evenings. Soon he had to take to his bed altogether; the discovery of a fistula in the rectum made an operation inevitable. The doctors, however, were afraid to operate in view of his extreme weakness and long-standing heart trouble. Finally, on the 3rd of November the operation was performed.

Rossini, surrounded by his most intimate friends and tended by his wife, who would allow nobody else to do the dressings, did not suffer much at first, though once again he practically refused to speak, except a few words of greeting to the four male nurses who came every morning to move him from one bed to another. No easy task! for he was not only abnormally corpulent but abnormally sensitive. Presently, however, symptoms of septic poisoning developed; his sufferings became acute; voluntary silence gave place to groans and cries. He had to endure, further, the torture of thirst, for the doctors refused to let him be given anything but the minimum quantity of ice for which he begged continually, using every artifice to try to persuade his various attendants to disobey their orders.

By this time the whole of Paris knew that Rossini was very ill; hundreds came to sign their names in the visitors' book at Passy; letters and telegrams poured in unceasingly. One day there arrived at the Villa the Papal nuncio, who, despite Olympe's protests and the strict orders of the doctors, insisted on being admitted to the sick-room, where he thought it his duty or his privilege to tell Rossini that he had come on purpose to bestow the Holy Father's benediction *in articulo mortis*. The effect on a man to whom the idea of death had always been a nightmare need not be stressed; mental was now added to physical, agony. So terrified was he that, when it became obvious that his hours were numbered, the doctors had considerable difficulty in persuading him to let a priest come and administer the Last Sacraments. Finally, he consented, and everything passed off unexpectedly well. The priest seems to have shown tact and kindness; Rossini liked his voice, and told him that, had the Italian clergy been as the French, he himself would have been a better Christian. He even begged him earnestly to return.

He lingered on for a day or two, still in great pain but far more at ease in his mind. The watchers by his bed-side often heard him murmuring prayers. As is not infrequently the case, his whole mentality seems to have reverted to that of the stock from which he came, for in the late hours of the night he would address the Virgin Mary in the most primitive terms: "What are you doing, Blessed Virgin? Here am I suffering the torments of Hell and I have been calling you since nightfall! You hear me! you can do it if you like; it all depends on you. Come on now, be quick . . ." We seem to be listening once more to old Vivazza cursing the saints on the day of his birth!

At the end he was unconscious, the last sound he uttered being the name of his wife, who, poor woman, had been roused from a few moments of hastily snatched sleep to be present at the passing of her husband. When the doctor had satisfied himself that life was extinct, he turned to her and said: "Madame, Rossini has ceased to suffer." She threw herself upon the body and, embracing him for the last time, exclaimed: "Rossini, I shall always be worthy of you." So closely,

Gewandhaus Society of Leipzig shed an official tear. Needless to say, the great cities of Italy did not lag behind, but, appropriately, the most successful celebrations took place at Pesaro, which had donned municipal mourning on the day of the funeral. Typically Rossinian was the tragi-comic fiasco of Verdi's greathearted, if misguided, attempt to induce the Italian composers to collaborate in a Requiem Mass to his memory. In the intervals of listening to Mozart's music in Paradise Rossini may have found a moment to view with cynical amusement the optimism of one who thought it possible to unite thirteen musicians—ah that thirteen again!—in any successful endeavour whatsoever.

The public spirit manifested in his will must have come as a surprise to the many who viewed him merely as a cynical wag. He left two and a half million francs (about a hundred thousand pounds) invested in property, Government stocks and, strange to relate, railway shares. In the circumstances it seems a lot of money, but, despite the protests of one of his biographers who insists that Rossini exclusively managed his own affairs, it is impossible not to think that the knowledge and advice of his three intimate banker-friends were of great service to him. Most of it, originally earmarked for the Liceo Musicale at Bologna, was devoted to the foundation of a Music School at Pesaro. In gratitude to France for her hospitality two annual prizes of three thousand francs each were established for French subjects; the best lyrical or religious composition of the year to win the one, the best libretto in prose or verse, the other. The composition was to be distinguished by melody, "so neglected nowadays"; the libretto by those precepts of morality "by which authors do not always set sufficient store". It seems possible, therefore, that a subject such as the Life of Rossini might have been automatically disqualified from winning the second of the two prizes! He arranged, too, that sufficient capital should eventually be provided to found a Home for aged French singers, or Italian singers who had made their careers in France. Appropriately enough, it was built at Passy where it still performs valuable service.

Needless to say, these various bequests only took effect after the death of Olympe who was left in enjoyment of all her husband's estate until her death, which took place ten years later. She cannot have been sorry to die. The war of 1870 made havoc with the house at Passy, not to say her whole life; she missed Rossini constantly, acutely; her sole comfort was the certainty of their reunion in another and better world where everybody, doubtless, would unite to pay homage to the unapproachable greatness of his genius.

Her last act showed that she herself was not incapable of greatness in a certain measure. For some time the city of Florence had desired that Rossini's body should be removed from Père Lachaise to lie with Galileo, Michelangelo and Machiavelli in the church of Santa Croce, the Westminster Abbey of Italy. The decision rested with her, for by the terms of Rossini's will she was the sole arbiter in the matter. She consented, but with the stipulation that when her time, too, came to die, her body should accompany his. It might be placed in as humble, as inconspicuous a position as they liked, but go it must. The Italian Government felt obliged to refuse her terms; so there, for a time, the matter ended. Later, however, she came to see the reasonableness of the refusal, agreeing to make what must have appeared to her the supreme sacrifice of separation. Before her death, no; that was too much. But after . . . let them have him. "I make this sacrifice in all humility," she wrote in her will; "I have been sufficiently honoured by the name that I bear."

Owing to the laziness or the indifference of the Italian officials she was left for eight years with Rossini in Père Lachaise. But on the 30th of April, 1887, they took him from her. The embalmer had done his work well. When the coffin was opened for purposes of recognition the face of Rossini was almost as it had been nineteen years previously. There were more speeches as the body was handed to the representatives of Italy; from Massenet, Ambroise Thomas, the Prefect of the Seine on the French side; from the Marchese Torrigiani on the Italian. In Florence, again more speeches, but of greater intimacy; for somebody had had the felicitous idea of asking Michotte and the tenor Tamberlick, long associated with roles in many of Rossini's operas, to take part in the ceremony. A procession of six thousand persons, headed by a squad of *carabinieri* and four military bands, escorted him to his last resting place in Santa Croce. On the steps of the church a chorus of three hundred voices, accompanied by the massed bands, sang the famous Prayer from *Mosè*. The effect on the huge crowd, which thronged the square in front of the church, was electric. They clapped, they shouted, they cheered; nothing but the repetition of the piece would satisfy them.

And thus, in a crescendo of applause and the climax of an encore, the tragi-comedy of Gioacchino Rossini reached its apposite and ultimate conclusion.

MAINLY FOR MUSICIANS

IT has been said that Rossini, despite the brilliance of his genius and the greatness of his popularity, exercised little influence on the main current of music, that his whole career was, in fact, a kind of backwater. No attentive reader of this book is likely to share this illusion but, even at the risk of a certain amount of repetition, the various reasons for holding a contrary view may with advantage be summarised.

Curiously enough, it was not, I think, the Italian operatic stage where his influence was most felt except, of course, in a general sense. His young contemporary, Bellini, shows a marked reaction against Rossinian *fioritura*, and, except in that little gem, *Don Pasquale*, there is not, perhaps, very much in common between Rossini and Donizetti beyond a certain conventional lay-out of arias and ensembles. Verdi owed him more. Not to mention the early arias and ensembles, the splendid choruses of *Nabucco* and *I Lombardi* suggest the influence of *Mosè;* the "Miserere" in *Trovatore* was clearly inspired by the finale of the first act of *Semiramide;* various devices in the vocal parts of the early and middle-period operas had been anticipated by Rossini. Moreover, though Verdi, in *I Vespri Siciliani, Don Carlos,* and perhaps *Aïda,* indulged in a definite flirtation with Meyerbeer, he never quite forgot his *William Tell,* while *Falstaff* is definitely a pendant to *The Barber.*

A case might be made out, too, for considering *La Gazza Ladra* as the ancestor of the realistic school of opera associated with Puccini, Mascagni and Co. Here, however, it is the subject rather than the musical treatment which is in question. The lighter operas of Wolf-Ferrari also derive to a large extent from Rossini.

As regards French Opera, Rossini's great influence can scarcely be questioned. *William Tell* has been described as the foundation stone of French Grand Opera. This is incorrect, because Auber's admirable *Masaniello*, though it may have been written about the same time, was in fact produced a year earlier. The era of Grand Opera was, as we have seen, inaugurated by *Le Siège de Corinthe*, closely followed by *Moïse*. But it may truthfully be said, I think, that *William Tell*, owing to its great merit, standardised the form; without it Meyerbeer, the protagonist *par excellence* of French Grand Opera, could scarcely have written *Robert le Diable* and *Les Huguenots;* while, incidentally, the influence of the earlier Rossini on Meyerbeer's Italian operas seems to have been far more potent than is usually supposed.

Nor was Rossini's imprint on French music confined to Grand Opera. *Le Comte Ory* proves that much. It may have owed a good deal to Gallic predecessors but it gave back more than it borrowed. Traces of its influence may be observed in all the masters of French Comic Opera, notably Offenbach and Lecocq. Our own Sullivan, consciously or not, was affected by it, though the characteristic patter songs are, in fact, based on the Italian operas of Rossini rather than on the French. The derivation of a certain school of modern French composition from the miscellaneous pieces written in his old age has already been commented on.

Even in Germany and Austria Rossini left deeper traces than is sometimes thought. Wagner has himself told us how, after conducting *William Tell* at Dresden, he could not get the tunes out of his head for days, and a reader of my chapter on that opera will see that he remembered one, if not two, of them to very good purpose! Professor Dent has further shown that Rossini's influence on Schubert is by no means confined to the comparatively unimportant Schubertian operas but is distinguishable in the great C Major Symphony, where, he says, the opening theme of the andante is a reminiscence of "Di Tanti Palpiti," and the rattle of the rhythm in the last movement comes direct from Rossini. "The whole of the Symphony shows the conflicting influences of Rossini and Beethoven." According to Dent, too, many characteristic devices in Weber, despite his antagonism, are of Rossinian origin, and I have myself noticed this in *Oberon*. The cases of Spohr, Nicolai (who made no secret of his indebtedness) and Hiller may perhaps be dismissed in a mere sentence. Sufficient evidence, I trust, has already been adduced to show that Rossini's importance as a formative influence is very far from negligible. Nevertheless, influence of this kind must always remain to a large extent a matter of opinion and necessarily conflicting judgments. In our consideration of Rossini as a musician we now, for a few pages, at any rate, enter the realm of stark facts.

It is not usually considered that Rossini achieved anything revolutionary in music, but such was by no means the opinion of his contemporaries. One of the principal reasons for the success of *Tancredi* was that the public felt for the first time a new sense of ease in the hitherto so stilted *opera seria*. Indeed, Rossini, quite apart from a new freshness in his style as a whole, must have the credit of having grafted on to *opera seria* many of the more elastic conventions of *opera buffa*, the employment of an important bass soloist being one notable instance. Nor must it be imagined that Rossini's innovations in this respect did not meet with opposition. Many cultured amateurs shared Lord Mount Edgcumbe's dislike of the fusion of the two styles; both courage and genius were necessary successfully to carry through such a reform. Once started on the road, Rossini progressed with rapidity, arriving not only at an unprecedented complexity in ensemble writing and at operatic Prayers with the backing of a full chorus, but at the introduction of a military band on the stage.

Further, the reader will have noted that at the very outset of his career Rossini had trouble with his singers on account of the unprecedented importance he attached to the orchestra. I am not concerned at the moment to stress the orchestral progress shown in his Paris operas, even though *William Tell* may have been, as Edwardes claims, the first opera in which the cornet was used. There was nothing particularly remarkable in writing well for the orchestra in a city familiar with Gluck and Weber, not to mention Habeneck's Conservatoire concerts. But in Italy it was different. There was no encouragement, rather the reverse, for Rossini to take trouble with the orchestra, to enlarge, as he did, the role played by the wood-wind, especially the clarinets. To use the orchestra for the accompaniment of recitatives, as was done for the first time in *Elisabetta*, must have seemed a veritable revolution. Indeed, we know that the traditionalists of the Conservatoire at Naples, where most of his important orchestral experiments were made, did regard him as a wanton and dangerous revolutionary, who, not content with allowing himself the use of consecutive fifths and other harmonic and contrapuntal licences, actually wrote for a third and fourth horn and no less than three trombones! To them he was the apostle of noise and chaos. As a matter of fact, almost, if not absolutely, everything that Rossini asked from the Italian orchestras had already been done by Mozart. But Mozart was scarcely known in Italy, so that Rossini, even if he must be admitted to have profited by Mozart's example, as he further did by Spontini's, should at any rate be given the credit for having translated his admiration into practical terms; and that, moreover, in his own way and in the face of definite hostility.

The question of Rossini's reform in the matter of writing down for the first time the actual *fioriture* to be performed by his singers is, needless to say, of the first importance. Here, too, it must not be imagined that the innovation commanded universal acceptance. Many of his contemporaries, including Stendhal, deplored the passing of the improvisations which had been the singers' prerogative. Rossini's method, they argued, tended to crystallise these ornaments; no scope was left for the singer to vary, as he or she used to do, the ornament or the cadenza according to the circumstances and his or her mood. It was not quite such a foolish attitude, I think, as is often assumed, particularly in view of the extreme musical and technical skill of many of the singers. Those of us who suffer from the stereotyped cadenzas, laboriously evolved, of the countless violinists and pianists who play concertos, must often have felt, either that the cadenza is a superfluity, or that it should return to its original function as a test and display of the executant's musicianship. Once again, moreover, it must be emphasised that these ornaments were not merely what we call "fireworks." To contemporary audiences they possessed a definite expressive value, difficult though it may be for us to appreciate the fact.

Rossini, who beyond question understood the human voice as few other composers have understood it, appears to have thought that he could obtain the same results without the musical sense being endangered by some singer incompetent to grasp it. He took for granted the high level of technical ability usual in those days, and, be it remembered, he wrote less and very different *fioritura* when he had to deal with French singers whose technique was not so brilliant. A strong case, indeed, could be made out for eliminating most of the ornamentation in a modern performance of a Rossini opera, for modern singers are mere novices compared with the singers of his day, and all he did was, so to say, to standardise the ornaments that they and the public considered indispensable. By a curious paradox Rossini, who may, if anything, have limited rather than extended vocal ornament, stands to-day for the very embodiment of elaborate, highly embroidered vocal music. The reason is, of course, that, before his reform, composers left passages of this kind to the fancy of the singers. In performance, however, *Don Giovanni*, *Figaro*,* *Il Matrimonio Segreto*, the operas, even possibly the oratorios, of Handel, would have been at least as florid as *The Barber* and *Cenerentola*. Probably the operas of Weber and the French operas of Gluck were a little less so, partly because of the difference in French and German taste, but mainly because the technical capacity of the singers was inferior. Poor Rossini! It seems hard that one of the few matters in which he showed comparative austerity should have earned him a reputation for licence!

---

*There is a place in "Dove Sono" in *Figaro*, just before the return to the theme, where, to me at any rate, it is obvious that a cadenza was intended. Nor can I believe that the words "Comfort Ye" at the beginning of *Messiah* were ever sung as simply as they are written. Our modern purists, especially in Germany, are a little silly in this matter. Is there any reason to think that Handel or Mozart objected to what the singers did?

The precise balance to be struck between the merits and defects of Rossini as a composer must always remain perforce a matter of opinion. His music will never appeal greatly to those who attach supreme value to profundity of feeling or intellect. The latter, at any rate, could scarcely be expected of him. Rossini was clear-headed, shrewd, urbane, but in no way intellectual. The extra-ordinary thing is rather, with an education so neglected, with a career during the first thirty years of his life so feverish and so vagabond, that he should have risen to the heights he did. Partly, no doubt, his lack of profound feeling can be ascribed to the same cause. Fétis observed with considerable perspicacity that, till he left Italy after *Semiramide,* Rossini never could have had the time even to cultivate a genuine friendship. Thrown constantly into contact with thousands of people in one town after another, his life must have been passed in a kind of delirium of sensations; and I think that this is reflected in his music. Doubtless, there was a great change in later life, when he made many real friends, but early habits leave an ineradicable mark, and, in any case, it must be remembered that he wrote very little music after the age of thirty-six.

Every student of Rossini has noticed, moreover, his comparative inability to portray the emotion of love in its more tender aspect. For my part, I doubt if he ever felt it. The countless amorous intrigues of his youth seem to have been nothing but the usual fleeting affairs of theatrical life. He must at one time have felt a certain amount of passion for Isabella Colbran, and she, poor woman, certainly grew to love him, but one has an uneasy suspicion that in that alliance material considerations counted at least as much as affection. In all probability he cared more deeply for Olympe Pélissier. By then, however, he had practically given up composition, and was, moreover, a sick man, full of self-pity, who needed protection and care, not stimulus to artistic creation. The most poignant emotion he ever knew was undoubtedly adoration of his mother, which some biographers have found reflected in certain pages of *William Tell*. It may be so. In any case, such filial devotion, however passionate, has nothing to do with the point.

To his faulty education, too, must be ascribed that indifference to the literary value of words and situations so noticeable in many of the operas. Any music would serve to express them provided it sounded agreeable in itself. His sluggishness and extraordinary facility combined further to induce in him a regrettable lack of self-criticism. Much of his subject-matter suffers from excessive similarity; he was far too easily satisfied with ideas as they first presented themselves, far too tolerant of repetitions and the continuous employment of stereotyped devices such as the famous crescendo. His excessive borrowings have been commented on already; they were in reality part and parcel of the same attitude of mind.

Rossini's operatic career might be summarised as a tragedy of bad librettos, for only once, in fact, was he really well served. But he must bear some of the responsibility. Had he, like Verdi, possessed the character and the determination to insist on his own way and reject even one-third of the fifteen librettos that he set to music in the space of four years; had he, like Beethoven, written three overtures for one opera instead of fitting one overture to three operas, there would have been a very different tale to tell. At the same time it must be remembered that the conditions of the Italian Theatre made any such proceeding exceedingly difficult. We should not so much blame Rossini as commiserate him on having been unable to rise above the handicaps of his life and circumstances. All things said and done, what he did in fact accomplish remains little less than a miracle.

Besides, as regards some of his defects there is, to say the least, another side to the medal. His carelessness in the setting of words, for instance, proceeded to some extent from the remarkably pure musicality of his inspiration. Music as pure sound, rhythm as pure rhythm, meant everything to him; words very little. "Give me a laundry list," he is reported once to have said, "and I will set it to music." He could, and did, compose music under any kind of conditions, amidst the chatter of friends, the clamour of copyists, out fishing and in bed. Now this musicality is, perhaps, his principal attraction; to it must be ascribed the spontaneity, the vivacity, the charm which are characteristic of his work. He did not always make the best of his extraordinary natural gift in this respect, but he rarely allows us to forget that he possessed it. His music is never anything but indisputably musical, the precise reverse of Meyerbeer's; indeed, that is why most musicians have kept somewhere in their hearts a warm spot for Rossini, be his faults what they may. The "storms" in some halfdozen of his operas provide a good instance of this musicality. They are never just imitative, but always translated into purely musical terms, often subtly attuned, as, for instance, in *La Cenerentola*, to the psychology of that particular score. In fact, one of the very few abstract principles which he laid down as a dogma was that music should be "ideal and expressive", not imitative.

Generally speaking, however, Rossini never dogmatised; his approach to music was instinctive rather than intellectual. This is shown in his famous saying that there are only two kinds of music, the good and the bad; or that other, less known, where he states that every kind of music is good except the boring kind. These are scarcely the utterances of a man who attached any value to æsthetic theories as such. The fact of the matter is that Rossini regarded himself as an artist-craftsman producing music when and where required, entirely devoid of the pretensions invented subsequently by the Romantic Movement, which at no time affected Italy as it affected Germany, France or England, and, before he went to Paris, had made no impression whatever south of the Alps. Besides, there is always a tendency to forget that for all practical purposes Rossini's musical career ended in 1829. To some extent, therefore, he remains in essence more akin to an eighteenth-century, than to a nineteenth-century, composer.

As regards Rossini's technical ability there can scarcely be two opinions. No man not a consummate technician could have written *William Tell*, while the wonderful ensembles in the earlier operas suffice by themselves to attest his mastery. These ensembles lack as a rule the power of characterisation later attained by Verdi, but as examples of skill and effectiveness in vocal part writing they are supreme. Yet Rossini always professed indifference to scholastic ingenuity as such. "Voilà du temps perdu", he added in pencil after writing some eight-part contrapuntal essay or other. He disliked the pedants as much as they disliked him, and I have a shrewd suspicion that many of the "irregularities" in his music were due as much to a wanton pleasure in annoying them as to carelessness and indifference.

His excellence in orchestration, too, has not, I think, been sufficiently emphasised. None of his Italian contemporaries, not even Verdi till the *Ballo in Maschera* period, scored as well as he did. It has been said, indeed, that, with his retirement in 1829, Italian writing for the orchestra took a definite step backward. All through the Rossini operas we find instruments treated with great skill, with an unerring instinct for their potentialities of expression. The overtures, in particular, deserve the highest praise in this respect. Take, for instance, the writing for the 'cellos in the *William Tell* overture. It is so masterly that the famous 'cellist Servais told Rossini that he had no need to be informed that the composer had himself studied the 'cello in his youth. And for sheer brilliance and effectiveness the rest of the orchestration is equally remarkable. Nor should the comparative simplicity of the effects in the earlier overtures such as *L'Italiana*, *The Barber*, *La Gazza Ladra* and *Semiramide* blind us to the surety of touch, the felicity of inspiration, that were necessary to invent them at that time. Everything "comes off" as well to-day as ever it did. Nobody who has heard them played by a Toscanini or a Beecham is likely to stand in need of conversion on that score. As a matter of fact, these overtures are little masterpieces from every point of view. In them we find displayed to the best advantage that rhythm in which Rossini so excelled and to which he attached so much importance, saying that in it resided all the power and expressiveness of music. The subject-material itself is nearly always excellent and highly individual; the form is as clear as the treatment. Possibly the very attractiveness of these overtures has led some of our musicians unduly to underrate them.

Finally, Rossini's exceptional knowledge and love of the human voice cannot be too strongly insisted upon. Himself a singer from childhood, he understood it as scarcely any other composer has understood it, and his writing for it sets a standard. There is no question here of demanding effects, as Verdi too often does, mainly from notes at the extremity of the singer's compass; the whole range of the voice is expected to pay its due contribution, while it is scarcely possible in all the operas and songs to find a vocal phrase which, granted the technique prevalent at the time, is not delightfully singable. It is not surprising that he should have excelled in this respect, for, of all forms of musical expression, Rossini loved singing the best. Inevitably, such enthusiasm on the part of so famous a composer produced its effect, particularly in France, where Rossini's influence is said to have altered for the better the whole style of French singing. The gradual decline of the art during the last thirty years of his life (a decline that has been progressing with increasing rapidity ever since) filled him with dismay. He told Michotte, indeed, that his main ambition in the *Petite Messe* was to leave a final legacy which might serve as an example of how to write for the voice. Yet he never willingly suffered the tyranny of singers, and he refused to allow that they had any share in the work of artistic creation. "A good singer", he wrote in 1851, "should only be the conscientious interpreter of the composer's ideas, endeavouring to express them as effectively as possible and to present them as clearly as they can be presented. . . . In short the composer and the poet alone have any serious claim to be regarded as creators."

In view of all the reproaches that have been levelled at Rossini for writing solely to show off the virtuosity of his singers, this insistence is decidedly interesting. There is no reason to think that he did not in the main succeed in putting it into practice, though there were occasions, in particular where Isabella Colbran was concerned, when he certainly did not. In fact Isabella, quite unintentionally, did him definite harm, in that in all probability a desire to minister to her particular talents led him to write *opera seria* when, as Beethoven suggested and he himself admitted, he would have been better employed in writing *opera buffa*. A man of stronger character would have noted the pitfall, to bridge or avoid it, but once again it must be insisted that there was nothing grand or heroic about Rossini; for him the easiest path was the obvious, the only path. Can one imagine Verdi advising a young friend, as Rossini did, to get out of a difficulty by a lie, if necessary? His general attitude towards music has not unfairly been described as indicative of a pronounced taste rather than passion or semi-religious veneration. His real justification is that he possessed in an exceptional degree the most essential attributes of a composer, melodic and rhythmical inventiveness, and that he brought into music a great healthy laugh which will always endear him to the artist if not to the educationalist. Wagner, who, as we have seen, described him as the first man he had met in the world of art who was truly great and worthy of reverence, wrote after his death an epitaph that was alike kind, wise and just:

"Rossini can scarcely be handed to posterity in a more false guise than by stamping him as a hero of Art on the one hand or degrading him to a flippant wag on the other. . . . No; Rossini will never be judged aright until someone attempts an intelligent history of the culture of our current century. . . . Were this character of our age correctly drawn, it would then be possible to allot to Rossini also his true and fitting station in it. And that station would be no lowly one, for, with the same title as Palestrina, Bach and Mozart belonged to their age, Rossini belongs to his. . . . Then, and not till then, will it be possible to estimate Rossini at his true and quite peculiar worth; for what fell short of full dignity would have to be accounted to neither his natural gifts nor his artistic conscience, but simply to his public and environment, which made it difficult for a man of his nature to raise himself above his age and thereby share the grandeur of the veritable art-heroes."

THE END

LIST OF ROSSINI'S COMPOSITIONS

STUDENT WORKS

Title	*Date of Performance or Composition*
Se Il Vuol la Molinara	
Duets for Horn	
Demetrio e Polibio (opera)	Rome, 18th May, 1812 (comp. 1806?)
Mass for Male Voices	Ravenna, 1808
Il Pianto d'Armonia sulla Morte d'Orfeo	Bologna, August, 1808
Two Overtures	
Five String Quartets	
Quartet for Wind Instruments (?)	
Varia	

OPERAS

La Cambiale di Matrimonio	Venice, 3rd November, 1810
L'Equivoco Stravagante	Bologna, 29th October, 1811
L'Inganno Felice	Venice, 8th January, 1812
Ciro in Babilonia	Ferrara, Lent, 1812
La Scala di Seta	Venice, 9th May, 1812
La Pietra del Paragone	Milan, 26th September, 1812
L'Occasione fa il Ladro	Venice, 24th November, 1812
Il Signor Bruschino	Venice, January, 1813
Tancredi	Venice, 6th February, 1813

Title	Date of Performance or Composition
L'Italiana in Algeri	Venice, 22nd May, 1813
Aureliano in Palmira	Milan, 26th December, 1813
Il Turco in Italia	Milan, 14th August, 1814
Sigismondo	Venice, 26th December, 1814
Elisabetta, Regina d'Inghilterra	Naples, 4th October, 1815
Torvaldo e Dorliska	Rome, 26th December, 1815
Il Barbiere di Siviglia	Rome, 20th February, 1816
La Gazzetta	Naples, 26th September, 1816
Otello	Naples, 4th December, 1816
La Cenerentola	Rome, 25th January, 1817
La Gazza Ladra	Milan, 31st May, 1817
Armida	Naples, 11th November, 1817
Adelaide di Borgogna	Rome, 27th December, 1817
Mosè in Egitto	Naples, 5th March, 1818
Adina	Lisbon, 12th June, 1826 (comp. 1818)
Ricciardo e Zoraide	Naples, 3rd December, 1818
Ermione	Naples, 27th March, 1819
Edoardo e Cristina	Venice, 24th April, 1819
La Donna del Lago	Naples, 24th September, 1819
Bianca e Falliero	Milan, 26th December, 1819
Maometto II	Naples, 3rd December, 1820
Matilde di Shabran	Rome, 24th February, 1821
Zelmira	Naples, 16th February, 1822
Semiramide	Venice, 3rd February, 1823
Il Viaggio a Reims	Paris, 19th June, 1825
Le Siège de Corinthe	Paris, 9th October, 1826
Moïse	Paris, 26th March, 1827
Le Comte Ory	Paris, 20th August, 1828
Guillaume Tell	Paris, 3rd August, 1829

PASTICCIOS

Title	*Date of Performance or Composition*
Ivanhoe	Paris, 15th September, 1826
Le Testament	Paris, 22nd January, 1827
Cinderella	London, 13th April, 1830
Robert Bruce	Paris, 30th December, 1846
Andremo a Parigi	Paris, 26th October, 1848
Un Curioso Accidente	Paris, 27th November, 1859
La Boutique Fantasque (ballet)	London, 5th June, 1919
Rossini (operetta)	Rome, 18th May, 1922

SACRED MUSIC

Messa Solenne	Naples, March, 1820
Stabat Mater	Paris, 7th January, 1842
La Foi, L'Espérance, La Charité	Paris, 20th November, 1844
Petite Messe Solennelle	Paris, 14th March, 1864
Varia	

MISCELLANEOUS

Esle e Irene (cantata)	Milan, 1814
Inno dell' Indipendenza	Bologna, April, 1815
Le Nozze di Teti e di Peleo (cantata)	Naples, 24th April, 1816
La Morte di Didone (cantata)	Venice, 2nd May, 1818 (comp. 1811)
La Riconoscenza (cantata)	Naples, 27th December, 1821

Title	Date of Performance or Composition
Il Pianto delle Muse in Morte di Lord Byron (cantata)	London, 9th June, 1824
Soirées Musicales (songs and duets)	Paris, 1835
Le Chant des Titans	Paris, 22nd December, 1861
Hymne à Napoléon III, etc.	Paris, 1st July, 1867
A National Hymn	Birmingham, 1867
"Péchés de Vieillesse" (piano pieces, songs, etc.)	Paris, 1857—1868
Varia (cantatas, songs, marches, etc.)	

INDEX

ACCADEMIA dei Concordi (Bologna), 12
Accademia Filarmonica (Bologna), 12–13
Addio ai Viennesi, 105
Adelaide di Borgogna, 77, 86
Adina, 84
Africaine, L', 172
Agolini (composer), 68
Aguado (a banker), 133–5, 137–9, 154–5, 159, 166, 180, 182, 190–1
Aïda, 243
Aix-les-Bains, 156
Albertazzi (contralto), 186
Alboni, 239
Allgemeine Musikalische Zeitung, 132
Almack's, 118
Almaviva (see *Barber*), 55
America, South, 111
Andromaque (Racine), 85
Anna (Rossini's Mother, *see under* Rossini)
Antwerp, 163, 170
Apollo Theatre (Rome), 92
Arditi, 57 *note*
Argentina Theatre (Rome), 54, 58, 77
Aria Buffa, 116
Arie di bravura (Rossini on), 27
Arie del sorbetto, 26, 31–2, 68
Armida, 76–7, 86, 129
Artaria (publisher), 103
Auber, D. F., 113, 128, 136, 138, 205–6, 213, 215, 226, 244
Aulagnier (publisher), 183, 186
"A un Dottor," 56
Aureliano in Palmira, 30 *note*, 44, 52, 56–7
Australia, 231
Austria, Austrians, etc., 40, 77, 107, 124, 141, 148, 196, 201, 245

BACH, J. S., 12, 163–4, 215, 218, 228, 257
Baden, 207
Balfe, M. W., 119
Ballo in Maschera, Un, 135, 138 *note*, 254
Balocchi (librettist), 126, 129
Balzac, H. de, 131

Barbaia (impresario), 48–50, 53, 77, 79, 93–6, 100, 180
Barber of Seville, The, v, vii, xiii, 19 *note*, 30 *note*, 44, 46, 54–62, 66, 69, 71, 97, 99, 102–4, 108, 113, 118, 123, 133, 139, 150, 151 *note*, 155, 207, 211 *note*
Barbier de Séville, Le (Beaumarchais), 61
Barbiere di Siviglia, Il (*see under* Barber), 115
Bassi, Father Ugo, 198–9
Bayonne, 154
Beaumarchais, C. de, 55–6, 61–2, 71
Beckmesser, 215
Beecham, Sir Thomas, 254
Beethoven, L. van, 12, 14, 60, 87, 94, 100–5, 109, 135, 137, 184, 216–8, 223, 233, 239, 245, 252, 256
Belgioioso, Count Pompeo, 224
Belgioioso, Princess, 44
Bellini, V., 146–7, 152, 160–2, 182, 239
Bergami, B., 83–4
Berio, Marchese, 64–6, 85
Berlin, 54, 96, 100, 190
Berlioz, H., ix, 60, 97, 135, 144, 147–8, 193, 232
Berners, Lord, 212
Berry, Duc de, 63
Berton (professor), 112
Berton (student), 87
Bianca e Falliero, 89, 90
Bigotini, 208
Birmingham Festival, 230, 232 *note*
Bis (poet), 138, 142–3
Bishop, Sir H. R., 119
Bizet, Georges, 215
Boadicea, 78
Boïeldieu, F. A., 113, 136, 223
Boito, 215
Bologna, viii, 10–14, 30, 46–7, 50, 72, 84, 95, 123, 132, 137, 140, 152, 157–8, 160, 163, 165–6, 174, 177, 179, 181, 187, 191–9, 213
Bonaparte, Prince Lucien, 44
Bordeaux, 149
Bouffes Parisiens, 38
Boutique Fantasque, La, ix, 128, 211

Braga ('cellist), 220
Brahms, J., 60, 175
Brighton, 115, 231
Brussels, 163, 170
Busoni, F., 181
Buzzi (horn player), 120
Byron, Lord, 64, 118

CALUMNY Song, the (*Barber*), 46, 61, 66
Cambiale di Matrimonio, La, 17, 20–1, 56, 78, 108
Cambridge, 120
Carafa, 205, 214–5, 226
Caress for My Wife, A, 210
Carpani, 81, 101, 103
Carpano, Adelaide (soprano), 20
Caruso, Enrico, 161
Castenaso, 106, 108 *note*, 152–3, 158, 165, 195–6
Castrati, 28, 168, 225, *and see* 116
Catalani (soprano), 120
Cavalli, Marquis (impresario), 19, 20
Cendrillon (Etienne), 69
Cenerentola, La, vii, 28, 63–4, 68–71, 92, 97, 117, 123, 150, 189, 234, 249, 253
Cera (impresario), 33, 36–7
Chabrier, 212
Chant des Titans, Le, 224
Charité, La (and see under La Foi), 194
Charles X, 124, 141, 152, 154
Cherubini, Luigi, 112, 132, 224, 239
Chopin, F., 239
"Chorus of Bards," 88, 192
Church Music, 184
Cimarosa, D., 21, 42, 47, 104, 113, 223
Ciro in Babilonia, 31
Civiale (surgeon), 191
Colbran, Isabella, 49, 50–1, 53, 63–4, 77–9, 82, 85–6, 88, 95, 102, 106–7, 190, 195, 251, 256
"Comfort Ye," 249 *note*
Comte Ory, Le, vii, 124, 133–4, 136–7, 207, 211 *note*, 244
Como, 14
Corona d'Italia (Order of), 234
Costa, Sir Michael, 230, 232 *note*, 239
Cotignola, 5
Coward, Noel, 138
Creation, The, 12, 30, 94, 186
Crescendo ("the famous"), 35, 46, 52, 109, 142, 202, 251 (*and see* 112)
Crescenti (teacher), 159
Crociato, Il, 124
Crystal Palace, 239

Curzon, Henri de, xi

DALL' Argine (composer), 55
Dante, 201–2
Danza, La, vii, 161
David (tenor), 86
Débats, Les, 186, 193
de Beriot, (violinist), 160
Debussy, C., 175, 211
Deep Sleep, A, 210
Dei Fiorentini Theatre (Naples), 63
Demetrio e Polibio, 14, 33–4, 179
Dent, Professor, 245
De Sanctis (painter), 168, 212, 223
Devonshire, Duke of, 114
Didone Abbandonata (see Morte di Didone, La)
"Di Tanti Palpiti," 35, 39, 40, 245
Don Carlos, 243
Don Giovanni, 109, 173, 249
Donizetti, G., 146, 181, 187, 202, 243
Don Pasquale, 243
Donna del Lago, La, vii, 76, 87–90, 192
Donzelli (tenor), 167, 201–2
"Dove Sono," 249 *note*
Dragonetti (double-bass player), 120
Dresden, 54–5, 80, 245
Drury Lane, 119
Du Barry, Countess, 156
Duval, Marguerite, 156

Edoardo e Cristina, 87
Edwardes (Rossini's English biographer), xi, 168, 246
Esle e Irene, 44
Ehrlich, P. (chemist), 170
Elisabetta, Regina d'Inghilterra, 30 *note*, 51–2, 57, 65, 94, 100, 102, 247
Emma di Resburgo, 87
England, 40, 111, 141
Entführung, 21
Equivoco Stravagante, L', 30
Ermione, 85–6
Eroica Symphony, 102
Etex (sculptor), 192, 195
Eugène, Prince, 36
Euryanthe, 49, 96

FACCIO, 215
Falliero, 89
Falstaff, 243
Fara, G., xi, 59
Farse (one-act operas), 19, 32, 36
Faure (baritone), 213, 234, 239
Faust, 153
Fenice Theatre (Venice), 36, 38, 46, 107

INDEX

Ferdinand VII, 63, 86, 155
Ferrara, 31–2, 38
Ferretti (librettist), 67–9, 92
Ferrucci, Professor, 230
Fétis, F. J., 131–2, 146, 182, 250
Fidelio, 87
Figaro, 249
Figlia dell' Aria, La, 118
Figlio per Azzardo, Il, 36
Filippi (critic), 212
Fioriture (excessive), 37, 79, 126, 135, 243, 247–8
Florence, 56, 85, 197, 199, 201, 204, 206, 242
Fondo Theatre (Naples), 48, 64
France, the French, etc., 40, 111, 249
Francis, the Emperor, 47
Frankfurt, 163
Freischütz, 96
Freudenberg (composer), 100
Funeral Ode for Meyerbeer, A, 210

GABRIELI, 215
Gabussi, 194
Galileo, 241
Gambaro (clarinettist), 113
Garcia, M. del P. V., 55–7, 113
Gazza Ladra, La, 72–6, 82, 84, 90, 99–101, 115, 123, 244, 254
Gazzetta, La, 63–4, 68, 76
George IV, 98, 114–7, 121, 155
Germany, Germans, etc., 39, 40, 73, 77, 91, 94, 97, 99, 100, 111, 139, 141, 147, 218, 222, 231, 233, 245, 249
Gewandhaus Society (Leipzig), 240
Gherardini, 72
Gill, André, iv
Giusti (engineer), 47
Gluck, C. W., 12, 29, 76, 85–6, 101, 113, 176, 217, 219, 247, 249
Goethe, J. W. von, 153
Goldoni, C., 64
Gounod, C., 213
Grand Opera (birth of), 128
Greece, Greeks, etc., 129 *note*, 190
Grenade, A, 201
Grétry, A. E. M., 136, 223
Grisi, G., 186, 213
Grove's Dictionary of Music, 57
Guillaume Tell (see William Tell), 54 *note*
Gustave III, 138

HABENECK, 137, 150, 247
Halévy, J. F., 169
Handel, G. F., viii, 12, 101, 129 *note*, 208, 249

Hanslick, Professor, 214–5
Harmonicon (periodical), 118
Haydn, J., 11, 16, 42, 94, 99, 184, 186, 199, 218, 223, 233
Hegel, G. W. F., 100
Heine, H., 173, 186, 192 *note*
Heller, S., 193
Hérold, L. J. F., 85, 93, 113, 123, 136
Hiller, F., 13, 18, 86, 115, 120–1, 153, 155, 163, 169, 206, 245
Holy Alliance, 106–7
"Home, Sweet Home," 119
Huguenots, Les, 149, 172, 244
Hunting Chorus, 224
Hygienic Prelude for Morning Use, A, 211
Hymn to Peace, 201

Inganno Felice, L', 30, 32
Inutile Precauzione, L' (see Barber), 55
Isabella (see under Colbran), 160
Italiana in Algeri, L', vii, 28, 41–5, 60, 72, 99, 133, 189, 200, 254
Italian Theatre (London), 123
Ivanhoe, 125
Ivanoff (tenor), 182, 187

JOUY (librettist), 129, 138, 142–3
Judith and Holofernes, 156
Juive, La, 138 *note*, 149
Juva, Signor and Signora, 203–4

KÄRNTHNERTHOR Theatre (Vienna), 93, 95–6
Kaune (composer), 101
Kent, Duchess of, 117
King's Theatre (London), 118
Kissingen, 207, 217 *note*
Kramer, C. (Master of Royal Band), 116

LA BOUILLERIE, 141
Lady of the Lake, The, 87
La Foi, L'Espérance, La Charité, 193, 232
"Largo al Factotum," 61, 102, 120
La Rochefoucauld, 140–1, 153
La Scala (Milan), 23, 34, 44–5, 48, 72, 74, 89, 90, 178
Lecocq, A. C., 136, 244
Leopold of Saxe-Coburg, Prince, 117
Le Soir, vii
Lesueur, J. F., 112
Letters to Haydn, 101
Liceo Musicale (Bologna), viii, 12–17, 180–1, 192, 199, 240; (Pesaro), 210
Liège, 163

Lieven, Count, 114–5
Lisbon, 84
Liszt, F., 161, 179, 213, 221, 224
Little Pleasure Trip in the Train, A,
211
Lombardi, I, 243
Lombroso, C., 202
London, 80, 93, 97, 112, 116–8, 121–3
Louis-Philippe, 154
Lucca, 204
Lucia, 188
Ludwig of Bavaria, King, 207
Lugo, 3

MACHIAVELLI, 241
Madrid, 54, 80, 154
Maffei, 167
Malanotte (prima donna), 39
Malerbi, Don Giuseppe, 11
Malibran, M. F., 54, 160
"Manca un Foglio," 56
Maometto II, 76, 91–2, 107, 118, 126,
128–9
Marcello, 129 *note*
Marcolini (prima donna), 34
Maria Cristina, Queen, 155
Marinai, I, 161
Mario, G., 213
Marionettes (London), 36 *note*
Mark Twain, 84
Marriage of Figaro, 61
Mars, Mlle, 113
Martini, Padre, 15, 184
Masaniello, 244
Mascagni, Pietro, 244
Massenet, J., 242
Matilde di Shabran, 92–3
Mattei, Padre, 12, 15–17, 223
Matrimonio Segreto, Il, 21, 32, 120,
249
Mayer (painter), iv
Mayr (composer), 90, 129 *note*
Mendelssohn-Bartholdy, J. F., 131,
147, 160 *note*, 163–4, 186
Mercadante, 181
Méry, 205
Messager, A., 136
Messiah, 249 *note*
Metternich, Prince, 105–7
Metastasio, P. (P. Trapassi), 55, 209
Mexico, 111
Meyerbeer, G., 87, 124–8, 145, 147, 169,
171–2, 190, 210, 211, 213, 226–9, 243–4,
252
Michelangelo, 241
Michotte, 81, 108 *note*, 172, 194, 216,
220, 242, 255
Mikado, The, 200

Milan, 44–5, 49, 72–3, 87, 89, 114,
148, 152, 177–9, 195 (*see also* La
Scala)
Milhaud, D., vii
Miscarriage of a Polka Mazurka, 211
"Miserere," 109, 243
Moïse, 80, 129–33, 136, 138, 140, 150,
244
Mombelli family, 14–15, 30, 33
Mont Cenis, 191
Montecatini, 204
Monti (librettist), 47
Morandi, 19, 20
Mordani, Professor, 202–3
Morlacchi (composer), 55, 78
Morning Post, The, 115, 118
Morte di Didone, La, 30
Mosca (musician), 35, 41
Moscow, 231
Moscheles, 232–3
Mosè in Egitto, 76, 79, 80, 82, 86, 89,
94, 97, 104, 129, 206, 217, 242–3
Mount Edgcumbe, Lord, 246
Mozart, W. A., viii, 11, 16, 21, 29,
42, 50, 61, 94, 99, 101, 104, 113,
128, 135, 162, 184, 199, 216, 218,
220, 223–4, 233, 239–40, 247, 249
note, 257
Munich, 80
Murat, 46
Musical World, 193
Musique Anodine, 209

Nabucco, 195, 243
Naples, 47–52, 63–4, 67, 72, 76, 78,
80–2, 85, 87, 90–5, 180, 247
Napoleon I, xiii, 13, 46, 111, 123
Napoleon III, 224, 231
Nash, J., 115
National Hymn, 231
Naumann, 220, 233
Neukomm, 168
Newman, Ernest, ix
Nicolai, 245
Niedermeyer (composer), 192
Nilsson, 239
Norma, 28
Nourrit, A. (tenor), 126, 129
Novello, Clara, 187
Nozzari (tenor), 82, 102
Nozze di Teti e di Peleo, Le, 63
Nuit de Noël, La, 224

OBERON, 97–8, 245
Occasione fa il Ladro, L', 36
Odéon (Paris), 125
Offenbach, J., 35, 38, 136, 208, 211,
244

INDEX

Olympe (*see* Pélissier), 156
Opéra, L' (Paris), 140–1, 154, 168, 171, 191, 193, 215–6, 232
Opera Buffa, 26, 41, 55, 80, 103, 246, 256
Opéra Comique (Paris), vii
Operas *di mezzo carattere*, 26
Opere serie, 26, 31, 33, 39, 44–5, 53, 77, 80, 86, 91, 104, 246, 256
Orleans, Duke of, 178
Orphée, 86
Ortigue (critic), 147
Otello, 49, 64, 67, 80, 85, 101, 104, 116, 123, 151 *note*, 153, 190, 203, 217

PACINI (composer), 90, 92, 167, 173
Paer 13, 87, 122–3
Paganini, N., 93, 210, 213
Paisiello, G., 50, 55–6, 58, 60, 113
Palestrina, G. P., 223, 257
Panseron, 112–3
Pappatacci, 41–2
Paris, 54, 80, 97, 122, 152, 159, 163, 174, 178, 186, 192–3, 206, 217, 222, 233, 239, 253
Parry, Sir C. H. H., x
Passy, 207, 222, 232, 234, 236, 241
Pasta, Mme., 113, 178
Patti, A. J. M. (Baroness Ceder-ström), 213, 239
Pau, 154
Pélissier, Olympe, 156–160, 165, 170, 177–8, 191, 193, 195, 197–8, 202–6, 209, 212, 222, 232, 234, 236, 241, 251
Pergolesi, G. B., 104, 184
Perticari, Count, 84
Peru, 174
Perugino, 31
Pesaro, 3, 5, 7, 47, 82–3, 240
Peter the Hermit (*see* Mosè), 80
Petit Bourg, 137
Petite Messe Solennelle, 224, 229, 255
Pianto delle Muse in Morte di Lord Byron, 118
Pianto d'Armonia sulla Morte d'Orfeo, 17
Pietra del Paragone, La, 30, 35–6, 39, 56
Pillet-Will (banker), 205, 208, 213, 229
Pillet-Will, Countess, 226
Pirata, Il, 152
Pius IX, Pope, 192, 196, 230
Planquette, R., 136
Poniatowski, 201, 215
Ponselle, Rosa (singer), 28

Posillipo, 180
Prague, 80
Prinetti, 10
Prophète, Le, 172
Prussia, 149, 190
Puccini, G., 244
Puritani, I, 161–2

"QUAL mesto gemito," 190

RACINE, J. B., 85
Radiciotti, xi, 33, 37, 69, 76, 85, 88, 97, 105, 108 *note*, 118, 143, 147, 170–1, 180, 211, 224
Radishes, The, 211
Raimondi, 90
Ranz des Vaches, 144
Raphael, 31
Ravenna, 16
Recess, the (English novel), 51
Regata Veneziana, La, vii, 210
Requiem (Verdi), 184
Respighi, O., 211
Return of Ulysses, The, 82
Ricciardo e Zoraide, 85–6, 88
Riconoscenza, La, 94
Ricordi, 215
Riga, 161
Righetti, G. (mezzo-soprano), 58–9
Rigoletto, 66, 213
Ring, The, 145
Robert Bruce, 192–3, 232
Robert le Diable, 149, 244
Rochefoucauld(*see* La Rochefoucauld)
Romani, F. 56, 89, 203, 215
Rome, 33, 53–6, 67, 71–2, 77, 93
Rossi, G. (poet), 106, 108
Rossini, Gioacchino Antonio, 3; birth, 27; counterpoint, 14, 34, 94; death, 238; earnings, 62, 82, 107, 129; education, 9–14; expressive-ness, 255; father, 5–8 (*and see* "Vivazza"); harmony, 94; inven-tiveness, 256; Italia, Order of Corona d', 234; Legion of Honour, 150; local colour, 88; marriage (1st), 95 (*and see* Colbran); marriage (2nd), 195 (*and see* Pélissier); mother, 123, 132, 158, and *passim*; nature, feeling for, 88; opera, in-fluence on French, 244; orchestra-tion, 73–4, 80, 94, 230, 246–7, 254; origin of family, 5; overtures, attractiveness of, 255; plagiarism, charged with,129 *note*; romanticism, 88; *Rossiniani a Parigi, I* (vaude-ville), 179; *Rossini à Paris* (vaude-ville), 114

INDEX

Rothschilds, 163–4, 213, 224
Rubens, 163
Rubinstein, A., 213
Russia, 107, 111, 149

St. François de Paule marchant sur les Flots, 213
St. Paul (Mendelssohn), 186
Saint-Saëns, C. C., 213, 215
Salieri, 103, 162
Sampieri, Marchese Francesco, 72, 153
San Benedetto Theatre (Venice), 41, 86
San Carlo Theatre (Venice), 23, 30, 48–9, 63–4, 76, 78, 87, 91, 93, 95, 99
San Mosè Theatre (Venice), 19, 32, 36
Santa Alleanza, La, 106
Satie, Erik, 212
Sax, Adolphe, 230, 239
Sax, Mme., 214
Scala di Seta, La, 32–3
Scheffer, Ary, 192
Schiller, F. von, 138, 142–3
Schmitt (librettist), 77
Schopenhauer, A., 100 *note*
Schubert, F. P., viii, 100, 245
Schumann, R., 234
Scott, Sir Walter, 67, 87
Scribe, E., 114, 134, 138
Semiramide, 108–11, 118, 128, 149, 153, 155, 204, 243, 250, 254
Serenata, La, 161
Servais ('cellist), 213, 254
Serva Padrona, La, 104, 184
Severini, 165, 178–9
Sforza-Cesarini, Duke Francesco, 54, 58
Siège de Corinthe, Le (*see* Maometto II), 91, 126–7, 129–31, 136, 138, 244
Sigismondo, 45, 56
Signor Bruschino, Il, 33 *note*, 36, 38, 56
Sinclair (tenor), 107
Sinigaglia (theatre at), 20
Sins of My Old Age, 210
Sitwell, Osbert, ix
Soirées Musicales, 161, 210
Song of Farewell, 152
Soumet (librettist), 126
Spohr, L., 50, 52, 245
Spoleto, 72
Spontini, F. C., 90, 125, 247
Stabat Mater (Pergolesi), 104, 155, 184

Stabat Mater (Rossini), 155–6, 160, 182–6, 190, 194, 206, 212, 222, 228, 231, 239
Stendhal, Henri Beyle, xi, 14, 18, 23, 31–2, 34, 39, 41, 44, 52, 57, 64, 67, 74, 77–8, 80, 85, 90, 94, 111, 126, 247
Sterbini, 53, 55, 57–8, 60, 68
"Storms," 252
Strasbourg, 207
Sullivan, Sir A., 244
Supervia, Conchita (singer), 28, 71

Tadolini (conductor), 156, 183, 185
Taglioni, Maria, 191
Talma, F., 113
Tamberlick (tenor), 242
Tamburini (bass), 186, 239
Tancredi, 35, 38–9, 40, 43–4, 63, 80, 82, 97, 99, 101, 104, 108, 150, 153, 246
Tannhäuser, 216–8, 221
Tartar Bolero, 211
Tasso, T., 38, 77, 192
Teatro Comunale (Bologna), 153
Tesei, Angelo, 12
Thalberg (pianist), 213
Théâtre Italien (Paris), 122–5, 140, 153–4, 156, 160, 165, 179, 198, 206, 226
Theatres (*see under* La Scala, San Carlo, etc.)
Thomas, Ambroise, 226, 242
Tolentino, Peace of, 7
Tonino, 205
Torrigiani, the Marchese, 242
Tortured Waltz, 211
Torvaldo e Dorliska, 53–5
Toscanini, A., 254
Tottola (librettist), 79, 81, 85, 87, 94
Tournedos Rossini, xiii, 174
Traviata, La, 28
Tristan, 100 *note*, 218
Troupenas (publisher), 160, 183, 185, 194
Trouville, 206
Trovatore, Il, 109
Turco in Italia, Il, 45, 53, 63, 230
Turkey, Sultan of, 111, 201
Tuscany, Grand Duke of, 201

Ugo, Re d'Italia (?), 118

Valle Theatre (Rome), 53–4, 58, 67, 163
Varela, 182–3
Vatielli, Professor (Bologna), xiii
Veau-qui-Tette, Le (restaurant), 113

INDEX

Velluti (male soprano), 45, 52–3
Venice, 19, 31, 38, 40–3, 50, 86–7,
    107–8 *note*, 110, 181
Ventadour, the Salle, 185
Ventignano, Duca di (librettist), 91
Vêpres Siciliennes, Les, 206
Vera Cruz, 54
Verdi, G., xi, 29, 44, 50, 58, 66–7,
    109, 128, 138, 140, 145, 147, 152
    note, 173, 184–5, 195, 200, 206, 213,
    229, 231, 240, 243, 251, 253–6
Vernet, H., 113, 156
Vernon, Lord (Dante scholar), 201–2
Verona, 106, 114
Vero Omaggio, Il, 107
Vespri Siciliani, I, 149, 243
Viaggio a Reims, Il, 124–5, 134–5
Victor (French general), 7
Victor Emmanuel, King, 234
Vie de Rossini (Stendhal), xi
Vienna, 48–9, 54, 80, 93–4, 96, 99,
    102, 105, 149, 162, 224
Vigano (choreographer), 14
Vitali ('cellist), 187, 191
"Vivazza" (*see under* Rossini), 19, 47,
    123, 132, 137, 152, 158–9, 168, 177,
    180, 237

Voltaire, 38, 91, 108

WAGNER, R., x, 15–16, 19 *note*, 27,
    57, 60, 97, 103–4, 128, 137, 144–5,
    147, 161, 164, 168, 173, 185–6, 196,
    216–21, 234, 245, 256
Wales, Princess of (Caroline of
    Brunswick), 83–4
Walton, William, 212
Wassermann, 170
Weber, K. M. von, 49, 96–9, 125,
    164, 173, 217, 219, 233–5, 247, 249
Weigl (conductor), 99
Wellington, Duke of, 107, 121
Wesley, Samuel, 119
Wildbad, 207
William Tell (Guillaume Tell), vii, x, xii,
    xiii, 9, 74, 88, 106, 138–43, 146, 148–52,
    166, 169–71, 176, 191, 199, 200, 207, 210,
    212, 219, 227–8, 234, 243–6, 253–4
Winter, 73, 92
Wolf-Ferrari, E., 244
Word to Paganini, A, 210

Zelmira, 94, 99, 101–2, 104, 118
Zingarelli (Naples Conservatoire), 50

A CATALOG OF SELECTED
DOVER BOOKS
IN ALL FIELDS OF INTEREST

A CATALOG OF SELECTED DOVER
BOOKS IN ALL FIELDS OF INTEREST

DRAWINGS OF REMBRANDT, edited by Seymour Slive. Updated Lippmann, Hofstede de Groot edition, with definitive scholarly apparatus. All portraits, biblical sketches, landscapes, nudes. Oriental figures, classical studies, together with selection of work by followers. 550 illustrations. Total of 630pp. 9⅛ × 12¼.
21485-0, 21486-9 Pa., Two-vol. set $25.00

GHOST AND HORROR STORIES OF AMBROSE BIERCE, Ambrose Bierce. 24 tales vividly imagined, strangely prophetic, and decades ahead of their time in technical skill: "The Damned Thing," "An Inhabitant of Carcosa," "The Eyes of the Panther," "Moxon's Master," and 20 more. 199pp. 5⅜ × 8½. 20767-6 Pa. $3.95

ETHICAL WRITINGS OF MAIMONIDES, Maimonides. Most significant ethical works of great medieval sage, newly translated for utmost precision, readability. Laws Concerning Character Traits, Eight Chapters, more. 192pp. 5⅜ × 8½.
24522-5 Pa. $4.50

THE EXPLORATION OF THE COLORADO RIVER AND ITS CANYONS, J. W. Powell. Full text of Powell's 1,000-mile expedition down the fabled Colorado in 1869. Superb account of terrain, geology, vegetation, Indians, famine, mutiny, treacherous rapids, mighty canyons, during exploration of last unknown part of continental U.S. 400pp. 5⅜ × 8½. 20094-9 Pa. $6.95

HISTORY OF PHILOSOPHY, Julián Marías. Clearest one-volume history on the market. Every major philosopher and dozens of others, to Existentialism and later. 505pp. 5⅜ × 8½. 21739-6 Pa. $8.50

ALL ABOUT LIGHTNING, Martin A. Uman. Highly readable non-technical survey of nature and causes of lightning, thunderstorms, ball lightning, St. Elmo's Fire, much more. Illustrated. 192pp. 5⅜ × 8½. 25237-X Pa. $5.95

SAILING ALONE AROUND THE WORLD, Captain Joshua Slocum. First man to sail around the world, alone, in small boat. One of great feats of seamanship told in delightful manner. 67 illustrations. 294pp. 5⅜ × 8½. 20326-3 Pa. $4.50

LETTERS AND NOTES ON THE MANNERS, CUSTOMS AND CONDITIONS OF THE NORTH AMERICAN INDIANS, George Catlin. Classic account of life among Plains Indians: ceremonies, hunt, warfare, etc. 312 plates. 572pp. of text. 6⅛ × 9¼. 22118-0, 22119-9 Pa. Two-vol. set $15.90

ALASKA: The Harriman Expedition, 1899, John Burroughs, John Muir, et al. Informative, engrossing accounts of two-month, 9,000-mile expedition. Native peoples, wildlife, forests, geography, salmon industry, glaciers, more. Profusely illustrated. 240 black-and-white line drawings. 124 black-and-white photographs. 3 maps. Index. 576pp. 5⅜ × 8½. 25109-8 Pa. $11.95

THE BOOK OF BEASTS: Being a Translation from a Latin Bestiary of the Twelfth Century, T. H. White. Wonderful catalog real and fanciful beasts: manticore, griffin, phoenix, amphivius, jaculus, many more. White's witty erudite commentary on scientific, historical aspects. Fascinating glimpse of medieval mind. Illustrated. 296pp. 5⅜ × 8¼. (Available in U.S. only) 24609-4 Pa. $5.95

FRANK LLOYD WRIGHT: ARCHITECTURE AND NATURE With 160 Illustrations, Donald Hoffmann. Profusely illustrated study of influence of nature—especially prairie—on Wright's designs for Fallingwater, Robie House, Guggenheim Museum, other masterpieces. 96pp. 9¼ × 10¾. 25098-9 Pa. $7.95

FRANK LLOYD WRIGHT'S FALLINGWATER, Donald Hoffmann. Wright's famous waterfall house: planning and construction of organic idea. History of site, owners, Wright's personal involvement. Photographs of various stages of building. Preface by Edgar Kaufmann, Jr. 100 illustrations. 112pp. 9¼ × 10.
23671-4 Pa. $7.95

YEARS WITH FRANK LLOYD WRIGHT: Apprentice to Genius, Edgar Tafel. Insightful memoir by a former apprentice presents a revealing portrait of Wright the man, the inspired teacher, the greatest American architect. 372 black-and-white illustrations. Preface. Index. vi + 228pp. 8¼ × 11. 24801-1 Pa. $9.95

THE STORY OF KING ARTHUR AND HIS KNIGHTS, Howard Pyle. Enchanting version of King Arthur fable has delighted generations with imaginative narratives of exciting adventures and unforgettable illustrations by the author. 41 illustrations. xviii + 313pp. 6⅛ × 9¼. 21445-1 Pa. $5.95

THE GODS OF THE EGYPTIANS, E. A. Wallis Budge. Thorough coverage of numerous gods of ancient Egypt by foremost Egyptologist. Information on evolution of cults, rites and gods; the cult of Osiris; the Book of the Dead and its rites; the sacred animals and birds; Heaven and Hell; and more. 956pp. 6⅛ × 9¼.
22055-9, 22056-7 Pa., Two-vol. set $20.00

A THEOLOGICO-POLITICAL TREATISE, Benedict Spinoza. Also contains unfinished *Political Treatise.* Great classic on religious liberty, theory of government on common consent. R. Elwes translation. Total of 421pp. 5⅜ × 8½.
20249-6 Pa. $6.95

INCIDENTS OF TRAVEL IN CENTRAL AMERICA, CHIAPAS, AND YUCATAN, John L. Stephens. Almost single-handed discovery of Maya culture; exploration of ruined cities, monuments, temples; customs of Indians. 115 drawings. 892pp. 5⅜ × 8½. 22404-X, 22405-8 Pa., Two-vol. set $15.90

LOS CAPRICHOS, Francisco Goya. 80 plates of wild, grotesque monsters and caricatures. Prado manuscript included. 183pp. 6⅜ × 9⅜. 22384-1 Pa. $4.95

AUTOBIOGRAPHY: The Story of My Experiments with Truth, Mohandas K. Gandhi. Not hagiography, but Gandhi in his own words. Boyhood, legal studies, purification, the growth of the Satyagraha (nonviolent protest) movement. Critical, inspiring work of the man who freed India. 480pp. 5⅜ × 8½. (Available in U.S. only)
24593-4 Pa. $6.95

ILLUSTRATED DICTIONARY OF HISTORIC ARCHITECTURE, edited by Cyril M. Harris. Extraordinary compendium of clear, concise definitions for over 5,000 important architectural terms complemented by over 2,000 line drawings. Covers full spectrum of architecture from ancient ruins to 20th-century Modernism. Preface. 592pp. 7½ × 9⅝. 24444-X Pa. $14.95

THE NIGHT BEFORE CHRISTMAS, Clement Moore. Full text, and woodcuts from original 1848 book. Also critical, historical material. 19 illustrations. 40pp. 4⅝ × 6. 22797-9 Pa. $2.25

THE LESSON OF JAPANESE ARCHITECTURE: 165 Photographs, Jiro Harada. Memorable gallery of 165 photographs taken in the 1930's of exquisite Japanese homes of the well-to-do and historic buildings. 13 line diagrams. 192pp. 8⅜ × 11¼. 24778-3 Pa. $8.95

THE AUTOBIOGRAPHY OF CHARLES DARWIN AND SELECTED LETTERS, edited by Francis Darwin. The fascinating life of eccentric genius composed of an intimate memoir by Darwin (intended for his children); commentary by his son, Francis; hundreds of fragments from notebooks, journals, papers; and letters to and from Lyell, Hooker, Huxley, Wallace and Henslow. xi + 365pp. 5⅜ × 8. 20479-0 Pa. $5.95

WONDERS OF THE SKY: Observing Rainbows, Comets, Eclipses, the Stars and Other Phenomena, Fred Schaaf. Charming, easy-to-read poetic guide to all manner of celestial events visible to the naked eye. Mock suns, glories, Belt of Venus, more. Illustrated. 299pp. 5¼ × 8¼. 24402-4 Pa. $7.95

BURNHAM'S CELESTIAL HANDBOOK, Robert Burnham, Jr. Thorough guide to the stars beyond our solar system. Exhaustive treatment. Alphabetical by constellation: Andromeda to Cetus in Vol. 1; Chamaeleon to Orion in Vol. 2; and Pavo to Vulpecula in Vol. 3. Hundreds of illustrations. Index in Vol. 3. 2,000pp. 6⅛ × 9¼. 23567-X, 23568-8, 23673-0 Pa., Three-vol. set $36.85

STAR NAMES: Their Lore and Meaning, Richard Hinckley Allen. Fascinating history of names various cultures have given to constellations and literary and folkloristic uses that have been made of stars. Indexes to subjects. Arabic and Greek names. Biblical references. Bibliography. 563pp. 5⅜ × 8½. 21079-0 Pa. $7.95

THIRTY YEARS THAT SHOOK PHYSICS: The Story of Quantum Theory, George Gamow. Lucid, accessible introduction to influential theory of energy and matter. Careful explanations of Dirac's anti-particles, Bohr's model of the atom, much more. 12 plates. Numerous drawings. 240pp. 5⅜ × 8½. 24895-X Pa. $4.95

CHINESE DOMESTIC FURNITURE IN PHOTOGRAPHS AND MEASURED DRAWINGS, Gustav Ecke. A rare volume, now affordably priced for antique collectors, furniture buffs and art historians. Detailed review of styles ranging from early Shang to late Ming. Unabridged republication. 161 black-and-white drawings, photos. Total of 224pp. 8⅜ × 11¼. (Available in U.S. only) 25171-3 Pa. $12.95

VINCENT VAN GOGH: A Biography, Julius Meier-Graefe. Dynamic, penetrating study of artist's life, relationship with brother, Theo, painting techniques, travels, more. Readable, engrossing. 160pp. 5⅜ × 8½. (Available in U.S. only) 25253-1 Pa. $3.95

HOW TO WRITE, Gertrude Stein. Gertrude Stein claimed anyone could understand her unconventional writing—here are clues to help. Fascinating improvisations, language experiments, explanations illuminate Stein's craft and the art of writing. Total of 414pp. 4⅜ × 6⅜. 23144-5 Pa. $5.95

ADVENTURES AT SEA IN THE GREAT AGE OF SAIL: Five Firsthand Narratives, edited by Elliot Snow. Rare true accounts of exploration, whaling, shipwreck, fierce natives, trade, shipboard life, more. 33 illustrations. Introduction. 353pp. 5⅜ × 8½. 25177-2 Pa. $7.95

THE HERBAL OR GENERAL HISTORY OF PLANTS, John Gerard. Classic descriptions of about 2,850 plants—with over 2,700 illustrations—includes Latin and English names, physical descriptions, varieties, time and place of growth, more. 2,706 illustrations. xlv + 1,678pp. 8½ × 12¼. 23147-X Cloth. $75.00

DOROTHY AND THE WIZARD IN OZ, L. Frank Baum. Dorothy and the Wizard visit the center of the Earth, where people are vegetables, glass houses grow and Oz characters reappear. Classic sequel to *Wizard of Oz*. 256pp. 5⅜ × 8. 24714-7 Pa. $4.95

SONGS OF EXPERIENCE: Facsimile Reproduction with 26 Plates in Full Color, William Blake. This facsimile of Blake's original "Illuminated Book" reproduces 26 full-color plates from a rare 1826 edition. Includes "The Tyger," "London," "Holy Thursday," and other immortal poems. 26 color plates. Printed text of poems. 48pp. 5¼ × 7. 24636-1 Pa. $3.50

SONGS OF INNOCENCE, William Blake. The first and most popular of Blake's famous "Illuminated Books," in a facsimile edition reproducing all 31 brightly colored plates. Additional printed text of each poem. 64pp. 5¼ × 7. 22764-2 Pa. $3.50

PRECIOUS STONES, Max Bauer. Classic, thorough study of diamonds, rubies, emeralds, garnets, etc.: physical character, occurrence, properties, use, similar topics. 20 plates, 8 in color. 94 figures. 659pp. 6⅛ × 9¼. 21910-0, 21911-9 Pa., Two-vol. set $14.90

ENCYCLOPEDIA OF VICTORIAN NEEDLEWORK, S. F. A. Caulfeild and Blanche Saward. Full, precise descriptions of stitches, techniques for dozens of needlecrafts—most exhaustive reference of its kind. Over 800 figures. Total of 679pp. 8⅛ × 11. Two volumes. Vol. 1 22800-2 Pa. $10.95
Vol. 2 22801-0 Pa. $10.95

THE MARVELOUS LAND OF OZ, L. Frank Baum. Second Oz book, the Scarecrow and Tin Woodman are back with hero named Tip, Oz magic. 136 illustrations. 287pp. 5⅜ × 8½. 20692-0 Pa. $5.95

WILD FOWL DECOYS, Joel Barber. Basic book on the subject, by foremost authority and collector. Reveals history of decoy making and rigging, place in American culture, different kinds of decoys, how to make them, and how to use them. 140 plates. 156pp. 7⅞ × 10¾. 20011-6 Pa. $7.95

HISTORY OF LACE, Mrs. Bury Palliser. Definitive, profusely illustrated chronicle of lace from earliest times to late 19th century. Laces of Italy, Greece, England, France, Belgium, etc. Landmark of needlework scholarship. 266 illustrations. 672pp. 6⅛ × 9¼. 24742-2 Pa. $14.95

ILLUSTRATED GUIDE TO SHAKER FURNITURE, Robert Meader. All furniture and appurtenances, with much on unknown local styles. 235 photos. 146pp. 9 × 12. 22819-3 Pa. $7.95

WHALE SHIPS AND WHALING: A Pictorial Survey, George Francis Dow. Over 200 vintage engravings, drawings, photographs of barks, brigs, cutters, other vessels. Also harpoons, lances, whaling guns, many other artifacts. Comprehensive text by foremost authority. 207 black-and-white illustrations. 288pp. 6 × 9. 24808-9 Pa. $8.95

THE BERTRAMS, Anthony Trollope. Powerful portrayal of blind self-will and thwarted ambition includes one of Trollope's most heartrending love stories. 497pp. 5⅜ × 8½. 25119-5 Pa. $8.95

ADVENTURES WITH A HAND LENS, Richard Headstrom. Clearly written guide to observing and studying flowers and grasses, fish scales, moth and insect wings, egg cases, buds, feathers, seeds, leaf scars, moss, molds, ferns, common crystals, etc.—all with an ordinary, inexpensive magnifying glass. 209 exact line drawings aid in your discoveries. 220pp. 5⅜ × 8½. 23330-8 Pa. $3.95

RODIN ON ART AND ARTISTS, Auguste Rodin. Great sculptor's candid, wide-ranging comments on meaning of art; great artists; relation of sculpture to poetry, painting, music; philosophy of life, more. 76 superb black-and-white illustrations of Rodin's sculpture, drawings and prints. 119pp. 8⅜ × 11¼. 24487-3 Pa. $6.95

FIFTY CLASSIC FRENCH FILMS, 1912–1982: A Pictorial Record, Anthony Slide. Memorable stills from Grand Illusion, Beauty and the Beast, Hiroshima, Mon Amour, many more. Credits, plot synopses, reviews, etc. 160pp. 8¼ × 11. 25256-6 Pa. $11.95

THE PRINCIPLES OF PSYCHOLOGY, William James. Famous long course complete, unabridged. Stream of thought, time perception, memory, experimental methods; great work decades ahead of its time. 94 figures. 1,391pp. 5⅜ × 8½. 20381-6, 20382-4 Pa., Two-vol. set $19.90

BODIES IN A BOOKSHOP, R. T. Campbell. Challenging mystery of blackmail and murder with ingenious plot and superbly drawn characters. In the best tradition of British suspense fiction. 192pp. 5⅜ × 8½. 24720-1 Pa. $3.95

CALLAS: PORTRAIT OF A PRIMA DONNA, George Jellinek. Renowned commentator on the musical scene chronicles incredible career and life of the most controversial, fascinating, influential operatic personality of our time. 64 black-and-white photographs. 416pp. 5⅜ × 8¼. 25047-4 Pa. $7.95

GEOMETRY, RELATIVITY AND THE FOURTH DIMENSION, Rudolph Rucker. Exposition of fourth dimension, concepts of relativity as Flatland characters continue adventures. Popular, easily followed yet accurate, profound. 141 illustrations. 133pp. 5⅜ × 8½. 23400-2 Pa. $3.50

HOUSEHOLD STORIES BY THE BROTHERS GRIMM, with pictures by Walter Crane. 53 classic stories—Rumpelstiltskin, Rapunzel, Hansel and Gretel, the Fisherman and his Wife, Snow White, Tom Thumb, Sleeping Beauty, Cinderella, and so much more—lavishly illustrated with original 19th century drawings. 114 illustrations. x + 269pp. 5⅜ × 8½. 21080-4 Pa. $4.50

SUNDIALS, Albert Waugh. Far and away the best, most thorough coverage of ideas, mathematics concerned, types, construction, adjusting anywhere. Over 100 illustrations. 230pp. 5⅜ × 8½. 22947-5 Pa. $4.00

PICTURE HISTORY OF THE NORMANDIE: With 190 Illustrations, Frank O. Braynard. Full story of legendary French ocean liner: Art Deco interiors, design innovations, furnishings, celebrities, maiden voyage, tragic fire, much more. Extensive text. 144pp. 8⅞ × 11¾. 25257-4 Pa. $9.95

THE FIRST AMERICAN COOKBOOK: A Facsimile of "American Cookery," 1796, Amelia Simmons. Facsimile of the first American-written cookbook published in the United States contains authentic recipes for colonial favorites— pumpkin pudding, winter squash pudding, spruce beer, Indian slapjacks, and more. Introductory Essay and Glossary of colonial cooking terms. 80pp. 5⅜ × 8½. 24710-4 Pa. $3.50

101 PUZZLES IN THOUGHT AND LOGIC, C. R. Wylie, Jr. Solve murders and robberies, find out which fishermen are liars, how a blind man could possibly identify a color—purely by your own reasoning! 107pp. 5⅜ × 8½. 20367-0 Pa. $2.00

THE BOOK OF WORLD-FAMOUS MUSIC—CLASSICAL, POPULAR AND FOLK, James J. Fuld. Revised and enlarged republication of landmark work in musico-bibliography. Full information about nearly 1,000 songs and compositions including first lines of music and lyrics. New supplement. Index. 800pp. 5⅜ × 8¼. 24857-7 Pa. $14.95

ANTHROPOLOGY AND MODERN LIFE, Franz Boas. Great anthropologist's classic treatise on race and culture. Introduction by Ruth Bunzel. Only inexpensive paperback edition. 255pp. 5⅜ × 8½. 25245-0 Pa. $5.95

THE TALE OF PETER RABBIT, Beatrix Potter. The inimitable Peter's terrifying adventure in Mr. McGregor's garden, with all 27 wonderful, full-color Potter illustrations. 55pp. 4¼ × 5½. (Available in U.S. only) 22827-4 Pa. $1.75

THREE PROPHETIC SCIENCE FICTION NOVELS, H. G. Wells. *When the Sleeper Wakes, A Story of the Days to Come* and *The Time Machine* (full version). 335pp. 5⅜ × 8½. (Available in U.S. only) 20605-X Pa. $5.95

APICIUS COOKERY AND DINING IN IMPERIAL ROME, edited and translated by Joseph Dommers Vehling. Oldest known cookbook in existence offers readers a clear picture of what foods Romans ate, how they prepared them, etc. 49 illustrations. 301pp. 6⅛ × 9¼. 23563-7 Pa. $6.00

SHAKESPEARE LEXICON AND QUOTATION DICTIONARY, Alexander Schmidt. Full definitions, locations, shades of meaning of every word in plays and poems. More than 50,000 exact quotations. 1,485pp. 6½ × 9¼. 22726-X, 22727-8 Pa., Two-vol. set $27.90

THE WORLD'S GREAT SPEECHES, edited by Lewis Copeland and Lawrence W. Lamm. Vast collection of 278 speeches from Greeks to 1970. Powerful and effective models; unique look at history. 842pp. 5⅜ × 8½. 20468-5 Pa. $10.95

THE BLUE FAIRY BOOK, Andrew Lang. The first, most famous collection, with many familiar tales: Little Red Riding Hood, Aladdin and the Wonderful Lamp, Puss in Boots, Sleeping Beauty, Hansel and Gretel, Rumpelstiltskin; 37 in all. 138 illustrations. 390pp. 5⅜ × 8½.   21437-0 Pa. $5.95

THE STORY OF THE CHAMPIONS OF THE ROUND TABLE, Howard Pyle. Sir Launcelot, Sir Tristram and Sir Percival in spirited adventures of love and triumph retold in Pyle's inimitable style. 50 drawings, 31 full-page. xviii + 329pp. 6½ × 9¼.   21883-X Pa. $6.95

AUDUBON AND HIS JOURNALS, Maria Audubon. Unmatched two-volume portrait of the great artist, naturalist and author contains his journals, an excellent biography by his granddaughter, expert annotations by the noted ornithologist, Dr. Elliott Coues, and 37 superb illustrations. Total of 1,200pp. 5⅜ × 8.
Vol. I 25143-8 Pa. $8.95
Vol. II 25144-6 Pa. $8.95

GREAT DINOSAUR HUNTERS AND THEIR DISCOVERIES, Edwin H. Colbert. Fascinating, lavishly illustrated chronicle of dinosaur research, 1820's to 1960. Achievements of Cope, Marsh, Brown, Buckland, Mantell, Huxley, many others. 384pp. 5¼ × 8¼.   24701-5 Pa. $6.95

THE TASTEMAKERS, Russell Lynes. Informal, illustrated social history of American taste 1850's-1950's. First popularized categories Highbrow, Lowbrow, Middlebrow. 129 illustrations. New (1979) afterword. 384pp. 6 × 9.
23993-4 Pa. $6.95

DOUBLE CROSS PURPOSES, Ronald A. Knox. A treasure hunt in the Scottish Highlands, an old map, unidentified corpse, surprise discoveries keep reader guessing in this cleverly intricate tale of financial skullduggery. 2 black-and-white maps. 320pp. 5⅜ × 8½. (Available in U.S. only)   25032-6 Pa. $5.95

AUTHENTIC VICTORIAN DECORATION AND ORNAMENTATION IN FULL COLOR: 46 Plates from "Studies in Design," Christopher Dresser. Superb full-color lithographs reproduced from rare original portfolio of a major Victorian designer. 48pp. 9¼ × 12¼.   25083-0 Pa. $7.95

PRIMITIVE ART, Franz Boas. Remains the best text ever prepared on subject, thoroughly discussing Indian, African, Asian, Australian, and, especially, Northern American primitive art. Over 950 illustrations show ceramics, masks, totem poles, weapons, textiles, paintings, much more. 376pp. 5⅜ × 8. 20025-6 Pa. $6.95

SIDELIGHTS ON RELATIVITY, Albert Einstein. Unabridged republication of two lectures delivered by the great physicist in 1920-21. *Ether and Relativity* and *Geometry and Experience*. Elegant ideas in non-mathematical form, accessible to intelligent layman. vi + 56pp. 5⅜ × 8½.   24511-X Pa. $2.95

THE WIT AND HUMOR OF OSCAR WILDE, edited by Alvin Redman. More than 1,000 ripostes, paradoxes, wisecracks: Work is the curse of the drinking classes, I can resist everything except temptation, etc. 258pp. 5⅜ × 8½.   20602-5 Pa. $3.95

ADVENTURES WITH A MICROSCOPE, Richard Headstrom. 59 adventures with clothing fibers, protozoa, ferns and lichens, roots and leaves, much more. 142 illustrations. 232pp. 5⅜ × 8½.   23471-1 Pa. $3.95

PLANTS OF THE BIBLE, Harold N. Moldenke and Alma L. Moldenke. Standard reference to all 230 plants mentioned in Scriptures. Latin name, biblical reference, uses, modern identity, much more. Unsurpassed encyclopedic resource for scholars, botanists, nature lovers, students of Bible. Bibliography. Indexes. 123 black-and-white illustrations. 384pp. 6 × 9. 25069-5 Pa. $8.95

FAMOUS AMERICAN WOMEN: A Biographical Dictionary from Colonial Times to the Present, Robert McHenry, ed. From Pocahontas to Rosa Parks, 1,035 distinguished American women documented in separate biographical entries. Accurate, up-to-date data, numerous categories, spans 400 years. Indices. 493pp. 6½ × 9¼. 24523-3 Pa. $9.95

THE FABULOUS INTERIORS OF THE GREAT OCEAN LINERS IN HISTORIC PHOTOGRAPHS, William H. Miller, Jr. Some 200 superb photographs capture exquisite interiors of world's great "floating palaces"—1890's to 1980's: *Titanic, Ile de France, Queen Elizabeth, United States, Europa,* more. Approx. 200 black-and-white photographs. Captions. Text. Introduction. 160pp. 8⅜ × 11¼. 24756-2 Pa. $9.95

THE GREAT LUXURY LINERS, 1927–1954: A Photographic Record, William H. Miller, Jr. Nostalgic tribute to heyday of ocean liners. 186 photos of Ile de France, Normandie, Leviathan, Queen Elizabeth, United States, many others. Interior and exterior views. Introduction. Captions. 160pp. 9 × 12. 24056-8 Pa. $9.95

A NATURAL HISTORY OF THE DUCKS, John Charles Phillips. Great landmark of ornithology offers complete detailed coverage of nearly 200 species and subspecies of ducks: gadwall, sheldrake, merganser, pintail, many more. 74 full-color plates, 102 black-and-white. Bibliography. Total of 1,920pp. 8⅜ × 11¼. 25141-1, 25142-X Cloth. Two-vol. set $100.00

THE SEAWEED HANDBOOK: An Illustrated Guide to Seaweeds from North Carolina to Canada, Thomas F. Lee. Concise reference covers 78 species. Scientific and common names, habitat, distribution, more. Finding keys for easy identification. 224pp. 5⅜ × 8½. 25215-9 Pa. $5.95

THE TEN BOOKS OF ARCHITECTURE: The 1755 Leoni Edition, Leon Battista Alberti. Rare classic helped introduce the glories of ancient architecture to the Renaissance. 68 black-and-white plates. 336pp. 8⅜ × 11¼. 25239-6 Pa. $14.95

MISS MACKENZIE, Anthony Trollope. Minor masterpieces by Victorian master unmasks many truths about life in 19th-century England. First inexpensive edition in years. 392pp. 5⅜ × 8½. 25201-9 Pa. $7.95

THE RIME OF THE ANCIENT MARINER, Gustave Doré, Samuel Taylor Coleridge. Dramatic engravings considered by many to be his greatest work. The terrifying space of the open sea, the storms and whirlpools of an unknown ocean, the ice of Antarctica, more—all rendered in a powerful, chilling manner. Full text. 38 plates. 77pp. 9¼ × 12. 22305-1 Pa. $4.95

THE EXPEDITIONS OF ZEBULON MONTGOMERY PIKE, Zebulon Montgomery Pike. Fascinating first-hand accounts (1805-6) of exploration of Mississippi River, Indian wars, capture by Spanish dragoons, much more. 1,088pp. 5⅜ × 8½. 25254-X, 25255-8 Pa. Two-vol. set $23.90

A CONCISE HISTORY OF PHOTOGRAPHY: Third Revised Edition, Helmut Gernsheim. Best one-volume history—camera obscura, photochemistry, daguerreotypes, evolution of cameras, film, more. Also artistic aspects—landscape, portraits, fine art, etc. 281 black-and-white photographs. 26 in color. 176pp. 8⅜ × 11¼. 25128-4 Pa. $12.95

THE DORÉ BIBLE ILLUSTRATIONS, Gustave Doré. 241 detailed plates from the Bible: the Creation scenes, Adam and Eve, Flood, Babylon, battle sequences, life of Jesus, etc. Each plate is accompanied by the verses from the King James version of the Bible. 241pp. 9 × 12. 23004-X Pa. $8.95

HUGGER-MUGGER IN THE LOUVRE, Elliot Paul. Second Homer Evans mystery-comedy. Theft at the Louvre involves sleuth in hilarious, madcap caper. "A knockout."—Books. 336pp. 5⅜ × 8½. 25185-3 Pa. $5.95

FLATLAND, E. A. Abbott. Intriguing and enormously popular science-fiction classic explores the complexities of trying to survive as a two-dimensional being in a three-dimensional world. Amusingly illustrated by the author. 16 illustrations. 103pp. 5⅜ × 8½. 20001-9 Pa. $2.00

THE HISTORY OF THE LEWIS AND CLARK EXPEDITION, Meriwether Lewis and William Clark, edited by Elliott Coues. Classic edition of Lewis and Clark's day-by-day journals that later became the basis for U.S. claims to Oregon and the West. Accurate and invaluable geographical, botanical, biological, meteorological and anthropological material. Total of 1,508pp. 5⅜ × 8½. 21268-8, 21269-6, 21270-X Pa. Three-vol. set $25.50

LANGUAGE, TRUTH AND LOGIC, Alfred J. Ayer. Famous, clear introduction to Vienna, Cambridge schools of Logical Positivism. Role of philosophy, elimination of metaphysics, nature of analysis, etc. 160pp. 5⅜ × 8½. (Available in U.S. and Canada only) 20010-8 Pa. $2.95

MATHEMATICS FOR THE NONMATHEMATICIAN, Morris Kline. Detailed, college-level treatment of mathematics in cultural and historical context, with numerous exercises. For liberal arts students. Preface. Recommended Reading Lists. Tables. Index. Numerous black-and-white figures. xvi + 641pp. 5⅜ × 8½. 24823-2 Pa. $11.95

28 SCIENCE FICTION STORIES, H. G. Wells. Novels, *Star Begotten* and *Men Like Gods,* plus 26 short stories: "Empire of the Ants," "A Story of the Stone Age," "The Stolen Bacillus," "In the Abyss," etc. 915pp. 5⅜ × 8½. (Available in U.S. only) 20265-8 Cloth. $10.95

HANDBOOK OF PICTORIAL SYMBOLS, Rudolph Modley. 3,250 signs and symbols, many systems in full; official or heavy commercial use. Arranged by subject. Most in Pictorial Archive series. 143pp. 8⅛ × 11. 23357-X Pa. $5.95

INCIDENTS OF TRAVEL IN YUCATAN, John L. Stephens. Classic (1843) exploration of jungles of Yucatan, looking for evidences of Maya civilization. Travel adventures, Mexican and Indian culture, etc. Total of 669pp. 5⅜ × 8½. 20926-1, 20927-X Pa., Two-vol. set $9.90

DEGAS: An Intimate Portrait, Ambroise Vollard. Charming, anecdotal memoir by famous art dealer of one of the greatest 19th-century French painters. 14 black-and-white illustrations. Introduction by Harold L. Van Doren. 96pp. 5⅜ × 8½.
25131-4 Pa. $3.95

PERSONAL NARRATIVE OF A PILGRIMAGE TO ALMANDINAH AND MECCAH, Richard Burton. Great travel classic by remarkably colorful personality. Burton, disguised as a Moroccan, visited sacred shrines of Islam, narrowly escaping death. 47 illustrations. 959pp. 5⅜ × 8½.   21217-3, 21218-1 Pa., Two-vol. set $17.90

PHRASE AND WORD ORIGINS, A. H. Holt. Entertaining, reliable, modern study of more than 1,200 colorful words, phrases, origins and histories. Much unexpected information. 254pp. 5⅜ × 8½.   20758-7 Pa. $4.95

THE RED THUMB MARK, R. Austin Freeman. In this first Dr. Thorndyke case, the great scientific detective draws fascinating conclusions from the nature of a single fingerprint. Exciting story, authentic science. 320pp. 5⅜ × 8½. (Available in U.S. only)   25210-8 Pa. $5.95

AN EGYPTIAN HIEROGLYPHIC DICTIONARY, E. A. Wallis Budge. Monumental work containing about 25,000 words or terms that occur in texts ranging from 3000 B.C. to 600 A.D. Each entry consists of a transliteration of the word, the word in hieroglyphs, and the meaning in English. 1,314pp. 6⅜ × 10.
23615-3, 23616-1 Pa., Two-vol. set $27.90

THE COMPLEAT STRATEGYST: Being a Primer on the Theory of Games of Strategy, J. D. Williams. Highly entertaining classic describes, with many illustrated examples, how to select best strategies in conflict situations. Prefaces. Appendices. xvi + 268pp. 5⅜ × 8½.   25101-2 Pa. $5.95

THE ROAD TO OZ, L. Frank Baum. Dorothy meets the Shaggy Man, little Button-Bright and the Rainbow's beautiful daughter in this delightful trip to the magical Land of Oz. 272pp. 5⅜ × 8.   25208-6 Pa. $4.95

POINT AND LINE TO PLANE, Wassily Kandinsky. Seminal exposition of role of point, line, other elements in non-objective painting. Essential to understanding 20th-century art. 127 illustrations. 192pp. 6½ × 9¼.   23808-3 Pa. $4.50

LADY ANNA, Anthony Trollope. Moving chronicle of Countess Lovel's bitter struggle to win for herself and daughter Anna their rightful rank and fortune— perhaps at cost of sanity itself. 384pp. 5⅜ × 8½.   24669-8 Pa. $6.95

EGYPTIAN MAGIC, E. A. Wallis Budge. Sums up all that is known about magic in Ancient Egypt: the role of magic in controlling the gods, powerful amulets that warded off evil spirits, scarabs of immortality, use of wax images, formulas and spells, the secret name, much more. 253pp. 5⅜ × 8½.   22681-6 Pa. $4.00

THE DANCE OF SIVA, Ananda Coomaraswamy. Preeminent authority unfolds the vast metaphysic of India: the revelation of her art, conception of the universe, social organization, etc. 27 reproductions of art masterpieces. 192pp. 5⅜ × 8½.
24817-8 Pa. $5.95

CHRISTMAS CUSTOMS AND TRADITIONS, Clement A. Miles. Origin, evolution, significance of religious, secular practices. Caroling, gifts, yule logs, much more. Full, scholarly yet fascinating; non-sectarian. 400pp. 5⅜ × 8½.
23354-5 Pa. $6.50

THE HUMAN FIGURE IN MOTION, Eadweard Muybridge. More than 4,500 stopped-action photos, in action series, showing undraped men, women, children jumping, lying down, throwing, sitting, wrestling, carrying, etc. 390pp. 7⅞ × 10⅝.
20204-6 Cloth. $19.95

THE MAN WHO WAS THURSDAY, Gilbert Keith Chesterton. Witty, fast-paced novel about a club of anarchists in turn-of-the-century London. Brilliant social, religious, philosophical speculations. 128pp. 5⅜ × 8½. 25121-7 Pa. $3.95

A CEZANNE SKETCHBOOK: Figures, Portraits, Landscapes and Still Lifes, Paul Cezanne. Great artist experiments with tonal effects, light, mass, other qualities in over 100 drawings. A revealing view of developing master painter, precursor of Cubism. 102 black-and-white illustrations. 144pp. 8¾ × 6⅝. 24790-2 Pa. $5.95

AN ENCYCLOPEDIA OF BATTLES: Accounts of Over 1,560 Battles from 1479 B.C. to the Present, David Eggenberger. Presents essential details of every major battle in recorded history, from the first battle of Megiddo in 1479 B.C. to Grenada in 1984. List of Battle Maps. New Appendix covering the years 1967–1984. Index. 99 illustrations. 544pp. 6½ × 9¼. 24913-1 Pa. $14.95

AN ETYMOLOGICAL DICTIONARY OF MODERN ENGLISH, Ernest Weekley. Richest, fullest work, by foremost British lexicographer. Detailed word histories. Inexhaustible. Total of 856pp. 6½ × 9¼.
21873-2, 21874-0 Pa., Two-vol. set $17.00

WEBSTER'S AMERICAN MILITARY BIOGRAPHIES, edited by Robert McHenry. Over 1,000 figures who shaped 3 centuries of American military history. Detailed biographies of Nathan Hale, Douglas MacArthur, Mary Hallaren, others. Chronologies of engagements, more. Introduction. Addenda. 1,033 entries in alphabetical order. xi + 548pp. 6½ × 9¼. (Available in U.S. only)
24758-9 Pa. $11.95

LIFE IN ANCIENT EGYPT, Adolf Erman. Detailed older account, with much not in more recent books: domestic life, religion, magic, medicine, commerce, and whatever else needed for complete picture. Many illustrations. 597pp. 5⅜ × 8½.
22632-8 Pa. $8.50

HISTORIC COSTUME IN PICTURES, Braun & Schneider. Over 1,450 costumed figures shown, covering a wide variety of peoples: kings, emperors, nobles, priests, servants, soldiers, scholars, townsfolk, peasants, merchants, courtiers, cavaliers, and more. 256pp. 8⅜ × 11¼. 23150-X Pa. $7.95

THE NOTEBOOKS OF LEONARDO DA VINCI, edited by J. P. Richter. Extracts from manuscripts reveal great genius; on painting, sculpture, anatomy, sciences, geography, etc. Both Italian and English. 186 ms. pages reproduced, plus 500 additional drawings, including studies for *Last Supper, Sforza* monument, etc. 860pp. 7⅞ × 10¾. (Available in U.S. only) 22572-0, 22573-9 Pa., Two-vol. set $25.90

THE ART NOUVEAU STYLE BOOK OF ALPHONSE MUCHA: All 72 Plates from "Documents Decoratifs" in Original Color, Alphonse Mucha. Rare copyright-free design portfolio by high priest of Art Nouveau. Jewelry, wallpaper, stained glass, furniture, figure studies, plant and animal motifs, etc. Only complete one-volume edition. 80pp. 9⅜ × 12¼. 24044-4 Pa. $8.95

ANIMALS: 1,419 COPYRIGHT-FREE ILLUSTRATIONS OF MAMMALS, BIRDS, FISH, INSECTS, ETC., edited by Jim Harter. Clear wood engravings present, in extremely lifelike poses, over 1,000 species of animals. One of the most extensive pictorial sourcebooks of its kind. Captions. Index. 284pp. 9 × 12. 23766-4 Pa. $9.95

OBELISTS FLY HIGH, C. Daly King. Masterpiece of American detective fiction, long out of print, involves murder on a 1935 transcontinental flight—"a very thrilling story"—NY Times. Unabridged and unaltered republication of the edition published by William Collins Sons & Co. Ltd., London, 1935. 288pp. 5⅜ × 8½. (Available in U.S. only) 25036-9 Pa. $4.95

VICTORIAN AND EDWARDIAN FASHION: A Photographic Survey, Alison Gernsheim. First fashion history completely illustrated by contemporary photographs. Full text plus 235 photos, 1840–1914, in which many celebrities appear. 240pp. 6½ × 9¼. 24205-6 Pa. $6.00

THE ART OF THE FRENCH ILLUSTRATED BOOK, 1700–1914, Gordon N. Ray. Over 630 superb book illustrations by Fragonard, Delacroix, Daumier, Doré, Grandville, Manet, Mucha, Steinlen, Toulouse-Lautrec and many others. Preface. Introduction. 633 halftones. Indices of artists, authors & titles, binders and provenances. Appendices. Bibliography. 608pp. 8⅜ × 11¼. 25086-5 Pa. $24.95

THE WONDERFUL WIZARD OF OZ, L. Frank Baum. Facsimile in full color of America's finest children's classic. 143 illustrations by W. W. Denslow. 267pp. 5⅜ × 8½. 20691-2 Pa. $5.95

FRONTIERS OF MODERN PHYSICS: New Perspectives on Cosmology, Relativity, Black Holes and Extraterrestrial Intelligence, Tony Rothman, et al. For the intelligent layman. Subjects include: cosmological models of the universe; black holes; the neutrino; the search for extraterrestrial intelligence. Introduction. 46 black-and-white illustrations. 192pp. 5⅜ × 8½. 24587-X Pa. $6.95

THE FRIENDLY STARS, Martha Evans Martin & Donald Howard Menzel. Classic text marshalls the stars together in an engaging, non-technical survey, presenting them as sources of beauty in night sky. 23 illustrations. Foreword. 2 star charts. Index. 147pp. 5⅜ × 8½. 21099-5 Pa. $3.50

FADS AND FALLACIES IN THE NAME OF SCIENCE, Martin Gardner. Fair, witty appraisal of cranks, quacks, and quackeries of science and pseudoscience: hollow earth, Velikovsky, orgone energy, Dianetics, flying saucers, Bridey Murphy, food and medical fads, etc. Revised, expanded In the Name of Science. "A very able and even-tempered presentation."—The New Yorker. 363pp. 5⅜ × 8. 20394-8 Pa. $5.95

ANCIENT EGYPT: ITS CULTURE AND HISTORY, J. E Manchip White. From pre-dynastics through Ptolemies: society, history, political structure, religion, daily life, literature, cultural heritage. 48 plates. 217pp. 5⅜ × 8½. 22548-8 Pa. $4.95

SIR HARRY HOTSPUR OF HUMBLETHWAITE, Anthony Trollope. Incisive, unconventional psychological study of a conflict between a wealthy baronet, his idealistic daughter, and their scapegrace cousin. The 1870 novel in its first inexpensive edition in years. 250pp. 5⅜ × 8½. 24953-0 Pa. $4.95

LASERS AND HOLOGRAPHY, Winston E. Kock. Sound introduction to burgeoning field, expanded (1981) for second edition. Wave patterns, coherence, lasers, diffraction, zone plates, properties of holograms, recent advances. 84 illustrations. 160pp. 5⅜ × 8¼. (Except in United Kingdom) 24041-X Pa. $3.50

INTRODUCTION TO ARTIFICIAL INTELLIGENCE: SECOND, EN-LARGED EDITION, Philip C. Jackson, Jr. Comprehensive survey of artificial intelligence—the study of how machines (computers) can be made to act intelligently. Includes introductory and advanced material. Extensive notes updating the main text. 132 black-and-white illustrations. 512pp. 5⅜ × 8½. 24864-X Pa. $8.95

HISTORY OF INDIAN AND INDONESIAN ART, Ananda K. Coomaraswamy. Over 400 illustrations illuminate classic study of Indian art from earliest Harappa finds to early 20th century. Provides philosophical, religious and social insights. 304pp. 6⅛ × 9⅜. 25005-9 Pa. $8.95

THE GOLEM, Gustav Meyrink. Most famous supernatural novel in modern European literature, set in Ghetto of Old Prague around 1890. Compelling story of mystical experiences, strange transformations, profound terror. 13 black-and-white illustrations. 224pp. 5⅜ × 8½. (Available in U.S. only) 25025-3 Pa. $5.95

ARMADALE, Wilkie Collins. Third great mystery novel by the author of *The Woman in White* and *The Moonstone*. Original magazine version with 40 illustrations. 597pp. 5⅜ × 8½. 23429-0 Pa. $7.95

PICTORIAL ENCYCLOPEDIA OF HISTORIC ARCHITECTURAL PLANS, DETAILS AND ELEMENTS: With 1,880 Line Drawings of Arches, Domes, Doorways, Facades, Gables, Windows, etc., John Theodore Haneman. Sourcebook of inspiration for architects, designers, others. Bibliography. Captions. 141pp. 9 × 12. 24605-1 Pa. $6.95

BENCHLEY LOST AND FOUND, Robert Benchley. Finest humor from early 30's, about pet peeves, child psychologists, post office and others. Mostly unavailable elsewhere. 73 illustrations by Peter Arno and others. 183pp. 5⅜ × 8½. 22410-4 Pa. $3.95

ERTÉ GRAPHICS, Erté. Collection of striking color graphics: *Seasons, Alphabet, Numerals, Aces* and *Precious Stones*. 50 plates, including 4 on covers. 48pp. 9⅜ × 12¼. 23580-7 Pa. $6.95

THE JOURNAL OF HENRY D. THOREAU, edited by Bradford Torrey, F. H. Allen. Complete reprinting of 14 volumes, 1837–61, over two million words; the sourcebooks for *Walden*, etc. Definitive. All original sketches, plus 75 photographs. 1,804pp. 8½ × 12¼. 20312-3, 20313-1 Cloth., Two-vol. set $80.00

CASTLES: THEIR CONSTRUCTION AND HISTORY, Sidney Toy. Traces castle development from ancient roots. Nearly 200 photographs and drawings illustrate moats, keeps, baileys, many other features. Caernarvon, Dover Castles, Hadrian's Wall, Tower of London, dozens more. 256pp. 5⅜ × 8¼. 24898-4 Pa. $5.95

CATALOG OF DOVER BOOKS

AMERICAN CLIPPER SHIPS: 1833–1858, Octavius T. Howe & Frederick C. Matthews. Fully-illustrated, encyclopedic review of 352 clipper ships from the period of America's greatest maritime supremacy. Introduction. 109 halftones. 5 black-and-white line illustrations. Index. Total of 928pp. 5⅜ × 8½.
25115-2, 25116-0 Pa., Two-vol. set $17.90

TOWARDS A NEW ARCHITECTURE, Le Corbusier. Pioneering manifesto by great architect, near legendary founder of "International School." Technical and aesthetic theories, views on industry, economics, relation of form to function, "mass-production spirit," much more. Profusely illustrated. Unabridged translation of 13th French edition. Introduction by Frederick Etchells. 320pp. 6⅛ × 9¼. (Available in U.S. only)
25023-7 Pa. $8.95

THE BOOK OF KELLS, edited by Blanche Cirker. Inexpensive collection of 32 full-color, full-page plates from the greatest illuminated manuscript of the Middle Ages, painstakingly reproduced from rare facsimile edition. Publisher's Note. Captions. 32pp. 9⅜ × 12¼.
24345-1 Pa. $4.50

BEST SCIENCE FICTION STORIES OF H. G. WELLS, H. G. Wells. Full novel The Invisible Man, plus 17 short stories: "The Crystal Egg," "Aepyornis Island," "The Strange Orchid," etc. 303pp. 5⅜ × 8½. (Available in U.S. only)
21531-8 Pa. $4.95

AMERICAN SAILING SHIPS: Their Plans and History, Charles G. Davis. Photos, construction details of schooners, frigates, clippers, other sailcraft of 18th to early 20th centuries—plus entertaining discourse on design, rigging, nautical lore, much more. 137 black-and-white illustrations. 240pp. 6⅛ × 9¼.
24658-2 Pa. $5.95

ENTERTAINING MATHEMATICAL PUZZLES, Martin Gardner. Selection of author's favorite conundrums involving arithmetic, money, speed, etc., with lively commentary. Complete solutions. 112pp. 5⅜ × 8½. 25211-6 Pa. $2.95

THE WILL TO BELIEVE, HUMAN IMMORTALITY, William James. Two books bound together. Effect of irrational on logical, and arguments for human immortality. 402pp. 5⅜ × 8½. 20291-7 Pa. $7.50

THE HAUNTED MONASTERY and THE CHINESE MAZE MURDERS, Robert Van Gulik. 2 full novels by Van Gulik continue adventures of Judge Dee and his companions. An evil Taoist monastery, seemingly supernatural events; overgrown topiary maze that hides strange crimes. Set in 7th-century China. 27 illustrations. 328pp. 5⅜ × 8½. 23502-5 Pa. $5.00

CELEBRATED CASES OF JUDGE DEE (DEE GOONG AN), translated by Robert Van Gulik. Authentic 18th-century Chinese detective novel; Dee and associates solve three interlocked cases. Led to Van Gulik's own stories with same characters. Extensive introduction. 9 illustrations. 237pp. 5⅜ × 8½.
23337-5 Pa. $4.95

Prices subject to change without notice.

Available at your book dealer or write for free catalog to Dept. GI, Dover Publications, Inc., 31 East 2nd St., Mineola, N.Y. 11501. Dover publishes more than 175 books each year on science, elementary and advanced mathematics, biology, music, art, literary history, social sciences and other areas.